For Karen
with gratitude for your
support and friendship
with all my heart,
            Nadia

DOUBLE EXPOSURE

From Russia Cross-Country Through Time

NADIA SHULMAN

ISBN: 978-1-4834-8942-1 (sc)
ISBN: 978-1-4834-8941-4 (e)

Library of Congress Control Number: 2018909153

Lulu Publishing Services rev. date: 09/20/2018

To Dad, my love and inspiration.

To my fellow Jews, Russian, American, and Israeli,

who fought for our freedom.

Acknowledgement

With Deepest Thanks

I want to thank my sons, Igor and Alex, for their support and encouragement, my sister Ellen for the many shared memories, and the beautiful progeny of Lenya-Junior, the Kantors clan, especially his daughter Marina. Most of all, a big kiss to my husband Romen, who bravely endured our 50 years together.

My deepest gratitude goes to all who believed in me and supported the pre-order program. Thanks to everyone on my email list, friends on Facebook, and to all who came to the readings and expressed interest.

Special thanks to Caroline, our Virtuoso travel agent (carolinetravel.com), and 2MG (helpme2mg.com) for all the publishing and marketing efforts behind bringing the book to its readers. Appreciation to Framingham Access Television "Travel With Jack Show." Cover photo by SPUTNIK / Alamy Stock Photo. Cover design by Oliviaprodesign.

Please follow my adventures on nadiashulman.com.

FAMILY TREE

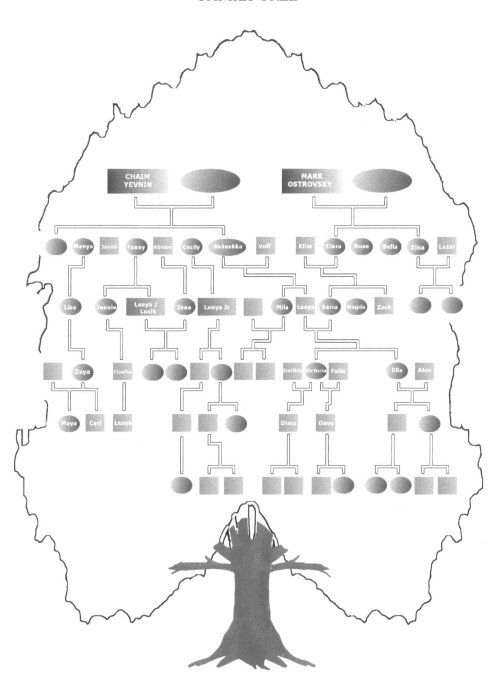

Contents

Day 1, Aug 28: Framingham, MA – Hubbard, Oh 1
   Dmitry: Kiev, Ukraine 1960s 2
   Dmitry: Kiev, Ukraine 1960s 10
Day 2, AUG 29: Indianapolis, IN, Omni Severin Hotel 16
   Babushka, Gorbashovka, Ukraine 1920s 17
Day 3, Aug 30: Indianapolis, IN - St. Louis, MS,
   Hamptons Inn 21
   Babushka, Uzbekistan 1940s 22
   Babushka, Kiev, Ukraine 1940 24
   Babushka, Kiev, Ukraine 1960 30
Day 4, Aug 31: St. Louis, MS - Kansas City, KS, Hilton
   President 33
   Lenya Junior: Kharkov, Ukraine 1950s 33
Day 5, Sept 1: Kansas City, KS, Hilton President 40
   The Family: Moscow, Russia 1960 41
Day 6, Sept 2, Labor Day: Kansas City, KS, Hilton President 44
   Volodya, Kiev, Ukraine 1970s 45
Day 7, Sept 3: Kansas City, KS - Kearney, NE, Best Western .. 52
   Volodya: Kiev, Ukraine 1970s 53
Day 8, Sept 4: CUSTER STATE PARK, SD, State Game Lodge 61
   Childhood: Kiev, Ukraine 1940s 62
Day 9, Sept 5: CUSTER STATE PARK, SD, State Game Lodge 70
   The Girlfriends: Kiev, Ukraine 1940s 71
Day 10, Sept 6: Cody, WY, Chamberlain Inn, Hemingway
   suite 78
   Boris Babich: Kiev, Ukraine 1950s 81

Day 11, Sept 7: Yellowstone National Park, WY, Lake
    Yellowstone Hotel 88
    The Golden Anniversary: Kiev, Ukraine 1960s....................89
    The Golden Anniversary: Kiev, Ukraine 1960s....................93
Day 12, Sept 8: Yellowstone National Park, WY, Old
    Faithful Inn 98
    Sarra: Kiev, Ukraine, 1940s..99
    Efim: Kiev, Ukraine 1940s 105
Day 13, Sept 9: Jackson Hole, WY, Spring Creek Ranch 108
    Sarra: Kuybyshev, Russia 1940s.................................. 108
    Sarra, Kiev, Ukraine 1940s 111
Day 14, Sept 10: Jackson Hole, WY, Spring Creek Ranch.......117
    Aunt Rose: Kiev, Ukraine 1950s.................................. 119
Day 15, Sept 11: Jackson Hole, WY, Spring Creek Ranch...... 125
    The Last Train from Russia: Kiev, Ukraine 1970s 126
Day 16, Sept 12: Jackson Hole, WY, Spring Creek Ranch...... 133
    Emigration: Vienna, Austria 1970s............................... 133
Day 17, Sept 13: Park City, UT, Montage, Vista View Suite ... 138
    Emigration: Rome, Italy 1970s.................................... 140
Day 18, Sept 14: Elko, NV, Hilton Garden Inn 144
    Emigration: Rome, Italy 1970s.................................... 145
Day 19, Sept 15: Reno, NV, Peppermill Resort and Casino 148
    Emigration: Ladispoli, Italy 1970s................................ 149
    Emigration: Ladispoli, Italy 1970s................................ 152
Day 20, Sept 16: Yosemite National Park, CA, Ahwahnee
    Hotel 157
    Americana: Haverhill, MA, USA 1970s 159
Day 21, Sept 17: Yosemite National Park, CA, Ahwahnee
    Hotel 162
    Americana: Haverhill, MA 1970s 163
Day 22, Sept 18: Carmel, CA, Carmel Valley Ranch.............. 169
    Americana: Haverhill, MA 1970s 170
    Americana: Haverhill, MA 1970s 173
Day 23, Sept 19: Carmel, CA, Carmel Valley Ranch.............. 176
    Americana: Haverhill, 1970s 177
Day 24, Sept 20: Carmel, CA, Carmel Valley Ranch.............. 181
    Americana: Haverhill, MA 1980s................................. 182

Kids: Kiev, Ukraine 1960s..182
Americana: Haverhill, 1980s..183
Day 25, Sept 21: Santa Barbara, CA, Hotel Four Season
Biltmore...187
Zoya: Kiev, Ukraine, 1950s...187
Zoya: Kiev, Ukraine 1960s..190
Zoya: Kiev, Ukraine, 1970s...191
Emigration, Europe, 1970s..193
Zoya California, USA, 80s...194
Zoya California, USA 1990s...195
Zoya: Ladispoli, Italy, 1970s..197
Zoya, California, USA, 1970s...198
Day 26, Sept 22: Santa Monica, CA, Casa del Mar..............200
Kids: Kiev, Ukraine 1960s...201
Kids: Yalta, Crimea 1960s..207
Day 27, Sept 23: Santa Monica, CA, Casa del Mar..............210
Kids: Haverhill, MA, USA 1980s......................................211
Day 28, Sept 24: Santa Monica, CA, Casa del Mar..............214
Kids: Haverhill, MA USA 1980s.......................................216
Day 29, Sept 25: Santa Monica, CA, Casa del Mar..............220
Kids: Kiev, Ukraine, 1970s...221
Kids: Massachusetts, USA 1980s....................................221
Day 30, Sept 26: Santa Monica, CA, Casa del Mar..............227
Kids: Kiev, Ukraine, 1970s...228
Day 31, Sept 27: Las Vegas, NV, Hotel Vdara.....................231
Tales from Moscow: Moscow, Russia, 1950s....................232
Day 32, Sept 28: Las Vegas, NV, Hotel Vdara.....................237
Tales from Moscow: Moscow, Russia 1960s.....................239
Day 33, Sept 29: Springdale, UT, Zion National Park,
Hampton Inn & Suites...243
Moscow, Russia, 1970s...247
Kiev, Ukraine, 1970s..248
Day 34, Sept 30: Springdale, UT, Zion National Park,
Hampton Inn & Suites...252
Tales from Moscow: Moscow, Russia 1970s.....................253
Day 35, Oct 1: Big Water, UT, Lake Powell, Hotel Amangiri...258
Camaraderie: Kiev, Ukraine, 1940s................................259
Kiev, Ukraine 1950s...263
Day 36, Oct 2: Big Water, UT, Lake Powell, Hotel Amangiri...268

The Camaraderie: Kiev, Ukraine 1960s............................ 269

Day 37, Oct 3: Grand Canyon National Park, AZ, Hotel El
    Tovar 272
    Dad: Gorbashovka, Ukraine 1930s............................. 273
    Dad: Kiev, Ukraine 1940s 276

Day 38, Oct 4: Grand Canyon National Park, AZ, Hotel El
    Tovar 278
    Dad: Kiev, Ukraine 1940s 279
    Dad: Kiev, Ukraine 1950s 280

Day 39, Oct 5: Sedona, AZ, Enchantment Resort................. 284
    Dad: Kiev, Ukraine 1950s 285

Day 40, Oct 6: Sedona, AZ, Enchantment Resort 288
    Dad: Kiev, Ukraine 1970s 289

Day 41, Oct 7: Santa Fe, NM, The Inn of the Five Graces...... 294
    Victoria (Clothes): Kiev, Ukraine 1940s 295
    Victoria (Clothes): Kiev, Ukraine 1950 295
    Victoria (Clothes): Kiev, Ukraine 1960 297

Day 42, Oct 8: Santa Fe, NM, The Inn of the Five Graces 300
    Victoria: Kiev, Ukraine, 1950s 303

Day 43, Oct 9: Oklahoma City, Ok, Hilton Skirvin 306
    Felix (Romance): Kiev, Ukraine 1950s 306
    Victoria (Romance): Kiev, Ukraine 1960s.................... 309

Day 44, Oct 10: Hot Springs, AK, Embassy Suites Hotel....... 312
    Trains: Kiev, Ukraine 1940s 313
    Trains: Kiev, Ukraine 1950s 314
    Trains: Kiev, Ukraine 1950s 315
    Trains: Kiev, Ukraine 1960s 315
    Trains: Spain, Europe 1990.. 316

Day 45, Oct 11: Nashville, TN, Renaissance Hotel................. 318
    Grateful Dead: Maine, USA 1980s.............................. 319

Day 46, Oct 12: Walland, TN, Blackberry Farm.................... 324
    Babushka: Kiev, Ukraine, 1960s 325

Day 47, Oct 13: Walland, TN, Blackberry Farm 328
    ELLA: Kiev, Ukraine 1950s... 329
    ELLA: Kiev, Ukraine 1960s... 332

Day 48, Oct 14: Walland, TN, Blackberry Farm 335
    Victoria: PTSD 336

Day 49, Oct 15: Keswick, VI, Keswick Hall at Monticello 338

The Times. 338

Day 50, Oct 16: Framingham, MA 344

The places, Kiev, Ukraine 1940s..................................... 345
The places, Kiev, Ukraine 1950s..................................... 345
The places, Kiev, Ukraine 1960s..................................... 346
The places, Kiev, Ukraine 1970s..................................... 346
The places, Haverhill, MA USA 1970s 347
The places, Framingham, MA USA 1970s 347

DAY 1, AUGUST 28
FRAMINGHAM, MA – HUBBARD, OH

My heart jumped and made me lean on the corner of the house, next to the open garage door. The day excited and scared me at the same time.

The lazy, late August sun painted white streaks on my shiny car, crisp pre-fall coolness in the morning air.

The academic year at Russian colleges and universities began with students being sent to local collective farms to help with the crops. Since my college years, a dim September sunrise and sleepy early autumn mornings always reminded me of the bittersweet smoke of dying fires drifting slowly above foggy Ukrainian fields, and a city girl lost in the sad vastness.

My heart jumped again and returned to a slow trot. We were ready; the car was packed, and Felix just came out of the garage. We were at the start of the adventure of our lives.

"We are leaving. We are leaving!" I sang soundlessly.

We planned to drive from Massachusetts to Northern California visiting National Parks and Monuments on the way, then turn South onto Pacific Highway to Santa Monica and from there drive back to Massachusetts by the southern route visiting more parks and places of interest. We planned this trip around a family wedding in Kansas, a visit with our son and grandchildren in California and, the most of all, our Golden

Wedding Anniversary. We planned to travel one day for each year of our life together; it would be a long drive!

I looked at our car packed for the trip and thought about the anniversary; how did we get to this point? How did we manage to stay married for almost fifty years? How did our marriage survive a life packed with curveballs and high seas? How rocky was our boat through the emigration, a language barrier, culture shock and a penniless beginning?

Yet, on this beautiful August morning, I carefully navigated my X5 out of our circular driveway with an island full of blooming flowers to Mass Pike brimming with early morning traffic. Our route mapped out; we left Massachusetts behind in no time. We planned to stop in Ohio for our first night on the road toward Kansas.

Steamy downpours hit us somewhere in the hills of New Jersey, but we were on our way across America; what could a little rain do? I looked at Felix sleeping in the passenger seat. He was still weak and pale after double pneumonia. He opened his eyes as if feeling my concern.

"How are you doing, Victoria? I feel better; I think I can drive for a while."

I was happy to switch. From the passenger seat, I watched the road and stared at the wet windshield. It became chilly in the car.

DMITRY
KIEV, UKRAINE, THE 1960S

Victoria was wet and cold. Light rain seeped through her skin and chilled her to the core. She was standing in the shallow water of the river that just killed her husband.

She had been standing there for the last forty minutes that felt like an eternity. She just stood there, water to her knees, looking at the river. She was not frightened or sad. There were no thoughts in her head; she felt only wet and numb. She just wanted to survive.

She could not leave the river. Like a killer returning to the scene of the crime, she needed to be there, in the water, where it all happened.

She felt a kick in the stomach and brushed the feeling aside. Who, the hell, cares? Dima was dead. The river just took him and now she was all alone.

If not for a Good Samaritan on a small boat, who had jammed an oar into her hands thrashing violently in the water, she would not be here either. Maybe it would be better. She felt a kick again. The baby made it out of the river with her. However, it was not a comforting thought right now.

Only this morning, they were so happy. Victoria felt the first kick of the baby and Dmitry thought this kick was his personal achievement. Well, in a sense, it was. Their four-month wedding anniversary became very special with this tiny tap from the inside world.

The hybrid of a radio and a record player, their wedding gift called "Radiola" was spewing a loud western song, and they danced and jumped with the music.

Her Mom knocked on their door. "Vika, you will lose the baby, if you behave like that," she warned her crazy kids.

Only this morning they had agreed on the names, one for a boy and one for a girl, just in case. When was it? Not this morning, it was hundred years ago, in a different life, the past life. The life, which the river took, forever.

It all started last year, on a sunny, chilly November day, the holiday of the Great October Revolution.

"Only idiots could celebrate 'October Revolution' in November," thought Victoria. The streets were ablaze with red flags and portraits of the Communist Party leaders. Amateur orchestras headed home after playing all day at the parade, and the faint music was descending from downtown. Crowds were happy with a free day and good weather. Holiday dinners were waiting at homes.

Victoria spent the day on a blind date arranged by her girlfriend, Dora. They were friends since fifth grade and now married Dora wanted Victoria to date every single friend of her husband, even a distant cousin. Earlier, when she had met the young man, Victoria planned to walk downtown; however, many streets were closed by "militia" for the parade, and they were tired, walking all day. She decided that she had enough, enough of walking, Dmitry's stupid jokes, and even his good looks.

Victoria was a senior in Medical School, the graduation looming in a few months. Instead of being excited, she worried, she was afraid that after graduation she would have to leave Kiev and go to practice medicine in some remote area of Soviet Union. It was the school's right to decide where the graduate would have to go. However, she did not want to leave the city of her youth, her beloved Kiev.

She grew up on these green streets with elegant old buildings and beautiful parks, she went to the kindergarten and school here, and her family and friends were here. The only thing that could save her from exile to a remote village somewhere at the end of the world was a marriage. She urgently needed a husband who lived in this city and had a stamp in his passport confirming that. Then, the School would let her stay and find a job by herself. She was about to graduate from the same Medical School as both of her parents did, and they had plenty of friends in the medical world who would be able to help.

However, they could not help her to find a husband. She had plenty of blind and other dates but no good prospects to marry and she felt old at twenty-two.

Dmitry annoyed her, he was boring and provincial, and his good looks did not appeal to Victoria. She returned home, to her small room in a grand, imposing building, where she shared kitchen, bath, and toilet with two other families.

Before The Revolution, it was probably a lovely five-room apartment, but now these five rooms accommodated three different families. Each had a small table in the kitchen, a small shelf in the bath and a small handmade pocket with neatly cut newspapers or old textbooks in the toilet room.

Victoria was about twelve years old when she moved to this apartment with her parents. Her dad, the doctor, got a job at the River Navigation Administration. The position came with a perk, two rooms for his five-person family; it was a significant improvement in their previous living arrangements.

Back then, their neighbors, the Snisarenkos, was a family of three, parents and their daughter Elizabeth. The family occupied two beautiful rooms with two large very entertaining bay windows into the courtyard. They could see all the activity in the yard, who was coming to visit or going and to catch the mailman with a large blue linen cross body bag full of newspapers and letters.

There was a fountain in the middle of the courtyard, but, for all the years Victoria had lived here, the fountain had never worked, and its cement border had become a favorite place for the seniors. They would sit on cold cement, watching people, gossiping and making nasty remarks, yelling at the children and complaining to the parents.

Every summer, papa Snisarenko meticulously cut Elizabeth's textbooks from the prior year and stashed them in their toilet pocket embroidered by mama Snisarenko. Toilet paper did not exist yet in the Soviet Union.

Strangely, that was one of the reasons Victoria had all A's in school. That and her photographic memory.

Lizzy and Vika, as the parents lovingly called the girls, attended the same school. While using the toilet, Vika who was two years junior, preferred to put four small pieces of paper from Snisarenkos' pocket together, trying to restore the page and to read Lizzy's school textbook rather than The Soviet newspaper stored in her family's pocket. When two years later she caught up to Lizzy's grade, she knew the textbook by heart and got "A's" as a result.

By the time Victoria was in medical school, her family had moved out of the apartment, and her Dad managed to bend his employer's rules and to leave one small room to Victoria.

The Snisarenko family grew to four when Lizzy got married, and her husband moved in. The third neighbor, a riverboat captain with his wife, added Victoria parents' larger room.

All seven inhabitants of the apartment cooked on the same gas stove, bathed in the same bath, and sat on the same toilet. Everybody knew exactly what was cooking in every pot, what was hanging in every closet, who was visiting and who was staying for the night. There were no secrets in this communal living, and even though Victoria hated to share her life, her habits, and her secrets with the well-known strangers, she loved her own home.

She closed the door and looked at her small room.

A small elegant vanity desk with a flip top that hid a large mirror and her makeup stood under the window. To the left was a two-door wardrobe, which stored all her belongings, and next to it was the piano, a gift from her late Grandmother. The old bookcase left by her parents was in the right corner next to the window and something orange called "Recame," a sofa bed, which Victoria and her sister shared for many years, stood along the right wall. A piano stool and one chair completed the furnishing; it was all that room could accommodate.

Victoria was about to pull out a book when suddenly she noticed a piece of paper with an address on the table. She remembered running into her school teacher Mrs. Levin last week and her surprising invitation to a holiday dinner.

Mrs. Levin taught history for years. In the middle school, it was ancient, and world history and Victoria loved it. However, by high school, History of the Communist Party of Soviet Union was not among her favorite subjects. She finished school almost six years ago, and she saw her teachers only at the annual reunion.

When she met Mrs. Levin on the street, she did not expect the invitation for dinner. "Maybe she invited me because she is Jewish and I was the only Jewish girl in her class," contemplated Victoria. Not that it mattered to her; she did not feel she was any different. In the school, she had one single advantage; her Dad returned home alive from the war. Only two other kids in her class had fathers who survived the war. The rest lived with his or her mothers and resented anyone who had alive male in the family, even an uncle or a grandfather.

"Hmmm," she suddenly felt a hungry roar in her stomach and remembered the smiling face of Mrs. Levin. "Dinner is not such a bad idea." She looked at the address and saw that the teacher lived only two blocks away. "The book could wait," decided Victoria. "The holiday dinner and the company would be good for me, especially after this stupid blind date."

Then, she remembered the boots. Last summer she had begged her Dad for two hours to give her money for the new boots, and she stood in line for another four hours to get these, still-in-the-box boots. She was dying to wear them, and now she had a reason.

"What a great opportunity to ventilate my boots," she smiled.

She coated her lips with lipstick, took an enamored look at her feet now encased in the tall, stylish boots that cost more than a physician's salary and walked out into the early dusk of the familiar city.

Cold November wind tossed her hair and Victoria wrapped her scarf and coat tightly around her; she was late.

She rang one of the six buttons on the door and heard the bell somewhere in the distance. A drunken man in a torn sweater opened the door and silently pointed to one of the doors in a dark hallway. There were piles of coats, bikes, and shoes under every door. The smell of food floated in the air.

The large holiday table was too big for the small room. Plump Mrs. Levin hovered around the table while her husband opened a bottle of vodka and her two daughters helped to serve. There was one space on the sofa, and everybody had to get up to allow Victoria to her seat. Mrs. Levin made the introductions, and suddenly Victoria realized why she was invited. Next to her on the sofa was a young man, Mrs. Levin's nephew.

She could almost imagine the matchmaker's pitch, "Victoria is young and single, she is about to graduate from the medical school, and she has her own place." Maybe she even shared the info about the family, "Her both parents are well-known doctors."

The conversation at the table, interrupted by Victoria's arrival, was about her neighbor on the sofa who had moved to the city recently and stayed with the relatives. Just then, Victoria realized that his name was Dmitry.

"Please, call me Dima," he said.

"Another one," thought Victoria bitterly. "They are all the same; they even have the same name"! She swallowed a shot of vodka and ate silently.

A great variety of Russian, Ukrainian, and Jewish dishes were on the table. The mandatory salad "Olivie", just the fancy French name for a mayonnaise covered mixture of potato, peas, and mortadella, herring, pickled tomatoes and cucumbers, boiled potatoes, and the crown of any holiday table, "holodnoye", which meant "cold" and was merely beef in gelatin, were on a proud display.

Meanwhile, Mrs. Levin was reciting Victoria's achievements at the school. It is turned out, she was Victoria Dad's patient for many years, and she could not say enough about "the great doctor and, by the way, a very handsome man."

Dima had dark curly hair and a warm smile. His shoulders were broad, and he looked stocky. He had a charming slightly high-pitched voice that made Victoria think about singing. He saw to her glass and plate being full, asked about medical school and her parents, told her a little about himself, and was smiley and soft-spoken. He seemed like a nice guy.

She did not know what made her hot, her warm new boots, a few shots of vodka, or his unceasing attention. Dmitry, Dima as his aunt called him, was clearly so taken by her that Victoria allowed herself to have a good time. She was pleased when he volunteered to walk her home. He was funny and old-fashioned; he did not ask to come to her apartment, but instead gallantly asked for her phone number and permission to call her.

That night Victoria could not sleep, trying to figure out when he would call; she felt young and beautiful.

The next day was a busy day at school. Between lectures, sitting next to Ellen, her best girlfriend, Victoria was about to burst with the news.

"He is not very tall but, definitely, taller than I. He has the cutest dark curly hair! He graduated from Leningrad Politech, and the famous Director of the Kiev Computer Institute invited him to work here. He is so smart and funny! He plays the violin! And his name is Dmitry, but he prefers Dima."

After spending a mere two hours with him at the holiday dinner, it seemed to her that she knew him all her life and she wanted to know so much more.

Ellen was puzzled, "Dima? I thought you did not like him. You said he was boring."

"This is a completely different Dima, Ellen," Victoria could not sit still. The lecture was just about to start, and she had so many things to tell her girlfriend.

"I know it is confusing. I said goodbye to the first Dima after walking with him on Vladimir Hill and then went to see my old school teacher, who introduced me to her nephew. By coincidence, his name was Dima as well. Although the name was the same, he was a very different man. He walked me home, took my phone number, and he promised to call."

Ellen knew Victoria since high school, and they were the best friends through the medical school, but she could not recall the last time Victoria was so excited about the date. "What if he does not call, Vika?"

Only family and close friends could call her Vika. She was born during the Second World War and was named Victoria for the victory. She was also born right after her Grandfather Volf died and, by the Jewish tradition, she was named after him as well. She was not just Vika; she was Victoria, for sure.

"You only saw him once, Victoria, do not get so excited," cautioned Ellen. She was a year older and much more practical in the dating game than her enthusiastic girlfriend. Victoria bit her lip and clenched her teeth; she was not ready to confess even to herself that she hoped he would call tonight.

After canceling a planned dinner with her parents, Victoria went straight home after school. She was not hungry; she was afraid to miss his call. Thirsty, she stopped in the kitchen to get a glass of water. Pregnant Lizzy Snisarenko was cooking dinner and wanted to know what Victoria did for the Holidays.

Any other day, Victoria would be happy to chat with Lizzy, but not today; the telephone could ring any minute, and the hallway to her room was long. She got a glass of water and hurried back. She put the glass inside her vanity desk and examined her face in the mirror.

"Maybe twenty-two is not that old yet," she hoped. "I probably do not look that bad if he asked for my phone number right away".

The telephone rang and startled Victoria; she jumped to pick up the handset and the flip top of the desk closed with a sharp crack. The large mirror fell on the glass of water and both shattered.

"Hi, Dima," said Victoria cheerfully.

She looked with the sheer horror at the drawer where shards of glass and mirror sparkled, mixed with water and her makeup. It was an ominous sign; she felt it deep inside.

"But I am not superstitious," she tried to be optimistic and not give in to old women's tales.

"I will be ready in ten minutes," she heard her own voice.

Her mirror was broken, and her hands were shaking, but he called, and that was all that mattered.

November wind blew without mercy making street lamps bow to it gracefully and submissively as they were walking the cold streets of Kiev. Light rain, mixed with the first snow of the season, cruelly attacked Dmitry's glasses. Every few minutes he had to take them off trying to clean them clumsily with his fluffy wet scarf.

"This is terrible," thought Victoria. "I did not wait all day for the cold shower."

Dima's black curly hair was glistening under the rain.

"Tea," finally broke down Victoria "I can make us a tea."

To have her own room was a big convenience, especially on a night like this.

His lips were warm and soft, and his hands were cold and gentle. They forgot about the tea; they did not need food. They were falling in love.

*****

Felix was driving west to our first stop in Ohio. The rain stopped, and the sun was low, so low that the visors did not help. He was holding his hand up, blocking the sun with his palm. The last rays of sunset warmed the car, and I shed my light sweater. Through his glowing hand, Felix took a sideways look at me.

"Are you dreaming of somewhere hot, Victoria?" he asked.

I did not answer. I was not dreaming. I was somewhere a long time ago on the cold winter, in the heat of the night, in a tiny room in Kiev. With Dima ...

DMITRY
KIEV, UKRAINE, THE 1960S

Dima was five months old when the war shattered his big Jewish family with aunts and uncles, cousins and grandparents. Men went to fight, and women and children were evacuated to hot and not very welcoming Asian parts of the Soviet Union, mainly to Uzbekistan. The life there was all about survival.

His father perished in the very beginning of the war when Russians retreated and carried heavy losses.

After the war, his mother Maria, a young teacher with two small boys, returned to bombed and ruined Kiev. However, years of German occupation taught Ukrainians how to deal with Jews, and there was no job in Kiev for a Jewish teacher. Her younger brother David lived in the Western Ukraine, where he was teaching mathematics in the high school, so she took her boys and moved west. They settled with their busy Mom and uncle in Chernivtsi, a small old town that kept its European roots.

David took full responsibility for bringing up his two nephews. The boys, only a year apart, were inseparable. They were honor students and gifted violin players. Between the math and music lessons, the brothers did not have much time for anything else. Their occasional street activities usually ended up in a complete fiasco. Victor, the older brother, was a fighter; he tried to protect his bookish nearsighted younger brother, but both of them were frequently beaten up by the local boys.

One hot summer day, the brothers went for a swim to the small local lake, and Victor started to sputter and swallowed water. Terrified Dima tried to swim to help him, and both of them almost drowned. They were saved by adult bystanders, and their Mom never allowed them near water again. For the rest of their lives, their swimming skills remained on the same level as on that fateful day on the lake.

Now they were grown up; Victor was a physician working in a Leningrad and Dmitry, prodigy physicist, just moved back to Kiev. His uncle Matvey, the younger brother of his late father, survived the war and had his own family. He and the rest of Dmitry's aunts and cousins all around the city were happy to have him, for a while anyway.

Confused with their limited hospitality, he shuttled his folding bed between his uncle's dining room and an apartment of the third cousin.

It was not by accident that his aunt invited Victoria for the holiday dinner. Everybody rejoiced when Dima and Victoria took no time to fall in love and settled in her small room on her orange "recame".

Dima's family, all aunts, uncles, and cousins loved Victoria. His Mother died a few years before, and her brother David married and had a little daughter. He played father to his nephews for a long time and now when they were on their own feet, he built his own family.

Victoria's parents were pleasantly surprised when she brought Dmitry to meet them for the first time. They liked his looks and demeanor and were surprised by how much Dmitry resembled Victoria's father. Both were stocky, broad-shouldered men, both had dark curly hair, although her Dad's was a bit gray, they both had a warm, lovely smile and both were madly in love with Victoria. They looked like father and son.

The young couple was busy all winter; they went to concerts and movies, visited relatives and spent time with Dmitry's friends at the famous Kiev Computers Institute where they were designing the first Russian computer "Promin" that meant "Ray" in the Ukrainian language.

The computer was a five-story building and Dima, and his friends spent most of their time working on it with their tsar and god Academician Glushkov. They were fun, and exciting people and Victoria was proud of her perfect boyfriend.

In January, Dima surprised everybody, when, during a family dinner with Victoria's parents, he got on one knee and asked her father for Victoria's hand.

Victoria's jaw dropped, her Mom smiled, and her Dad cried; he was finally getting a son. Only Dima remained calm, he got up and presented Victoria's Mom with a small bunch of violets, which he hid in his coat pocket.

She planned the wedding, bought her dresses and arranged the festivities. They traveled to Leningrad to meet Dima's brother and to purchase some delicacies, which were rare in Kiev.

To Victoria's surprise, Victor was not thrilled; she could see it right away. "I will come to the wedding, of course," he promised, but she did not find him warm or happy about his brother's upcoming marriage. She could not understand why; everybody they knew told them they were a perfect couple.

"Maybe he worried that you are marrying first, before him?" she asked Dima.

"Forget about it," he reassured, explaining Victor's behavior by some old rift in the family.

They were busy with their love, plans for the big wedding, Dima's work and Vika's upcoming graduation. There was no time for anything else.

It was a rainy day in March when the wedding party arrived at the Palace of Marriage. Red carpet on the Grand Staircase, the March by Mendelssohn, white dress, wedding pictures, family, and friends -it was a fantastic day, rain or no rain.

The reception in Victoria parents' home was the epitome of elegance with the best cognacs from her dad's bar, black caviar, pates, smoked fish, and cheeses. Her parents served the best for their older daughter, who made the right choice at the right time. They celebrated for two more days. Everybody came, a close and distant family from Charkov and Chernivtsi, Leningrad and Moscow, friends of her parents and Dima's friends, Victoria's school and medical school classmates, old neighbors and colleagues; everyone toasted the young couple.

They moved in with Vika's parents. Her room was too small for two, and by May, Victoria knew she was pregnant.

Contrary to common sense, her father was not happy.

"It is too early for the child," he tried to convince Victoria. "You have to write your dissertation, build a career, and secure your future." As usually, her dad was in charge, he knew better what was right for his daughter and his family.

However, Dima disagreed. He was convinced it would be a boy and he wanted his son. He was incredibly excited; he told everybody that he was going to be a father. He did not remember his father, of course, but he knew he would be a great Dad, loving, understanding, and friendly, the best Dad in the world, a real Dad, not a substitute relative.

The future was beautiful; no war on the horizon and Vika, his Victoria, was right here, next to him, getting her Diploma and showing off her slowly growing belly.

They were married for four months, exactly, when on the splendid sunny day in July, their son kicked Victoria for the first time. It was an incredible strong kick, and Dima's hand almost jumped when he felt it. They laughed and danced, happy to love each other and their child. They went outside on the balcony. The weather was hot, and the city smelled like melted asphalt and sweat.

"Go to the park, you need some fresh air," suggested Victoria's Mom.

They decided to visit friends who lived across the river, at the "dacha" on the beach. They took a small river shuttle and stood at the closed gate that would open when they docked on the other side.

In the middle of the river, looking at the ill-fitted and buckling gate, Victoria joked, "What would happen if the gate opens now, Dima? Would you love me enough to save me in the middle of the river? Are you a good enough swimmer?"

She knew she was a decent swimmer, and would not need help, but she remembered the story of Dima's childhood accident on the lake and teased her husband.

12

Dmitry was unfazed, "I will be OK until the help would come; on the other hand, you, Victoria, would be on your own. Do not challenge me!"

The gate did not break, and they safely crossed the river. They visited with Victoria's Mom's girlfriend Cecily, and everybody except for Dima and Victoria drank beer.

Dima could not wait. "Let's go to the beach to wash off the sweltering city," he hurried everybody. They changed and went to a nearby beach.

Before the war, it was a beautiful beach; however, Germans bombed the area mercilessly, and sinkholes from the bombs created a bad vortex and undercurrents. The locals called it "The Devil's Dance."

The name stuck, but nobody remembered or knew where the name came from or what was in the name. Officially, it was a public beach with some booths, docks for the boats and a public phone.

By the time they reach the water, the weather changed, and very light rain hit the beach.

"Hurry up," yelled Dmitry. He took Victoria's hand, and they ran into the river, competing with the coming rain. They were not quite up to their chests as Victoria suddenly lost her footing and saw that Dima too was going under the water. His dark curly hair slowly disappeared into the deep. She felt he was taking her with him, but his hand opened, and she swam up, gasping for air, choking and losing her strength by the second. Suddenly, she felt an oar jamming in her hands. She held it, and the boat took her a few feet to the beach. She was in shallow waters and felt the sand under her feet, but she could not let the oar go, her fists clenched the wood. She was alone, although people started to gather around her.

She was standing in the water up to her knees. She was afraid to go any further. Somebody called the rescue. Somebody called her parents. The rain was cold and strong now. She was still in her bathing suit.

It took the Rescue team with aqualungs forty minutes to find Dima in the crater from the old bomb, not quite ten feet from the beach. She lost her hope. She lost her love. She lost her husband. She was standing in the water of the river that just killed him. She stood there for an eternity. She just stood there, water by her knees, looking at the river. She was not frightened or sad. She only felt wet and numb. She and the baby, they just had to survive.

*****

This is your Dad

Dusk spread its veil as the sun set down somewhere on the West ahead of us. We were coming to Hubbard, Ohio and I tried to shake off old stories and old pains. It was my turn to drive. I watched the road.

Something was wrong with the landscape. Every experienced traveler, every "good wisher" advised us to skip the drive to Chicago or Ohio or anywhere to the mid of the country: "America –the beautiful starts after the first two days of the drive," they assured us. Nevertheless, we decided on taking the very long drive, about six hundred miles, for the first day. Instead of the bleak landscapes, they promised, an incredible abundance of greenery, endless vistas, mountains and the roads delivering a grand view at every turn greeted us. We were happy we did not listen to anybody.

We prepared for this long drive with plenty of munchies,

numerous wailing Russian CDs, and sunglasses. We expected boredom galore, but time flew as I was thinking about the past. Somewhere in the trunk, we stashed the reward, an 18-year-old Macallan for the end of the day. We survived our first big day, day one of the trip of our lives.

DAY 2, AUGUST 29
INDIANAPOLIS, IN
OMNI SEVERIN HOTEL

W e started with a good breakfast and a beautiful three-hundred-and-fifty-mile-drive mostly through Ohio and Indiana. Endless road constructions and yellow hard hats became a familiar part of the landscape, and we waved each time they flagged us to slow down. Truck drivers with their truly noble driving habits surprised and pleased us. They never stayed in the left lane; they used it for passing and immediately got back into the long line on the right; every time another truck in front of me moved to the right, I said thank you and blew driver a kiss. Felix thought that I lost my mind, but this drive was as elegant as ballroom dancing compared to driving in Massachusetts. Divine fields of biblical proportions and calm, heavenly lakes surrounded the highway.

Appropriate signs were asking us to "Avoid Hell" and "Repent", to "Trust the Jesus " or to go to the best Antique Malls that were an integral part of the scenery. As I drove, the sun gently warmed up my left shoulder. It felt like a kind hug from childhood when I could snuggle up with my Grandmother.

BABUSHKA
GORBASHOVKA, UKRAINE, THE 1920S

Her name was Yaha Elya Chaimovna, but everybody called her Asya Efimovna. Nobody could survive with the name Yaha at any time or any place in the Soviet Union. She was one of the seven children of Victoria's paternal great-grandfather Chaim. The family with five daughters and two sons lived in a small village Gorbashovka, not far from Berdichev.

Chaim had a machine that weaved fabric; one horse and his kids pulled giant wheel of the engine by walking around and around all day.

Two boys went to Cheder, the traditional Jewish school and the only school in Gorbashovka before the Revolution. Girls did not need an education; they would get married and take care of the family.

After Cheder, the brothers left the house and moved to the city to study at the University. When her younger sisters started to date, Asya decided it was time for her to get married. She was a beautiful girl with soft wavy golden brown hair, hidden under a shawl, huge brown eyes and a roman straight nose. She had full lips, not touched by lipstick and an incredible ability to memorize her brothers' textbooks.

Volf was a shy and quiet young man. At the old porcelain factory in the dusty outskirt of Gorbashovka, he meticulously painted beautiful delicate flowers on the most elegant cups and plates. He had no chance to withstand the iron will call Asya.

They were married, and in no time, she had produced two beautiful children, a boy, and a girl. They gave the boy the Hebrew name Eleazar that would later become Lenya, and Leonid in his passport. Later, his wife would call him diminutive and gentle Leonichka. They named the girl Mila. Her mother and her husband would call her Milochka ("lovely"). Quiet Volf painted his flowers and did not interfere with Asya's rule.

This morning, Lenya was proud when his Grandfather trusted him, a little seven-year-old boy, to buy lard for greasing the weaving machine.

He clutched a few coins in his left fist and ran to the market. Asya caught him when he came back; she wanted to see what her little mischief brought back from the market. In the clean cloth was a piece of lard covered with coarse salt.

"O, my god," Asya rose her hands in bewilderment.

"Why, in the world, did you buy lard with salt on it? How would your Grandfather grease his machine with it?" She took scared Lenya to her dad.

Babushka

The Grandfather looked at the boy, "I told you that I needed the lard to grease my machine, Eleazar." He always called everyone in the family by their Hebrew names; the Revolution with its new rules did not impress old Chaim Yevnin.

"I know," Lenya loved his Zeide; he was afraid to upset him. "Remember, you always told me that salt was very expensive. At the market, a piece of lard cost the same as a piece of lard with salt on it, so I decided it was a better buy."

He almost cried by then, but grandfather lifted him on his knee and smiled.

"I always knew you are a very smart boy, Eleazar. Thank you for the lard, it would be fine. Just always remember to use your head."

"Mom, mom, I did fine, and Zeide called me a smart boy," proud Lenya was happy with his first financial decision.

The aroma of food cooking on a wood burning stove floated over a big dusty yard.

Asya with her husband and kids still lived with her parents in a big house in the back of the yard. During hot Ukrainian summers, Asya cooked on the outside stove, and the whole family gathered for dinner at the long table in the middle of the only green patch of grass in front of the house. In the left corner of the yard was a small shack that everybody grandly called "the stable." It housed the one horse, who worked all day turning the wheel.

The electrification did not reach the outskirts of the town where the big family lived in the sprawling house.

Every evening, Lenya had to take the horse to a nearby meadow. There, while the horse grazed, he could play with his friends. After the horse had her dinner, the boy had to take her back to the "stable." That was the time the family would have their dinner as well.

The sun was setting down, and kids were about to go home when Lenya's friend Petro wanted to ride the horse.

"No way," said Lenya. He was responsible beyond his age, even if the part of this responsibility was based on the fear of his big and tall grandfather. "You are too big for the horse."

"If you are so small why do not you ride the horse?" challenged Petro. The other boys laughed looking at tall, lanky Lenya and short, plump Petro.

"I will," angry Lenya got on the horse with no saddle and no stirrups. He hit the sunken sides of the horse with his bare heels and stirred the tired old horse on the path home. His friends yelled and whistled, and somebody slapped the horse, which remembered her way back, but all of a sudden forgot how old she was.

The low sun was blinding Lenya when the horse galloped into the yard at full speed. She lifted her front legs and dropped Lenya in the dust right before she got to the stable. There was almost no space between the doorframe and the horse's head. If Lenya were still up on the horse, he would lose his head flying full speed into the doorframe.

He was sitting in the dust swallowing his tears while at the dinner table, the whole family watched first in horror and then with smiles his misadventure. "Headless Horseman" was not Lenya's favorite book and for the rest of his life, he was afraid of horses.

All the five sisters got married and left the dusty Gorbashovka. Their mother and father Chaim were long gone; only Asya and Volf stayed behind in the family house.

*****

I am not a good liar! I am not going to lie that after we drove three hundred and fifty miles, we ran around to see every monument and every museum of a very beautiful Indianapolis, but we did our share.

The city looked spectacular from the car and even better on foot. We were staying in the elegant downtown hotel right in the very center of everything, including impressive monuments, museums, and well-known restaurants. Our hotel was connected to the lovely mall by the walking bridge, and we took a stroll. In a small store, Felix bought my favorite, hard to find perfume. Our golden anniversary was still a few days away, but we both were excited by the drive, our sexy hotel suite, unknown city and a real "date night." We dined at the famous Harry and Izzy's Restaurant, indulged in the enormous local 100% Black Angus steak and returned to our suite for the night.

Years before, I would try to lure my husband to bed; instead, now I was on the computer to "google" Indianapolis. In my nightly blog, I wanted to give a grand historical narrative of the city, however, thought better of it and advised my readers to google the history of Indianapolis themselves. Felix was still watching the news, and I had a plush bed all to myself.

DAY 3, AUGUST 30
INDIANAPOLIS, IN - ST. LOUIS, MS
HAMPTONS INN

"A beached whale is a whale that has stranded itself on land." That is what we were exactly, "beached" on the freshly made bed in our hotel room in the glorious city of Saint Louis, MO.

I felt bad for my car delivering us here in about hundred-degree heat. Even with the air conditioner blasting, we were hot all the way from Indianapolis; the area had not seen such a scorcher at the end of August since nineteen fifty-three.

We settled in our cool room with a view of the famous St. Louis arch, set the temperature to sixty-eight and spent most of the afternoon under the blanket. The Hamptons Inn was right in the middle of downtown, but there were no people on the hot streets of St Louis this Friday afternoon before the holiday weekend.

I remembered the old song about St. Lois and listened to the oozing saxophone that played the old tune in my head. I had many fun plans for this evening on the town, but the town looked deserted from our tenth-floor window.

Exhausted by the drive and heat, Felix was fast asleep. His breathing was still labored after pneumonia, and I felt a pang of guilt for dragging him onto this adventure so soon after being seriously ill.

Tomorrow, we will drive to Kansas City and stay there for

three days. There would be a family wedding and reunions with relatives and friends.

I closed my eyes and saw my beloved Babushka.

BABUSHKA
UZBEKISTAN, THE 1940S

She was only in her late forties when they met for the first time, but Victoria always remembered her as an old woman. Babushka was very thin and short because of a slight bend. She always wore a dark dress with a white collar and an old stretched cardigan on the top; her stockings and shoes were black. In her age, she was still beautiful with this classy, refined aura about her. She was not the woman to be rude with or to yell at; she was always collected and calm; she was in charge.

Asya was never sick, she never complained, she disregarded any aches, pains or signs of aging. She was always ready to help, to get, to fight for her children and grandchildren. She was a worrier.

WWII was raging all over the Soviet Union. Asya's son, Lenya, who she adored, was a doctor, a head of a large military hospital. His wife Sarra, his tall and beautiful medical school sweetheart, fought by his side as a surgeon. Unexpectedly, in the midst of the war, they found out she was pregnant.

Sarra's family was evacuated to Kuybyshev, the city on Volga –river, and Lenya decided that Kuybyshev would be a right place for his wife to deliver the baby. He settled his wife with her Mom and rushed off to check on his parents evacuated to Uzbekistan. He had only a few days before returning to the front.

The presents for his family filled the whole suitcase, food, food and more food; everybody knew that life in evacuation was bleak and hungry. Rations for the doctors and wounded soldiers were miserable, but Lenya always managed to get some food from the locals in exchange for medical help.

Asya was beaming with joy and pride. "Look at my son, just look at him," she wanted to scream into every face. "Look at this tall, handsome Officer! Not only he came to visit his family, but he also brought the food!"

Volf was quietly smiling while Asya cooked up a storm. The dinner was all Lenya's favorite dishes: sweet and sour stew, gefilte fish and honey cake. Lenya insisted on inviting the neighbors; his Mother was a great cook. Besides, everybody was anxious to hear news from the front.

It was a beautiful spring evening in the southern Republic of Uzbekistan, although one could already see the signs of an early drought in the wilted greenery. After the dinner, Asya cleaned the table and had a lengthy, much after midnight, conversation with her favorite son. They both loved these rare special times between them.

She was up for hours, cooking breakfast, washing the linens and laying the table outside in the backyard when Lenya returned from the morning walk. The world without bombs and shots was incredibly quiet, and for the first time in two years, he enjoyed his leisure morning.

"Leonichka," the diminutive from Lenya sounded like a song to him. "Can you, please, go to see why your Father is not up yet?"

"All your neighbors are pleased; they all thanked me for dinner, as if I cooked it, Mom," reported Lenya. He hugged and picked up his Mom; she was always thin, but now she weighted like a child.

"Stop it, Leonichka, please! Better, go wake up your Father; he never sleeps so late!"

"It's not that late, Mom. Let him sleep a bit later," Lenya vouched for his Dad, but Asya insisted; breakfast was almost ready.

Quiet and kind Volf had never changed, even in the death he was the same. He died the way he lived, in his sleep, not to disturb or inconvenience anyone. Lenya, the doctor, understood what happened right away, but Lenya, the son, was crushed by the grief.

He buried his Father later that day; he had to return to the Army. He could not find anybody to dig the grave. The local Uzbeks, even after a very sumptuous dinner, would not help evacuees. He dug his father's grave, and dry, dusty earth crawled into his nostrils, throat, and lungs. He felt and tasted this dust for a long time. Volf's death devastated him, and he felt guilty leaving his Mom and sister alone, without any help, but he had to return. To his wife. To his hospital. To the war.

Next month, in the middle of the brutal and unrelenting war, Lenya named his first-born daughter "Victoria" for his late father Volf and for so much wished victory in the Great War. Only then, he could breathe again.

BABUSHKA
KIEV, UKRAINE, THE 1940S

T he war ended on Victoria's second birthday, and the family returned to Kiev. Sarra's family stayed in Kuybyshev. Her Mom Clara and Sarra's younger sister Magda worked at the military plant, and Sarra's brother Zack was still in school.

There were three youth organizations in the Soviet Union preparing children as young as seven- year- old to be the real communists. They remained Octobrists until the age of nine when during a special ceremony they were accepted to be the Pioneers. They were continuously trained and brainwashed with the communist propaganda. At the age of fourteen until twenty-eight, most of them continued into Komsomol, the reserve of young ready-made communists. Almost every schoolchild and student in the Soviet Union belonged to these organizations.

Before the war, while studying in the medical school, Lenya was a Komsomol Secretary at the liquor producing plant and his family occupied two rooms in the drab five-story brick building owned by the plant. Returning from the war with his family, Lenya found his two-room- apartment taken. He could not find even one small room vacant in the building. They were among many families returning after years of war and looking for a roof above their heads, however, in the bombed and destroyed city every available living space was taken, mostly by the people who stayed in the town during the German occupation.

Tired and desperate Asya sat down in the middle of a small communal kitchen to rest for a second. Three women cooked something on a massive Russian stove in the corner.

It was a rainy day, and the family had nowhere to go. Lenya looked at his thin, tired Mother, his wife holding their little girl and pulled out his gun.

"Take your pots and get out of here. I am taking this room for my family. You can cook in your rooms," he aimed the gun at the women.

Scared, they scurried off with their pots and Lenya closed the door. They settled in this hundred-square-foot communal kitchen, listening to constant threats and screams of the neighbors.

Two days after the Army Major seized the kitchen, the director of the plant Tovarisch Podobed showed up at the door. He wanted to restore the order. Not that he offered to return the two-room apartment to its lawful owner; he suggested that major, who spent four years on the battlefront, should take his Jewish family somewhere else. Apparently, he had not seen an enraged Lenya before.

Victoria did not remember the actual fall of the Director from the third-floor staircase, but she saw her Babushka later, quietly drowning Lenya's gun in the communal toilet.

They lived in this tiny room, the former communal kitchen, for years. The room was so small that Asya slept on a thin blanket under the table, a small wooden chest was Victoria's bed, and her parents slept on the single bed Lenya found among the ruins next door. Lenya's sister Mila was sleeping on a small folding bed, and when it was open at night, nobody could walk by or make it to the toilet in the hallway.

Asya and young Mila survived in Uzbekistan, alone among strangers far from home; now under her Mom's sleepless eye, Mila graduated from the dental school and was about to marry a military doctor.

In the cold, starving after war Kiev, Asya dealt with an impossible task of planning the wedding.

"After the wedding," she would say dreamily, "I am going to sleep on Milochka's folding bed, and my blanket would go back on the bed where it belonged from the beginning."

One floor below was a spectacular two-room apartment with its own kitchen, long hallway and a bathroom. Victoria, who still had to use a night pot as not to take up the bathroom in case the neighbors would need it at night, never saw such a beautiful place. She was in awe of the sheer size of the rooms, furniture, and toilet. Another attraction of this apartment, occupied by the liquor plant's accountant Tovarisch Lipovetsky and his family, was the lacquered piano gleaming with ivories in the big main room.

The Lipovetsky's daughter Talla was Victoria's girlfriend. She was four years older than Victoria, a beautiful girl with two thick and long wheat color braids that reached below her waist.

Once a week, the music teacher Polina came to teach Talla to play the piano. She was a tired single woman, and she allowed Victoria to sit quietly on the chair under the window during the lessons.

For an hour, Victoria was afraid to breathe; she could smell the sound; she could inhale it, and she held her breath afraid to lose even one beautiful note. She could just touch the sideboard and feel the soft voice of the piano.

"Now I will be the teacher," Talla offered after Polina said her good-bye.

"Victoria, please do not play with the turning stool and be a good student." Talla was not only good at imitating her teacher; she was excellent in teaching; so good that soon Victoria could play an old military song "Polyushko-Pole" (Field, the lovely field).

She played it with such enthusiasm on and on again, singing about Red Army heroes that eventually her Babushka was summoned to pick her up.

Asya was the best friend with the accountant's mom Tina and his wife, Cecily. Tina looked like Asya's twin, thin and bent and she too, like Asya, took care of her family. They were evacuated like everybody else; however, her son was not in the army, and they lived together in the big southern city where her son and daughter-in-law worked. When they returned to Kiev, her son got this position at the plant, and their awesome apartment was a part of the deal.

Tina and Cecily offered their apartment for Mila's wedding. They convinced proud Asya that it would be their honor to have a Jewish wedding under the Chuppah at their place. Vika helped her grandmother to attach an embroidered velour tablecloth, part of Asya's own dowry, to four handmade wooden poles for the Chuppah. Grandma and Tina cooked up a storm in Tina's private kitchen with Talla and Vika running around, getting the first bite of such delicacies as a boiled potato, gefilte fish, and kasha with varnichkes.

Both girls got new dresses for the wedding.

Victoria's dress was a present from her Father's patient Tatiana Anisimovna. She was a young, big and soft woman with round face, sad smile and small knot of hair on the back of her head. She had progressive kidney failure, and her skin was pale and pasty. Her husband returned from the war a General only to find his wife sick with no hope to survive her disease, never mind to have a child. Tatiana showered Victoria with all her unspent love.

She was a great cook, and with her husband's combat ration, she often invited her young doctor with his family for lavish dinners. She taught Victoria the Ukrainian language and laughed heartily as the young girl tried to transform Russian words into Ukrainian.

"Aunty Tanya, Aunty Tanya, I understood," chirped Victoria. "You just change all "a"s to "e"s! Right?"

Aunty Tanya laughed with delight; she loved her doctor and his funny daughter. Suddenly, she got an idea.

In the city with bombed, crumbling buildings, closed stores, hunger and unthinkable poverty, she planned a surprise for her little friend.

It was a real undertaking; first, Tatiana seduced her husband, the decorated air force General to get her a parachute.

"Are you going to jump, Tanechka? What did I do?" teased the young General happy to fulfill his wife's any wish. When the beautiful white silk with the help of Tatiana's scissors and thread became a girl's dress, she embroidered the bottom and the sleeves with piercing blue cornflowers.

Victoria could not let her hands go. The warm neck of Aunty Tanya smelled like bread and flowers. She loved this woman so much. She never saw such a beautiful dress and Aunty Tanya said it was hers! Even Babushka cried when she saw her "maidele" in the new dress.

The dress

The big room with a tall window, high ceiling and beautiful piano, all courtesy of Babushka's neighbors, was way too small for the real Jewish wedding with Chuppah and music. Rabbi blessed the newlyweds standing under Asya's regal red tablecloth with gold monograms; Igor, the younger brother of Lenya's friend Jack, played the accordion and the food was incredible. Victoria had never seen so many people together. The relatives she had never known, friends of Mila and her parents came in their best pre-war attire; they ate, drank, sang "Lomir Ale", and danced "freilex". This was the first bright ray of peace and happiness, the first morsel of their faith and culture and everybody was happy in spite of small quarters, poverty and the gloom of anti-Semitism.

After the wedding, the family returned to live with Babushka in their three by three meters former communal kitchen. The newlyweds, Mila and her husband, a military dentist, were sent to serve in White Russia.

Sarra was finishing medical school and her younger brother, Victoria's uncle Zack, came from Kuybyshev to study at the Architecture Institute. He took Mila's bed, and Babushka still slept on the blanket under the table.

Every day Zack walked Victoria to kindergarten and back. Twice a day, on their way, they stopped in front of the bakery where Sofa, mother of Victoria's girlfriend Lina, was a saleswoman. Both of them were always hungry; it was almost painful to look at the plastic challah and bagels hung on the long strings in the bakery window.

"When I grew up I will be working here," proudly promised Victoria. "We will have plenty of bread, and every morning I will get you a fresh bublik, Zack. Bublik was just a hard, crunchy bagel.

While everybody worked or was in school and Babushka was busy cooking the dinner, Victoria was outside, free to play. There was plenty of excitement on the streets of the city; dusty columns of German prisoners of the war moved slowly by the bombed buildings, occasional horse-drawn-cart rattled by the street, trucks entered and exited the liquor plant.

Their building on Kudriavskaya Street, which meant "curly", was still the same, although plant recently built a new dormitory for the workers and opened a diner in the basement. Now the whole building smelled of sour borsch and potato peels.

In the long hallway of the apartment dimly lit with a small bulb, encased in the iron grate, everybody cooked now on the primus (kerosene stove). Small yellow and blue flames of this amazing invention lighted up the meager life like fireworks.

In the bad weather, Vika and her friends played on the wide windowsill between the second and the third floor at the huge window looking at the bleak industrial landscape of the liquor plant. In her nightmares, Vika was always falling from this windowsill back into the stairwell. She would wake up scared with wet patches of tears on her cheeks.

"You are growing, my girl," Babushka would try to calm her down.

Only years later, after her Grandmother Asya passed away and Victoria returned to visit one of the neighbors, she realized, that the windowsill was only a few inches high.

By the time Vika was ready for school, her parents were expecting another child and, although her Dad adored his tomboy daughter, this time he hoped for a real son.

He got a new job, and the family moved to a new apartment. It still was just one room, but they shared a bathtub, a toilet and a kitchen with only one other family.

Babushka stayed behind. She lived alone in her small room now mostly filled with the memories. She had the narrow single bed all to herself, primus that puffed happily on the wooden crate in the hallway and nobody to feed.

The newlywed Mila was expecting a baby. Babushka planned to take a train in the spring when the baby was due, and trains would be warmer.

The telephone on the wall rang on the snowy February morning; the news was horrible; Mila slipped on ice and was in premature labor.

The next day, in the heart of winter, Babushka took a cold train through Ukraine to the remote village in White Russia where Mila delivered a very premature boy.

"This baby is not-viable," was the gruesome verdict by the village doctor. He did not know Asya. For the long three months, while Mila was recuperating from the terrible delivery and shock, Babushka was the baby's incubator. She carried him constantly on her chest wrapped in the endless layers of gauze and cotton, she fed him from the dropper and when she finally came back to Kiev in June, she was all smiles. She saved her grandson's life and now she was back to take care of her granddaughter.

Victoria was about six when Babushka took her to "banya", the communal bathhouse. Individual shower cabins were more expensive, and Babushka bought tickets to public women's room with stone benches. Wall faucets were spewing hot water on the slippery tiled floor. With their tickets, they each got a tin basin, and Grandma filled them with hot water to wash Vika's short hair.

Victoria always wanted long braids, but lice was a terrible problem in the city stricken by poverty, lack of hygiene and medications. Long hair was not permitted at schools.

Babushka had a large dark rectangular piece of coarse soap, and after Victoria's hair was clean, Babushka let her stand in the basin, where she soaped her and then poured warm water all over her.

Steam was rising in the large room where next to them ten or fifteen women were washing themselves and their children in the similar basins or on the slimy stone benches. The floor was slippery, everybody was naked and wet, and Victoria felt woozy and weak in the hot fog.

When she fainted, everybody panicked; however, her Babushka never lost her cool. She dumped a full washbowl of icy water on green- looking Victoria, dried her up with a towel and brought her back home.

She never took Victoria to the banya again.

Hot steam was easy to blame, but that was not the reason. Victoria was scared when next to her own feet on the tiled floor she saw her grandmother's feet, and they were terrifying! Her toes, like the roots of an old tree, were all bent and coming on the top of each other, together, they formed wide, thick claws at the end of her feet. For the rest of her life, Victoria never forgot those feet on the slippery floor of the bathhouse. They scared little Victoria, and only later, she understood why her Grandmother wore two sizes larger men's shoes. She had never known what came first, poorly fit shoes or the disfigured toes.

BABUSHKA
KIEV, UKRAINE, THE 1960S

The big city that was rising from the ashes like the magic Phoenix. Trams and trolleys connected remote suburbs, stores were selling food and clothes, children were playing at the playgrounds, theaters were performing, and Victoria was a schoolgirl. Lenya with his family lived in another part of the city, however, in spite of the distance, Babushka was still watching over Victoria.

She was always arguing with Vika's parents about "the girl". They should pay more attention to "the girl". They should dress "the girl" better. Sometime in the heat of the argument, Asya spoke Yiddish to Lenya.

It was killing curious Victoria that she could not understand what adults were talking about. "Babushka, please, teach me Yiddish," she pleaded with uncompromising Asya.

"It's not good for a young pioneer to speak Yiddish" Asya was curt. Then she was back to her usual tune. They should teach "the girl" to play a piano.

It did not matter to her that in one room, where they all lived, was no place for a piano. In this room after the dinner, Lenya was seeing his private patients; at night, they all slept there and in the morning for a short time between family breakfast and the time Lenya had to leave for work, he saw his patients again.

The room was furnished with a narrow bed, small desk, table with chairs, built-in bookcase and a cot. They were family of five by now; Victoria had a new sister Ella who slept in her crib and Aunt Rose, Sarra's aunt who helped with a newborn Ella and slept on the folding bed opened at night. Nevertheless, Babushka was not willing to discuss with anybody, even with her son, her decision to buy a piano for her favorite granddaughter.

Lenya was a great doctor and in spite of his growing practice and popularity, and mainly because of it, he lived in permanent fear. Private practice, like everything else private, was illegal and punishable. His family well being depended on the loose tongues, word of mouth or a simple complaint from the neighbor.

On the positive note, there were no pianos to buy. The list of people wanting to buy pianos was a mile long; one would have to wait for years for the set of gleaming keys. However, this small problem would not stop Babushka.

Year after year, this loving woman got up before sunrise, put on her regular large black shoes with shoelaces and once a week, rain or shine, sun or snow, went to validate her place in the long line at the door of the furniture store. Where did she get the money? How did she manage to travel that early in the morning to the only store that sold pianos to confirm her place in line? She did. And eventually, she got a piano for Victoria.

It was a brand new shiny black lacquered piano named "Chernigov". The name of a small town with the only piano factory in Ukraine was written in gold letters under the top.

By the time Victoria got her piano, the family had moved to another "communal apartment", but this time they had two rooms, sharing all the conveniences with two other families.

Finally, the piano took its commanding place between the new breakfront and the sofa bed. In the room, that was simultaneously family/dining/living/children room, Vika gloriously drummed "Polyushko, pole" on her very own piano, the gift from her Babushka.

Both girls were taking music lessons and soon Victoria could play all Asya's favorite songs. An impossible pride and satisfaction lighted up Babushka's aging face when Victoria was playing.

Asya was still a matriarch of her extended family. Her brothers and sisters lived in the different Russian and Ukrainian cities but kept in touch, visiting and corresponding.

Babushka remembered all the important days, anniversaries and birthdays of her siblings, their children, and all the spouses. She was "a mensch" in the family, loved and respected and everyone, including her educated and successful brothers, sought her advice and approval.

She was a guest of honor at the weddings and family celebrations. The younger generation brought their spouses-to-be to Auntie Yaha for advice and permission. Her son was a pride of the family, and she was grooming her oldest granddaughter to reach the sky. Of course, Victoria had to play the piano!

*****

In my mind, I was still drumming "Polyushko, pole" on my old piano, when Felix turned and woke up. The third day was done, and we added two new states to our travel log. My neck was stiff and achy; was it from driving, from sitting at the computer writing my nightly blog or maybe my virtual piano playing made me stiff. Felix lightly massaged my neck and back, but slowly his hand grew heavy and found its resting place on my breast.

DAY 4, AUGUST 31
ST. LOUIS, MS - KANSAS CITY, KS
HILTON PRESIDENT

I t was already hot when we started early in the morning. In the traffic-free Saturday drive from St. Louis to Kansas City, I intended to refresh my husband's memory on who is who in the family, names of my cousins and their children, who and when and under what circumstances they met.

"Let's start from the beginning," I repeated for the twentieth time. "Felix, do you remember Lenya Junior? You had met him many times. His mom, Cecily, was a younger sister of my Babushka. Lenya is alive, and he lives now with his whole family in Kansas City."

LENYA JUNIOR
KHARKOV, UKRAINE, THE 1950S

T here were "Lenyas" galore in the family! Victoria had no idea why three out of the five Yevnins sisters, including Victoria's Babushka, named their sons Lenya. Did they, by Jewish tradition, name these boys after some dead ancestor, or just because Leonid was such a glorious name?

Asya's younger sister Cecily did good by the family measures. She married a very educated and intelligent, slightly older man.

Tall and handsome Moses had a bold head and assertive manners. He held a high position at work, and he moved his family to one of the big Ukrainian cities, Kharkov.

Babushka always kept a photo of her just married younger sister in her room. Cecily and Moses were photographed at a famous Russian resort; looking very elegant, wearing hats and matching oversized gray dusters.

Victoria remembered visiting Aunt Cecily with her grandmother. She loved everything, the apartment, the clothes, and a different lifestyle. She tried Cecily's high heels, so different from her Babushka's shoes and to the delight of the sisters walked all day in these incredibly beautiful but, oh, so big for her, shoes.

Cecily's son Lenya was younger than his first cousin, and when the sisters talked about their children, they called them "Lenya Senior" and "Lenya Junior". Sometime Cecily called her son Ilusha or Ilya; however, it seemed that just to say "Lenya" was a pleasure for both women.

No wonder Victoria was thrilled when, along with her parents and Babushka, she was invited to Lenya Junior's wedding.

It was a grand affair with a lot of people and music. Victoria remembered a night train to Kharkov and a very long wedding table, where she sat with her Babushka.

Both Lenyas were successful, both were married with children, and both stayed close to their mothers, who they adored. They looked very much alike, and they were more than first cousins, they were good friends who celebrated and mourned together.

Two Lenyas

They would get together in Kiev, Kharkov or Moscow, where another sister and two younger brothers put the anchor; they drank Russian vodka, ate Jewish food, danced the foxtrot and tango and sang traditional Yiddish song "Lomir Ale". The big family was scattered in Russia and Ukraine, but they would get together, talk about the war and the children, count their losses and teach the next generation to love, respect and cherish the family.

When Victoria was already married, she went to Lenya Junior's children weddings. By then, she knew them well, the parents and grandparents were still alive, and they kept the family traditions and ties.

*****

"The Kharkov branch of the family lives now in Kansas," I was about to repeat the family history to Felix. However, he chuckled smartly, "Is not that where we are going?"

"Oh, come on, Felix, have mercy! I still remember Lenya's wedding, and it was so long ago. I danced with my dad standing on the top of his shoes. I went to the weddings of Lenya's son and his beautiful daughter when we all still lived in Ukraine, and now his granddaughter is getting married."

"How many grandchildren does he have?" smiled Felix. "I am just thinking how many more weddings we would have to attend. I remember driving to his grandson's wedding about 4-5 years ago."

"Stop that, please!" I knew he was just kidding. I was proud that here, in the middle of America, my family tree had strong roots and beautiful flowers.

"You loved his Grandson's wedding, Felix. Now they have a little boy Jack, Lenya's first American-born Great-Grandson".

"I cannot believe you are so old Victoria," joked Felix. Obviously, he felt better in warm and sunny Kansas. "You know, when you are present at the weddings of three generations of the family, you are not just a guest anymore. You are an institution. I am not sure I want to be married to one".

I did not answer. I was happy to carry my family's duty

35

and to attend this wedding. I felt I was there for my own family. I carried the shield and the banner of the great clan of my Babushka's siblings, their children, and grandchildren. They were an intelligent, educated and handsome family. They survived the Revolution, the Great War and the rabid anti-Semitism of the Soviets. Finally, they uprooted the tree and replanted it in America, and it brought beautiful fruits.

We were driving on old route 66. We tried to see signs of a bygone era but saw only an incredible number of billboards.

"So much space, so few people," noticed Felix suddenly. "So different from Shanghai."

"Why did you think of Shanghai? " I looked at him, surprised.

"Was not it in Shanghai when we decided to travel cross-country one day and then we almost blew up the ship? It happened right after I quit smoking."

It was raining dogs and cats in Shanghai, one of the ports on our Southeast Asia cruise. In the pouring rain, we walked the main street, buying three- dollar- umbrellas sold on every corner.

"I bet they arranged for this, just to sell their umbrellas!" grumbled Felix. However, Chinese umbrellas were not a match to this downpour, and we had broken all three of them on our walk.

We were coming back to the port when a wrinkled old man on a bicycle stopped us at the entrance.

"Souvenir lighter, please, mister, buy the souvenir." Felix was already examining a large red lighter with a portrait of Mao.

"You just quit smoking," I reminded. "Why do you need a lighter, Felix?"

He clicked the lighter, and the sound of Chinese anthem poured over the port. The seller stopped the loud and forceful music with trembling hands and jumped on his bike ready to leave.

"Dima might like this," Felix always looked for a souvenir for our older son.

The frightened man looked around and pleaded "One dollar, please, give me a dollar." As if on command, both Felix and I put our right hands in our pockets, extracted one-dollar bills and simultaneously gave them to the seller. His bike sprayed us with dirty water from a puddle, as he sprinted out of the port, like a rocket, while the Chinese anthem played loudly in Felix's hand.

We passed port and ship securities with no problems, but back in our stateroom, we looked at the lighter again.

"It was a great bargain," reveled Felix. "Did you see how fast he rode away?"

"If it is too good to be true it is probably not good," I still had problems translating the Russian proverbs to English. "What if we brought a bomb on the ship?" I panicked, "Let's get rid of it, we can throw it overboard."

Felix would have none of it. We went to a dinner at the ship restaurant and all evening I was waiting for a blast from our room.

Next morning on our balcony, alive and well, we watched sunny Shanghai. The sprouting city below looked like an anthill. Hundreds of skyscrapers created an impressive picture of the modern city that housed thousands of tall cranes, the most cranes in the one city in the world.

Below us, on the pier, tourists assembled for the planned tour of old Shanghai. We rushed from the ship to catch our tour bus. Our driver and tour guide loaded a few wheelchairs.

Ancient core of the Old downtown was busy with the people. The sun finally shone over China, and the place was swarming with tourists, sellers of Chinese souvenirs, street jugglers, children, and workers in yellow construction hats. Walking in this constantly moving and unyielding crowd was impossible. We watched an elderly couple, our fellow passengers from the ship, navigating their wheelchairs in the

Shanghai heat and crowd, and we tried to rethink our plans to travel the world.

"We should travel far and away while we are still young and healthy before we would need wheelchairs," I created a strategy on the spot.

"We would travel America when we are old and in need of wheelchair ramps," added my pessimist husband.

We kept the promise and traveled far and away for the next thirty years. Now, finally, on our long awaited adventure, the cross-country drive, we planned to celebrate.

By the afternoon, we had arrived in impressive Kansas City and checked in a very "old money" Hilton President.

The world is incredibly small. Our beautiful corner room had a spectacular "city of lights" view, courtesy of the young men at the reception. Not only did he recognize the fellow New Englanders, but he also was born in the hospital where I attended for the last thirty years and where my friend, the obstetrician, delivered him; and that helped us secure the great room.

In the real Kansas heatwave, we showered and rested. When the hotel shuttle came to take us to the rehearsal dinner, we were ready to roll.

The famous Kansas barbeque mentioned in the invitation was indeed that, incredible, however, our hearts were melted not by the enormous dinner or drinks. My cousins, second or third, (does not matter what number is attached to the word) were all there. The family, people, who I knew since childhood and with whom I shared ancestors. Lenya Junior was now old and sick, but still full of chutzpah. He was the patriarch of a multigenerational family of capable and talented children, grandchildren and great-grandchildren, and every one of them was ready to pick up the family banner. Lenya, his wife, my cousins and their families were delighted to see us, appreciated our four-day drive to get there and melted our hearts with all the attention and the love of real family. The shadows of my dad and babushka stood behind me, peering over my shoulder at the descendants of Cecily, amazed and proud of the one big family in the new land. And the wedding was coming tomorrow.

DAY 5, SEPTEMBER 1
KANSAS CITY, KS
HILTON PRESIDENT

My babushka would be very happy. I was having breakfast surrounded by the familiar faces of my second and third cousins and not so familiar faces of their significant others and children. Everybody was wearing a green tee-shirt, emblazoned with the family name, and just looking at the crowd I felt home.

Between coffee and bagels ("bubliki"), we traced our family ties, learned who is who and how we were all related. There is always a discrepancy in family ties between Russians and Americans. Here, in our relatively new land, only siblings of your parents are your aunts and uncles, their cousins are your cousins as well. In Russia, at the moment you crossed generational lines, they are all your aunts and uncles, not your cousins, which caused much confusion during international introductions.

After all the cousins and "uncles" were sorted out, Felix and I went to explore Kansas City with its glorious high-rises, green streets, markets, and cafes. We came back early; I had to get dressed for the wedding to measure up to my younger relatives and to uphold the family standards.

The wedding was spectacular! Not like the old times, not like the old country. The Chuppah was beautiful, nothing like the old tablecloth improvised by my grandmother. The gorgeous white roses streamed down four poles. The bride's gown was classy, and the whole ceremony was all about love and commitment. It was fabulous!

However, the greatest surprise came during the reception. As we all sat down at our prearranged tables, boasting spectacular white roses centerpieces, the bride asked her Grandfather, Lenya-Junior, to sing. He got up, still tall in his late eighties, his baseball cap hiding chemotherapy-induced baldness. "Lo mir al, e nanem, e nanem" the voice was powerfully loud and clear, and it brought back memories and shadows of the people long gone. They were standing with us now; the cousins, tall and handsome, with gentle waves of slightly grey hair, their incredible mothers, who guided them out of Gorbashovka to the big world, and the whole clan of my large, tightly knit family. They were standing side by side, shoulder to shoulder, singing this old Yiddish song, just as they sang it years and years ago at the family gatherings, weddings and Jewish holidays back in Kiev, Moscow and Kharkov. I saw them clearly.

THE FAMILY
MOSCOW, RUSSIA, THE 1960s

When they were young, everyone tried to leave the hot city at least for a few days and to come to the dacha in Malachovka, near Moscow in the summer. The house was big, and the long table was welcoming.

When Vika's dad and his cousin Lenya Junior, were visiting, dacha was full of life and laughter. They were young and happy; they survived the war, and they believed in the happy future.

Three young men: Lenya, Lenya-junior and babushka's sister Fanny son Lusik looked amazingly alike, like brothers. Their mothers had a very little resemblance, but their sons, all named Lenya, were tall, handsome men with dark wavy hair and beautiful kind and thoughtful eyes; they were smart, intelligent, educated young Jews with big ambitions and plans for a better life. They were very much alike. They all got along and had fun; they were family, and they loved each other.

On a cold wintery day, Victoria came to Moscow to introduce her groom Dmitry and the whole family gathered to greet them. Babushka's sister Aunty Fanny, who stayed mostly with her daughter Jenny now, cooked the holiday dinner. The family crystal, silverware and old family's recipes graced the table. All the dishes that Victoria thought only her Babushka knew how to cook were on the table: chopped herring and potato salad, chicken liver pate and gefilte fish, kasha with varnichky and sweet and sour stew. Compote from dry fruits and honey cake crowned the meal.

Babushka's two younger brothers Yasha and Abram, their adult children Inna and Lusik and, of course, Jenny all promised to come to the wedding.

"Everybody loved Dmitry," smiled Aunty Fanny happily when Victoria helped her to undress at night. Victoria and Dima planned to stay with their friends, however, Jenny would not hear of it.

"We are the family, and you will stay right here with us," Jenny was adamant. She was soft spoken with a shy smile and nearsighted eyes twinkling behind her incredibly thick glasses. She was determined she could manage a difficult task to settle six people in one room for the night; even if it meant to undress in turns and to send men to wait in the hallway while women were changing into their nightgowns.

"Aunty Fanny, you are still wearing a corset!" Victoria could not believe. "And the ties; they are all twisted and knotted."

"That is for you, my dear, to untie and undo," Fanny was smiling, "especially now that you got engaged. If you do not have the patience to undo the knot, you are not ready to get married. There is also your wedding present under my pillow. I am very sorry I would not be able to dance at your wedding, Victoria".

They kissed, and Victoria looked at the present. Wrapped in the linen napkin were three huge silver spoons and three silver forks. "Oh, my god" smiled Victoria, "they are fit to feed Gulliver."

"You are lucky the KGB did not find them when they dug our yard at the dacha," smiled Aunt Fanny. "These belonged to mine and your Babushka's grandfather, and he was a big man. Just like your Uncle Markus who is also his grandson."

There are no secrets in the family that would not be unearthed eventually. Aunt Fanny and her husband Uncle Markus also were cousins, and now Victoria realized where Jenny and Lusik's thick glasses came from; their parents were first cousins.

They all kept the promise and came to the wedding. They were one big family, no matter how far apart they lived.

*****

Lenya Junior was singing for his beautiful Granddaughter at her wedding. My old, sick uncle, who was fighting the fight of his life against cancer, sang "Lo mir al, e nanem, e nanem". He sang this old Yiddish song to over 200 guests at the elegant ballroom in the middle of Kansas, United States of America. There was no dry eye in the huge festive room. For me, it was a very powerful and sentimental night. Tomorrow will be another exciting day.

DAY 6, SEPTEMBER 2, LABOR DAY
KANSAS CITY, KS
HILTON PRESIDENT

Time flies when you travel. We were on the road for six days, three of them in Kansas. We already fell one hour behind and had to change the disc in our GPS system for the western United States, although we did not even start our big trip yet.

On the Labor Day morning, we shuttled between Missouri and Kansas to have breakfast at the elegant house of my cousin and then had a lunch and a tour of beautiful Kansas City with an old friend from Kiev.

We walked the exotic Country Club Plaza with spectacular fountains and expensive stores. The exhaustive heat cut down our sightseeing, and after saying goodbye to our friend, we caught a taxi back to the hotel. The taxi driver, a gorgeous native woman, was happy to show her town off to the New Englanders; she narrated the history and architecture of the city all the way back to the hotel.

No wonder, after all that, we overslept and skipped the dinner. We had a tea at the hotel and packed our bags for the real stuff, the drive up North to Nebraska tomorrow. Felix was still coughing and wanted to get to bed early, but I could not sleep, of course.

VOLODYA
KIEV, UKRAINE, THE 1970S

E very marriage is like an onion. Look at the beautifully shaped, sun colored, glowing dome that smells fresh, and you would have no clue what is waiting for you inside. Nothing bad happens as you peel a few layers of the skins. There are first dates, tender smiles, batting eyelashes, light flirt, and happiness.

More layers down lay lust and passion, blood boiling lovemaking and jealousy, children and home chores and your eyes started to tear.

To get to the core, you have to cut the onion as it bleeds its corrosive juice. Even made-in-heaven marriages have this deep layer of angry whispers, gnawing hate, and broken promises.

That is where Victoria stood now, on her second marriage, with two small children and near separation.

The Holiday season was in full swing, and she needed to have a plan. The New Year, the most important holiday in the atheistic Soviet Union, was approaching fast, in a mere two weeks. The old belief was that the whole year would be exactly the way you celebrated New Year.

If at the twelfth stroke of the Kremlin currants you kiss the right man, it would be your happy year. If you met it alone, with no music and friends, sulking in your nightgown and hating your reflection in the mirror, the whole year would be a complete waste.

The meeting was at her girlfriend's Inessa apartment on the ninth floor. They planned a big party for the New Year, an A-list of attendees, music, spirits, and food. However, it was all for nothing; they could plan all they wanted- there was no food in the local stores, especially before the holidays. Victoria pursed her lips upset about ruined plans for the party.

Inessa and her boyfriend Tolya, both professors of Mathematics in Kiev Polytech Institute, had good salaries and one of the largest apartments in the high-rise condominium building, where Victoria lived. They had a perfect place for a big party but no "connections" to get food for a party table.

"I do not know the guy, but one of the guests, a friend of a friend, has 'connections' and can get everything," boasted Inessa. "His name is Volodya."

As if on cue, the doorbell rang. "This is our man," said Inessa. Impeccably dressed, handsome, if a bit short, the man was not alone. A beautiful blond woman in a stylish white fox hat and a full-length fur coat was on his arm. Victoria smiled to herself, "A dumb blond wife is a perfect accessory for a powerful man." However, even she had to admit they were a good-looking couple.

The blue-eyed stranger, indeed, had all the "connections". He promised Inessa to get whatever she wanted for the New Year party.

Victoria was writing the lists, the guests, the menu, the alcohol and Volodya moved his chair next to Victoria. He knew what and where to buy, what to serve and how much food and drinks they would need.

"You are very good in planning the party," he complimented Victoria. "Are you sure you are a doctor?"

"With your help, the party will be a hit," smiled Victoria. Volodya's wife Alla did not take off her fur hat and did not participate in any of the planning confirming Victoria's initial impression of her.

They discussed the menu and shopping list when suddenly Volodya changed the subject. "I have an uncle in Israel, he left two years ago, and he is doing great. He was a dentist, and he got a job in Israel. The life is good there, and he is making more money. He is very happy and he encourages me to come to Israel. And you can bet I would leave eventually".

"Uyehat'" ("to leave") was a code word in Russian. Everybody understood why you wanted to leave the country. If you would be lucky to get permission to leave, you could decide later where to go. It did not matter, actually, where; the most important step was "to leave" and everybody wanted "uyehat'".

Suddenly the room fell silent. The subject was dangerous. One could dream quietly about immigration to Israel, preferably when alone in the middle of the night. Leaving the country was everyone's dream, but too much was at stake; it was an incredibly difficult and unpredictable endeavor. You could lose your job and never get permission to leave the country. You could get imprisoned; your family could lose their livelihood forever, and you would be branded a traitor and a renegade.

"Stop this conversation Volodya, stop it right now!" Alla suddenly got her voice. "This is not a conversation to start with the strangers." She was furious. "We are leaving." Alla nodded to everybody at the table, got her fur coat and drew Volodya out of the apartment. It was clear that he wanted to stay.

"Wow!" thought Victoria. "She does not look Jewish and, obviously, does not cherish the opportunity. "

"Too bad he is married," she murmured as the charmer and his wife were out of the door.

"You are so right," exclaimed Inessa. "Alla, the girl that came with him, did you notice, she is not his wife. She teaches the law at the University, and she hoped he would divorce his wife". She thought for a minute. "I think I had heard something about his marriage and some story behind it. Nevertheless, it did not prevent him from spending his time and his nights elsewhere".

Victoria was shocked. First, Volodya was married but not to Alla. Second, he was going to celebrate the New Year not home, but with "the other woman". Third, why did she feel irritated to learn that blond Alla was not so dumb; she was a lawyer?

Inessa noticed a mischievous smile on Victoria's lips.

"Please, Victoria, stay as far from this guy as you can. You should try to repair your own marriage. Felix is a good man and a good father, and it would be a mistake to break the family. "

Inessa was an older and wiser friend. However, Victoria did not need anyone's advice. She was very angry with her soon to be ex-husband.

She returned to her empty apartment, put on an old sweater and decided to work on her thesis. The kids were staying with her parents, and she called her Mom to check if they were sleeping already. She got back to the table. The blue eyes of a stranger were looking from the pages of her dissertation.

This man was different, not at all like her friends. He was intriguing, especially with the idea of moving to Israel. She liked his demeanor, his self-confidence. Like her father, he was a man in charge.

She thought about the party and opened her narrow closet. For an unknown to her reason, suddenly she had to have a better dress for the New Year party. She was not sure if her old weekend dress was suitable. She fell asleep thinking about Alla's furs and Volodya's blue eyes.

The party was a great success. The holiday table was plentiful with all kinds of cold cuts, herring with boiled potatoes, "cholodnoe", preserved and marinated vegetables from Bulgaria, pate, and chickens and, finally, glorious desert. Volodya was a heart of the party; he was charming, generous and funny. Besides the food and gorgeous Alla, he brought western cassettes for the magnitophone ("tape player"), and everybody danced.

Victoria learned that he was managing a big dry cleaning atelier, right across a street from her parents' apartment. She even remembered bringing clothes for cleaning there not so long ago.

He sat next to her at the table, and they talked all evening. He invited Victoria to dance, and at the twelfth stroke of the Kremlin clock, he kissed her. Alla was not happy, and they left soon after.

"Well, maybe he goes home sometime," smiled Victoria. She was surprised when during the dance, Volodya had asked her for the phone number. However, she loved the sweet taste of attention and interest, and she was very angry with Felix.

The next morning she went to celebrate New Year with Dima and Dave staying with her parents. A few years ago, her dad bought one of the first condominiums in Kiev, the grand four-room apartment with no neighbors to share anything. Three large balconies were looking on three sides of the new boulevard. Victoria's sons, Dima and David were busy constantly running between large rooms and balconies unless Grandpa was working.

Lenya was seeing his patients now in his office. There were always two or three patients sitting in the long hallway, waiting for him before, and after his work and on the weekends.

Since Lenya was a teenager, he was in love with theater. He always wanted to be an actor, but his mom wanted him to be a doctor. Years before, he applied and was accepted to both, Kiev Theatrical School and Kiev Medical School. The life forced him to betray his dream and become a doctor. However, his love for the theater had never died.

He participated in every amateur performance at Medical School. He wrote his first play during the war, and the play won a prestigious award and the first place in the competition.

By now, he was a prominent playwright, a respected member of the Union of Soviet Writers. His plays were performed on many stages in Russian and Ukrainian theatres. He made it in Medicine and Literature, just like Chekov who called Medicine his wife and Literature his mistress.

He had fame and prestige in spite of living in a socialist state. Ukraine was the most anti-Semitic part of Russia; with a quota everywhere, in the University, Colleges and at work. The state did not have sovereignty, was ruled from Russia with the Russian language. Nobody would say he lives in Ukraine; the right answer would be, "We live in Russia; in Kiev, the capital of Ukraine."

Both his daughters were doctors. He and his family were well off with new private apartments. He loved his new car and a garage, a rarity in the USSR.

But all these were only things. Every morning before sunrise and late into the night Lenya was writing in his office. Plays and poetry, medical challenges and family, he could not choose between his callings.

Victoria nestled on her favorite stool at the kitchen window, staring down at the miserable looking boulevard. The recently trimmed almost to the naked trunks trees looked like old crosses on the graveyard. They were pitiful and reminded her of war. Across the street, she could see a shining, contemporary glassed storefront of a dry cleaning atelier and a lonely white "Pobeda" parked right next to it. She thought about Volodya, the man who kissed her at twelve o'clock on the New Year.

An early spring with its dirty half-melted snow added a gray background to black trunks without branches. Victoria felt terribly lonely. Felix moved out, her kids were with her parents, and she had never learned how to be alone. Volodya had never called. Almost every day she was looking out at this kitchen window; she did not understand. She tried to convince herself that he was a busy, married man, never mind his girlfriend. He was simply not interested.

A few days later, on the way home, contrary to her better judgment, Victoria took a brand new sweater to the dry cleaning shop, just to see if Volodya still remembered her.

It was a busy place with five or six workers and a pretty girl expertly managing a short line in the reception. Through the open door of the manager's office, she could see Volodya playing cards with a few men. Forever present blond Alla was watching the game.

He saw her right away and got out of the table. "Victoria! What are you doing here? Anything I can do for you?"

She felt like a fraud. Would Volodya notice that her sweater was new and did not need cleaning?

It was obvious that he was happy to see her. He pulled her out of the short line, took her new sweater and gave her a yellow slip. He was very friendly and very professional; however, that was it. She left upset and defeated.

The boys stayed with grandparents, Dave was sick again and could not go to the kindergarten tomorrow. She headed home, just four shortstops by the trolley. She missed her family, their dinners together and Felix's jokes, but her husband was nowhere in sight and tomorrow she had to be at work early, for the Grand Rounds. She had a quick dinner with her parents earlier; her small refrigerator at home was empty; Victoria suspected its empty stomach was growling at night.

She waited in a crowd for the trolley. Puddles from the melting snow were deep, and her boots were wet inside, she was cold, and her nose started to run. She hated this cold, wet spring, her life and the lonely evening ahead.

She saw a beautiful white car pulling out of Volodya's shop. It was an old 'Pobeda' with a shiny bumper; a private car that spoke of prestige and money. The car turned and passed the trolley stop, spraying pedestrians with gray slush. The woman in a beautiful white fox hat smiled behind the passenger window.

Victoria did not feel cold anymore; she was so angry she could kill. "I need to rebuild my life. I cannot hide behind Dad's back anymore; I need my children, my own family."

She tried to call Felix, but he did not answer the phone. He lived in his old bachelor's pad enjoying his newly found freedom.

She had to work on her theses. She had to, she had to … There was much more on her plate than she could bite.

She loved her work; it was amazing. After Dima's death and the fiasco of her marriage to Felix, the third floor of the State Institute of Mother and Child was the only place where she did not feel like a failure. Her Department was a unique place for pregnant women with medical problems not related to pregnancy. Every patient had two doctors, Gynecologist and Internist. There were patients with severe asthma, heart diseases, even heart attack during pregnancy. Chronic kidney problems, hunchbacks, and cancers were frequent diagnoses, and the women were pregnant. Gynecologists followed the pregnancy; Internists were responsible for the patient as a whole.

They were working in the uncharted territory, with no textbooks on the subject. They were pioneers in the field.

Victoria could talk about her patients forever. They were very sick and needed care, attention, and love. Her Dad's old friend Doctor Lena Gutman was her boss, and she was always ready to help Victoria with her patients and with her theses.

She was doing genetic research at the Institute's newly organized Genetic Laboratory, the very first attempt to introduce genetic teaching in Ukraine.

Only the Communist Party and its leaders could officially distinguish the real science from "the minion of Capitalism." According to the Party verdict, "Chez monk Mendel" was the "capitalistic Father of pseudoscience Genetic and a quack," hence, genetic was banned at schools and universities.

"I study 'the whore of Imperialism,'" mocked Victoria when she first met Felix. She was investigating genetic traits of heart diseases.

She did not have and could not afford the nanny without Felix's salary. Dave got sick every time he went to a kindergarten. Now, both her kids were staying mostly with the grandparents, and almost every day after work, she went to see them. The ride to work in the morning and back at night took about an hour, standing on one foot in the overcrowded bus, and she did not have time for anything else.

"My private life is nonexistent," Victoria complained to Inessa; they became closer after the New Year party. That Saturday, the two of them had "a girls' lunch" in Victoria's kitchen. For a change, Victoria's refrigerator was not empty. She had herring and the

Russian version of meat dumplings, called pelmeni, in the fridge and Inessa brought a half-a-liter bottle of vodka. They boiled pelmeni and fried potatoes.

They were brave Russian girls, and although, the first shots of vodka burned their throats, an almost empty bottle stood on the table now.

"What about Volodya," asked Inessa, "he was so taken by you at the New Year Party?"

"But you said he was married; what do I need him for?" Victoria sounded outraged. She did not feel like telling her girlfriend about her visit to the shop a few weeks back.

"Yes, but he is fun. What are your plans for tonight anyway? Why don't you give him a call?" challenged Inessa. After a few shots of vodka, she apparently forgot her own advice to stay away from the married man.

"I have no plans, none whatsoever; the kids are at my parents, and I planned to work at home," Victoria said with a sad smile.

She felt sleepy and slightly drunk. The lonely evening did not seem like a good idea. She picked up the phone and dialed the dry cleaning atelier. "Can I, please, speak to Volodya?" she heard her own wavering words.

The familiar soft voice was in her ear, "Victoria, what are we doing tonight? I will pick you up at seven at your place". Her trembling feet did not hold her, and she slowly dropped on the floor right there, in her small hallway next to the phone. She rested her head on the bathroom door. "Fine," she could hardly whisper the reply.

*****

Felix, about fifty years older Felix, turned on the plush hotel bed. "Victoria, why are you still awake? We have to get up early tomorrow. Please, try to sleep." His warm hand curled familiarly around me, and I felt content and happy. Through decades, I smiled at young, excited and worried Victoria on the threshold of a new chapter of her life. Finally, still smiling I fell asleep.

DAY 7, SEPTEMBER 3
KANSAS CITY, KS - KEARNEY, NE
BEST WESTERN

"A traveler is an artist painting life's canvas one remarkable journey at a time," wrote me our travel agent. Today we started to paint our canvas. Our first week was a long beautiful drive to a family reunion at the fabulous wedding. We had a wonderful time, delicious food and emotional conversations.

Early Tuesday morning we thanked our hosts, said good-bye to all forty-eight Kansas City's beautiful fountains, took some more pictures and drove off. We drove through three states on the way to Kearney, Nebraska, the place called a world capital of the Sandhill Cranes. In the spring, on the way from the South to Canada, Alaska and Siberia about half a million cranes converge on Nebraska's Platte River for the whole month. They would be back soon, on their way from the North breeding grounds to the South for the winter.

Why did they choose Nebraska? What prompted their ancestors about ten million years ago to pick this place for a short R&R during their twice a year travel? We did not see the cranes and Platte River was not especially impressive. Like most of the time in our own lives, we did not have answers to these eternal "whys?"

VOLODYA
KIEV, UKRAINE, THE1970S

"Why did I call him?" Victoria thought feverishly inspecting her limited wardrobe. "What am I going to wear?"

After the crash of their marriage, Fellx returned to his bachelor's pad, and Victoria with Dave stayed in their two-room- condominium in the center of the city.

Dima, named after his late father, stayed with her parents. When she was on call or when Dave was sick and could not go to the kindergarten, both kids stayed with her parents.

She was lucky today, the kids were at the grandparents and the evening was all hers.

She was so excited and panicky, her hands were shaking, and she could hear her heart thumping in her chest. "Where would we go? What should I wear? Skirt or pants, blouse or sweater, pumps or boots?" Looking at her, somebody could think she had a ton of choices. Actually, her closet fitted entirely into one narrow cabinet in a wall.

Finally, she decided on a short black dress and boots without heels; she remembered he was not very tall. Long coat and bright scarf finished the ensemble.

She was very nervous when her doorbell rang sharply at seven.

"Flowers!" Victoria gasped when she opened the door. The early spring did not give too many choices, but Volodya held a small bunch of the first fragile white snowdrops.

He wore a three-piece suit and a light overcoat. His eyes were piercing blue under strawberry blonde hair.

"I am sorry Victoria; these flowers are not much, but flower stores had nothing," he sounded embarrassed. "We have a reservation, and my car is downstairs."

He looked at her appraisingly, "You are a beautiful woman, Victoria." Apparently, the dress and the boots were lost on him.

She did not remember the last time she had dinner at the elegant "Swan". The new high-rise hotel graced a large square at the center of the city; its all-glass elegant restaurant on the second floor catered mostly to foreigners staying at the hotel. Funny, how it worked in Socialism: "Freedom, Equality and Brotherhood" were emblazoned in big scarlet letters on every building; however, a simple citizen, the "commoner", the "tovarishch" was left out everywhere: at the stores, restaurants, and theaters. Without "connections", there was no table at the restaurant, no ticket to the show and no pantyhose at a store.

It was clear that Volodya had connections. On Saturday night, they were treated like celebrities at one of the most elegant restaurants in the city. He did not even look at the menu, "Caviar, please."

Within minutes, the best French cognac, cheese, pate and tongue, all kinds of salads and smoked fish were on the table. Hot hors-d'oeuvre followed cold "zakuski", while the main course was prepared in the kitchen. He even remembered the song they danced to on the New Year, and he asked the band to play it for them.

All evening he did not take his eyes off Victoria. He was the best date, and it was a perfect romantic evening. As they danced, his lips gently brushed her cheek. Victoria was mesmerized; she wished this evening would never end. Only yesterday, she was sad and lonely, trying to call Felix and worrying about Dave spending yet another night with her parents.

Now, she felt young and free. She could see in Volodya's eyes how beautiful she looked and how much he tried to impress her.

She wanted to invite him to her apartment; "just for a nightcap" Victoria lied to herself. However, it was impossible; she had to return to her parents to spend the night with the kids.

Volodya was a real gentleman; he drove her to her parents' home and with a goodnight kiss handed her two boxes of chocolates he had bought at the "Swan".

"One is for you, Vika," he said softly. "I had a fabulous evening; and, please, pass that one to your Mom, as a thank you for babysitting your kids."

Her Mom smiled, she was pleased to see Victoria so happy. She wanted to know everything about this date and the evening. She poured a glass of milk for Victoria, opened the box of chocolates and sat down at the kitchen table across from her daughter to listen.

Sarra was still a strikingly good-looking woman. She did not look like a regular grandmother; she was stylish and elegant, but the most important, she had a special connection with her daughters. They were friends; they shared their secrets and stood by each other.

Victoria took a small heart shaped chocolate when a sudden thought stabbed her: "Did Volodya got a box of chocolates for his wife too?"

She did not know that the jealousy would haunt her for the next seven years.

Late spring lighted up white candles on chestnut trees all over the city. Lilies-of-the-valley and violets were sold on every corner, and the smell of lilac was in the air. The city looked clean and shiny trying to forget the drab and dreary winter. The sun was warm and tender, and Victoria was in love. She was the happiest women in the world. She had a new, very convenient life. No more lines in the empty stores, no overcrowded bus rides to work, no headaches what to cook for dinner. Volodya took care of everything.

It did not matter anymore, that he had a family somewhere; he spent every night with Victoria and drove her to work in the morning. It did not matter anymore, that he occasionally disappeared for two-three days to see his wife and his young son. It did not matter anymore, that her father did not talk to her and did not want to know him. Even her work, which she loved so much, was not that important anymore.

All her girlfriends envied her, her new boyfriend, her new clothes and her new lifestyle. She envied herself. Slowly, Volodya became indispensable. He picked up Dave from her parents or kindergarten, cooked the dinner, and had their friends over. He was seven years older than Victoria and had the experience to show for it. He knew so much more about life and love. With him, she felt like a little girl, loved and protected, and she trusted him to take care of her.

He was gentle and understanding. He always made Victoria unbelievably happy. It pleased him to make her happy, and he was comfortably convincing that nothing matter but love.

Volodya was on his third marriage. He had a misfortune to be born an entrepreneur in the country where to be one was a mortal sin and a crime.

His unstoppable energy gave some solace to his impoverished fatherless childhood. He married his first wife when they both were eighteen. The marriage lasted for about a year, and she left him for his best friend. When he was twenty, he married again, wiser this time. She was a nurse, older and much better educated. Within a year, they had a daughter. He did not need a professional career; he had an insane ability to make money.

"Leave Volodya in the empty room without clothes, and within fifteen minutes he would emerge in a tuxedo in a chauffeur-driven- limo with a stack of money in his pocket," his friends used to joke.

Volodya would do anything for Victoria. He adored her and was very proud of her. He lived in a different from Victoria world, and he wanted to show her the life she could never imagine.

"Yes, he is married, he does not know the difference between Bach and Beethoven, Monet and Manet, and Dad would not invite him to the table," Victoria recited her monologue to her friends, "but he lives in a real and much better world." At night, resting her head on Volodya's wide shoulder, she thought, "I would do anything for him. He makes me so happy; why would I care if he is married or not".

There were other problems, of course. Volodya dreamed about emigration, but he would not leave his family behind. He could not leave Victoria, he felt it would kill him, and he could not cut this Gordian knot.

His story started about fifteen years earlier when Volodya had his first problem with the Soviet law. He was sentenced to seven years in the labor camp for exercising his entrepreneurial skills. He never volunteered the details, but somewhere between the second and third year of imprisonment, he managed to seduce the sixteen-year-old-daughter of the camp's commandant. The young Ukrainian girl promptly got pregnant, and Daddy had to save the first love and the honor of his only daughter. Volodya got a quick divorce, and within two weeks, he was a married man again.

The newly minted couple got private living quarters outside of the camp's tall fence, and a short time later, after an early discharge, Volodya brought his new family to Kiev.

"I love my son, and I always will take care of him and his mother," was the only thing he would say. He never called her by name, and he never said "my wife" but he made it clear that he would never leave her and their son.

Victoria, meanwhile, completed her Ph.D. and made peace with her father. At last, he was proud of her.

Felix saw the boys often. He and Victoria tried to forget their bitter break; they kept their circle of friends, and they still liked each other, kind of. It was a separation, however, on the paper, they still were husband and wife, and nobody was in a hurry to rush for a divorce.

Volodya never stopped dreaming about the emigration. "You have to decide Victoria. I would get you ready to leave. We have all the information we need, and I would take care of everything." He was a strong man; he was ready to take two families.

Victoria, however, beside the invitation from Israel "to reunite with the family," needed the permission from Felix and her father.

Felix was easy, sort of. "Where is your common sense, Victoria? You cannot take the kids from me. You are insane if you think I would sign the paper!" Felix would not give up.

However, he hated the regime and wanted to leave just as much as she did. Nevertheless, he would not give the permission to take the kids out of the country until he will be able to leave.

"I will need to know where you would take the kids Victoria, and I would be there, if the Soviets would let me go, of course. I would never leave my sons," he pleaded with Victoria, but nobody had any answers.

The government made up every impossible rule to prevent emigration. The dreams and plans, desires and reality were hanging in the air, moving in different directions, depending on political winds and whims. Every possible document, inquiry, certificate, and form had to be submitted notarized in three copies. Including permission from Victoria's parents.

In his heart, Lenya was a convinced Zionist, and he knew that Victoria was right; they needed to leave the country where the Jews had no future.

"I wanted to immigrate to Palestine in 1948," Lenya reasoned with his stubborn daughter, "And for all my life I was sorry I didn't do it. Now is your chance, Victoria. Israel is the best place in the world for us; it is our Motherland, our destiny! If you want to leave Russia you must go to Israel."

"I would never take Dima and Dave to the country of ongoing war," Victoria argued with her father. "If allowed, we would go to America." Her heart was filled with fear and her eyes brimmed with tears thinking about Israel. The war was never forgotten in Russia. Most of the books Victoria had read, most of the movies she saw, plays, music, and memories were about tragedy and horrors of the Second World War.

"And what are you going to do in the United States, Victoria?" her Dad brought up the trump card. "Your Diploma of Medical Doctor from the Soviet Union would be an empty piece of paper there. However, in Israel, it would be a valid license, and you would be able to practice medicine right away."

Victoria had nothing to say; he was right. Her Dad was always right.

This time, he did not scream "Net!" He just said quietly, "Does not matter, America or Israel. I would never allow you and the children to leave with Volodya; you are completely out of your mind, Victoria!"

She did not have a coveted invitation from Israel yet, but everyone had an opinion what to do and where to take the kids, when and if they would ever leave the country.

Volodya grew more and more stressed; he was torn between his family and his love. He wanted the divorce, he wanted to leave the country; and he could not do either.

Their seventh anniversary, the seventh New Year, he spent with his family, but after the party, he quietly opened the door to Victoria's apartment with his own key and woke up sleeping Victoria. She tried to put on her robe when she suddenly realized that behind inebriated and crying Volodya was his wife, Galina.

"You tell her, Victoria," cried Volodya. "You tell her how much we love each other for all these years. Please, Vika, tell her that you would marry me and we would leave the country together," begged Volodya.

Terrified Victoria looked at his wife. Galina was young, tall and beautiful; she had this unique brand of Ukrainian beauty of a quiet strong woman. She was not shocked or surprised. It was clear that she knew about their seven-year-long affair and that she did not worry; she had an unbreakable hold on her husband. She owned him. Without a word, she took Volodya's hand, and they left together; they were a family after all.

Dismayed Victoria did not even cry; she had made up her mind instantly. She wanted a clean break and a new beginning. Her sons were growing up, and even if her life was not exactly in order, she saw the future clearly.

"It is so simple!" thought Victoria. "Felix," she said aloud as if trying to convince herself. Felix lived alone, and he loved her children, their children. She would not need to convince him to leave the country; they both hated antisemitism, communism, socialism and all the other "isms" that thrived in Soviet Russia.

She called him that morning. He came for dinner, and she never saw him happier. He had never asked for explanation; however, Victoria needed to clarify.

"You will provide for the family, while I would take the tests for my medical license," finalized Victoria. "When I would be able to work as a doctor, you would be free, and I would never ask you for any support."

"I will get my Medical License back, Felix!" she promised. "If I fail, I would do dishes at the restaurant or wash floors in the hospital," Victoria swore adamantly. "You know, in my whole life I had never failed an exam, and I would pass this one as well," she promised eagerly.

They drank champagne, kissed each other good night and for the first time in seven years, both of them were proud of their first coherent decision together.

*****

Felix drove through endless fields and vivid greenery of Missouri; mirrored manmade lakes and slowly rising hills of Iowa and irrigation machines looking like giant dragonflies in Nebraska. I closed my eyes.

Yesterday in Kansas City, much older Volodya took us out for lunch, showed off his latest Mercedes and drove us around the city. We shared a love story over forty years ago and remained friends ever since.

After leaving Russia, he settled his family in Kansas City where he had old friends. His children, the daughter from the second marriage and son from the third, were married and had children of their own. His wife recently retired, and they enjoyed their grandchildren and their life.

The dashing strawberry blond Casanova was gone, only blue eyes were still there. Neither three-piece Armani suit nor a grey ponytail could hide the slight limp and arthritic hands. The dental work distorted his previously beautiful smile. He worried about some mundane family chores and hurriedly suggested we would continue sightseeing on our own. My heart never skipped a beat. There were no feelings. Seven years of my previous life disappeared as a small puff of hot air somewhere in the middle of Kansas City.

The spell of the past was broken; another door closed. I was proud and happy with the decision I had made in Kiev so many years ago.

"Let's go to a supermarket and buy champagne," I suggested. After days of the wedding festivities, we planned to shop for our dinner tonight.

Back at our hotel, we toasted our approaching golden anniversary with cheap champagne. We shared roasted chicken and memories.

I was glad we had never subtracted the years of separation, and why would we? We stayed friends, took care of our children, helped each other, drank together and partied just the same. We tried to be civil and, in some strange way, we continued to love each other. We just did not want to confess that we did.

It was my Dad, who had the foresight. Among hundreds of forms and documents for emigration was the affidavit my parents had to sign, the permission for their daughter to leave the country.

"I would never do this, Victoria," my Dad threatened. "I

would never let you and the boys leave; I would let you go only with your husband and the father of your children."

He was always right. In all his life, he had made only two mistakes, first, when he did not go to Israel in nineteen-forty-eight and the second when he did not leave with us.

The bed in the middle of Nebraska was comfortable; we curled into each other and fell asleep at no time. Onto Dakota tomorrow.

DAY 8, SEPTEMBER 4
CUSTER STATE PARK, SD,
STATE GAME LODGE

I t was not a very promising morning - chilly and grey, it was, actually, perfect for driving. We had to beat four hundred and fifteen miles to Custer State Park, imprinting the rest of Nebraska and some of South Dakota with our tired tires. Our GPS did not behave; it got funny idea that we would want to drive extra three hundred and fifty miles, just for the fun of it. We did not; sometimes it pays off to be an old-timer and to know how to use the real map and directions. Especially, directions from our trip advisor.

Nebraska greeted us with the birds already flying south, gorgeous hills and small canyons, evergreens and the real American prairies. For the last three days, we wondered how anyone in the world could be hungry with all the endless fields of our blessed country.

The local radio station played Tchaikovsky; it was the "Swan Lake".

CHILDHOOD
KIEV, UKRAINE, THE 1940S

Victoria adored her Dad. Mom finishing her Medical School was never home; Babushka was constantly nagging and reprimanding her "little maidele", and her jobless father was Victoria's best friend. Lenya invented and played with her funny games, told her amazing stories and wrote for her a short poem on every occasion.

One day he even took her to the Opera Theater to see a ballet, "Swan Lake". Their seats were few floors above the stage, but Victoria loved it. She was enamored with the story, the music, and the beautiful ballerinas. Getting out of the famous Kiev Opera Theater, still in the impressive lobby with a painted high ceiling, in the crowd of the adoring parents and well-behaved children dressed in their best holiday outfits, she explained to her "forgetful" Dad about Odette and Odile. She remembered the name of Tchaikovsky who wrote the music, and she made her Dad infinitely proud of his little girl.

"Let's stop by uncle Naum," he smiled. "He would be delighted to learn from you about the 'Swan Lake'. It will be fun, Vika, I promise," he added when there was no answer.

Young Doctor Naum Polissky was one of Lenya's best friends; they moonlighted together at the same clinic. Naum, a great doctor with a kind smile, recently married and Lenya wanted to brag and show off his smart daughter.

The adult conversation about work and patients bored Victoria, and she wanted to go home. Siegfried and Odette did not excite her anymore; she just needed to go back to her Babushka.

"Victoria loved ballet," suddenly remembered Lenya. "Why don't you tell us about it, Vika?"

He tried with other questions, with kisses and threats, with begging and bribes; there was no answer. His stubborn five-year-old daughter had never said a word; she just wanted to go home. Naum was not convinced that children were a good idea. Looking at Victoria, he and his young wife decided to wait with children.

On their way home, Victoria did not want to walk trying to postpone punishment. Sudden rain washed the dusty streets, and Victoria in her beautiful new dress sat in every puddle as her angry Dad refused to carry his stubborn daughter and simply pulled her on the wet asphalt all the way home. She did not cry and did not say a word.

Lenya's nights on call and his first private patients fed the family. Patients did not mind to come to see the doctor in his small room, to lie down on the blanket over his own bed or to sit at the family table for IV injections. When Lenya had a patient, Babushka and Victoria would go for a walk.

The most luxurious moonlighting was in medical aviation. The war destroyed roads and railways and often the only mean to get to the patient was a small military biplane called a "Cornhusker". Lenya flew to remote villages to treat big bosses, and they sent him back with fresh eggs and chickens, occasional moonshine and fruits for the doctor's kid.

"Victoria, do you want to fly?" Dad asked one morning. Alarmed Babushka looked at her son with suspicion.

"You are not taking Vika with you on call; no way!"

"Mom, the village is nearby, it is a short flight. There are an orchard and beehouses, and fresh milk".

There was no argument after this, and glowing Victoria took her Dad's hand. Oh, if she only knew!

The pathetic "Stop the plane!" scream would not stop. Victoria's fingers were white from holding to her seat; her face was green from nausea and fear. She has never stopped screaming at the top of her lungs, "Stop the plane! I want out!"

Lenya was right, after all, milk and honey were on the table, and he told his little girl to play outside while he was taking care of the patient.

"I am not flying back," said Victoria.

"We will talk about this later, please." Lenya needed to examine the patient.

"I am not going on this plane again," insisted his daughter.

"Victoria, please, go outside, we will talk later," Lenya raised his voice.

"I will not, I will not," Victoria started to cry. "I will not go outside, and I will not fly the plane, and I do not love you anymore!" With these sacrilegious words, Victoria ran to the orchard and leaned on the thick apple tree to cry.

Her right foot landed straight in the wasp nest, and a small army of flying warriors attacked her with a vengeance.

The small biplane, which took severely beaten Victoria and her Dad straight to Kiev hospital, saved her life.

Their small room was hot in the summer and cold in the winter. A big Russian stove was useless behind a curtain, which Babushka had fashioned from the old piece of gauze. There were no fire logs to start the stove; no matter how cold it was, so they used it as a kitchen counter. Victoria slept on the old wooden trunk with uneven hard planks. Babushka always folded a thin blanket a few times, to make Victoria's bed a bit softer. Sometimes, especially in winter, she tried to sneak her own blanket to cover

Victoria, but Lenya watched over and would not allow this. He was a head of his large family, and he did everything he could, teaching, moonlighting, and writing. Still, all five of them and sometimes six, when Zack slept over, had to fit in this small room with no place for an extra bed; they could not afford even a simple luxury of an extra blanket.

It was the middle of the cold winter night when Victoria suddenly felt very warm. She loved the feeling. Quietly she threw her blanket on the floor over Babushka and went barefooted behind the curtain to get some water. Babushka got up and put the light on to see what was going on. There was only a single bulb hanging on a cord from the ceiling and, of course, everybody woke up.

"What are you doing, Vika?" asked Lenya blinded by the light.

"O my God!" whispered Babushka "Look at the girl!"

By then, everybody was up looking at Victoria. Lenya was already lifting Vika even closer to the light.

"Open your mouth Vika" he commanded. "Turn around, lift your shirt!" He examined his scarlet red daughter and finally, put her back into her so-called bed barricaded by the family table for safety.

"Nothing bad," he tried to calm his family. "It is scarlet fever. In the morning, Sarra and I will take Victoria to the Hospital".

He did not mention that scarlet fever required twenty—one- day quarantine hospitalization without visitation and "no hair" policy to prevent the spread of lice in the Pediatric department.

"The children's Department is on the third floor, doctor," a soft hearted nurse took a pity on stricken Lenya and crying Sarra after she took a shaved and terrified Victoria to the Infectious Ward. "You will be able to see her in the window."

They went through the war, they lost loved ones, and they lived in terrible conditions. They fought for their future and the future of their child. Now, for the first time, Victoria was taken from them. They were heartbroken when her shaved bald head disappeared in the dark hospital corridor.

They stopped at the corner shop to buy "the pencils", long- striped colored hard candies, which kids called "karandash".

With the same kind nurse, they sent candies upstairs to Victoria and went outside. They joined a group of parents looking at the third-floor windows.

A gloomy cold day hung above the fresh snow. Deformed branches of the single tree touched the dirty brick wall of the building. The bold heads of children were in every window.

"We would never recognize Vika from here!" Sarra was inconsolable. "They all look the same with their bald heads!"

Indeed, they saw a few kids in every window, and they all looked the same. However, only in one of the windows, every child held a long striped hard candy, and her parents recognized Victoria in the center of the group. The kids were smiling, and so were Lenya and Sarra, they were glad they taught their daughter to share.

Winters were long and boring and summers were short and exciting for Victoria; she was convinced that all-important things always happened in the summer. Indeed, they did!

During her last summer before school, an amazing newcomer settled in a small room on Kudryavsky Street. It was black and rectangular, and it resided high on the wall, specifically, out of Victoria's reach. Its name was telephone, and it could ring and talk.

In the Russian language, every thing has a gender; the imposing black box on the wall was a definite male, big, and black it dominated the wall right next to the window with a very industrial view of the liquor plant.

Victoria was not afraid; she bravely climbed on the old stool and put a receiver to her ear. A small black piece was attached to the telephone by the long wire, and it looked just like her Dad's stethoscope.

"Amazing!" Victoria was definitely not afraid of her Dad's stethoscope.

Lenya loved the phone and its convenience while his daughter was in love with a round black and white dial, which made loud clicking sounds when she put her little finger in the hole with the number and turned the dial.

"Victoria, stop touching the phone, please," everybody begged, but Lenya had an idea.

"Remember Alla and Lena?" he asked his daughter. Victoria was precisely the same height as her Dad when she stood on the old stool next to the phone, and they looked very much alike.

"You can call them, you know?" Lenya did not suspect that at this moment he let the Genie out of the bottle.

Alla was one year older than Victoria, Lena was one year younger, and they were daughters of Victoria parents' friends. They lived on the other end of a big city and Victoria did not see the girls often. She loved to play with Lena and always begged her parents to take her with them when they went to visit their friends.

It was a rainy summer, and there was nothing to do outside under the dreary rain. But Victoria had the telephone to play with. She would start and end the day with the conversations with Lena. They both behaved like adults on the phone, and everybody loved to listen to their incredibly important but always the same, conversations.

"Can I please speak to Lena?" Victoria would call. "Privet, Lena, how are you?"

"I am fine, thank you, our cat got lost, and I am very sad."

"Very sorry, Lena. If you are busy now, I will call later".

Their telephone friendship lasted for a few years.

They were already in the school when Lena's parents invited Victoria to spend the summer at their dacha in the suburb. The girls remembered this summer as the summer of the total eclipse of the sun.

Preparations started weeks ahead. Everybody was looking for a piece of glass to smoke on the open fire; broken bottles became precious. Victoria even dropped her father's tea glass trying to break it. When smoked on the fire, the piece of this glass would be perfect to watch the eclipse. She was lucky the glass did not break.

The daily tea drinking ritual was one of the best times of the day. Early in the morning and after dinner, Babushka placed the dry tea leaves inside of the small porcelain kettle and covered it with a small amount of boiling water. Then she set this little teapot on the top of the larger boiling kettle to steep. The adults drank tea from the clear glasses in the metallic glass holders. Tea could be strong or weak depending on how much boiling water one would prefer to add to his brew.

Victoria fitted a piece of glass into a long split tree branch and smoked the glass on the open fire until it became black. Sometimes, the branch would catch on fire, and the girls would run around wildly screaming and waving the burning branch. They had so much fun staying outside and preparing pieces of glass for the big day. They did not know about sunglasses and had never seen them.

On the day of the eclipse, they were ready. Slowly, it became darker and darker. First, a small sliver and then a larger part of the sun disappeared from the sky. Suddenly, night fell all around them. They did not expect it; they were supposed just to watch the sun.

They were not allowed outside when it was dark, and they tried to figure out what they should do. Cows at the farm next door seemed scared too as they "mu-u'ed" to no end, and young Lena started to cry.

In the darkness, Victoria stepped on her smocked glass and cut her foot. She did not pay any attention; she was in the magic kingdom where everything was possible. It was still daytime, but she could see the stars! And she did not need any glass for that.

She turned to Lena, "Do not cry, Lenochka. I am going to be an astronomer." She was so excited; she felt she would be able to solve all the problems of the world.

*****

Our Hotel in the Custer State Park, State Game Lodge, hosted Presidents Calvin Coolidge and Dwight Eisenhower and preserved their original rooms. I hoped they changed the linens, as we were staying in "The Coolidge Room".

We did not explore our beautiful suite or unpack. The day was growing short, and we planned to see the light show at the Mount Rushmore. We wanted to leave while it was still daylight.

It was a great idea until I took the wrong turn and drove on the mountains road instead of a better but longer route. The Black Hills were alive and beautiful in the warm rays of the retiring sun. We stopped at every turn enjoying the view and solitude. We were alone, high in the mountains, because these were not hills, for sure.

The dusk slowly descended, and annoying slippery rain arrived with the darkness. Many years ago, back in Russia, I was in the Caucasus Mountains. They were tall, ominous peaks; however, they were a child's play compared to the road we took. It left us speechless and scared as we passed through unlit one-lane tunnels and took sharp, slippery turns on the cliffs.

I asked Felix to find my phone in my purse.

"Going to call somebody?" he asked smiling.

"No," I replied with an equally brave smile. "But if we would tumble down to one of these ravines where nobody would ever find us or wild animals would want to have us for their dinner, I would be happy to have a phone with me, if we would survive the fall, of course."

He did not smile; he put his warm hand on my knee. "Do not worry, Victoria, we survived much more dangerous roads. There is nothing these wet hills could do to us. Especially on the Eve of Rosh Hashanah."

We made another sharp turn, the rain still dancing a wild

swing in our headlights, and stopped astonished by the view. In the distance, across the Black Hills, the high beam lit up the heads of four Presidents. Invited by it, wet, hungry, and shaken, we followed the beam until we reached the Mountain Rushmore.

We had some time before the lighting ceremony, and it was the Holiday, the eve of Jewish New Year. In the crowded Restaurant, we ordered our holiday meal.

We did not see any Jewish faces around; South Dakota had only about 400 Jews, less than any other state. On the walls, all around us were the pictures and art depicting the history and the heritage of the country. We were not born here; we had chosen our new Motherland. We became newly born citizens and patriots decades ago, and it took us almost forty years to get to the Mount Rushmore. It was a perfect place to celebrate Rosh Hashanah.

It was dark, and the Black Hills were just that, pitch black. The non-stop rain pounded our umbrellas as we sat in the impressive amphitheater for the light show on Mount Rushmore.

"Four hundred people worked on the Mountain for fourteen years; with an average pay of about one dollar per hour; the total cost of the project was under one million dollars," narrated the young Ranger on the stage.

As he told the story, busts of four Presidents: George Washington, Thomas Jefferson, Theodore Roosevelt and Abraham Lincoln were lit up. The clouds and fog surrendered to modern technology, and the faces of the fathers of the country were bright and powerful. It was awesome!

Hundreds of people were sitting in silence paying tribute to the foresight of the Presidents. The Ranger invited all the veterans in the audience on the stage. Slowly, gray-haired people, some in wheelchairs, some with canes, walk up the stage. One by one, the veterans recited their names, ranks, time and place of service.

There was a woman who stood in for her father who died in the WWII, a man named Michael Greenwald, who served in Vietnam and the people with last names Goldman and Rothman, and Cohen, and Shapiro. The small Jewish population of South Dakota was growing before our eyes, and we were incredibly proud to celebrate Rosh Hashanah in their company.

As the flag was lowered, everybody stood up to sing the National anthem. Suddenly, the light beam left the dead Presidents and lighted up faces of the men and women on the stage, the real heroes who believed in this country and fought for its freedom and liberties. There was no dry face in the audience, and I did not think it was the rain.

In complete darkness, we followed the line of the cars out of the Park. It seemed that the other drivers knew where to go. Our navigation system was looking for the fastest route and tried to lure us back through the Black Hills on the same insane road. Fortunately, Felix would not have any of this. We turned around and tried to figure our way through the dark and empty roads of South Dakota. The rain finally stopped, but the road constructions and detours had not.

We got back to our Lodge at the State Park around two in the morning. Massive buffalo greeted us at the gate.

"Take a picture, take a picture," shouted Felix, but the cell phone in my pocket lost its charge a long time ago. Insomniac antelopes escorted us to the Lodge. What a day! Shana Tova and a Happy and Healthy New Year!

DAY 9, SEPTEMBER 5
CUSTER STATE PARK, SD
STATE GAME LODGE

T he first rays of sun in the veranda window woke me up. We were at the White House circa 1927 located in South Dakota. It was not the Lincoln bedroom, but it was the very same room President Calvin Coolidge and his wife Grace spent the summer of 1927.

A four- poster bed prominently occupied the small room. Calvin Coolidge's photo with his signature on the official White house stationary hung above the stone fireplace. A small washbasin was right next to the bed and at the door to veranda was a small bureau.

Did he write The Entablature there?

The story about the supposed letter to the future carved into Mount Rushmore was incredible. By the idea of the sculptor Gutzon Borglum, a five hundred–word history of the United States written by President Coolidge would be carved into the mountain to accompany Washington's, Jefferson's, Lincoln 's and Roosevelt's images. The inscription would be in three languages: English, Latin, and some Asian language; Borglum had a Sanskrit in mind. When Calvin Coolidge finished the first two paragraphs, Borglum changed original work and released it to the public. Immediately every newspaper criticized and mocked the President's writing. Borglum had to admit that he had edited Coolidge's work.

With time, the whole idea almost died out, but not for the creator of the Mount Rushmore monument. Years later, with the help of the publisher William Randolph Hearst, Borglum announced a contest to write the Entablature and Franklin Roosevelt, himself, agreed to head the judging committee. Young Nebraskan William Burkett won the competition and went to college on the prize winnings. He became a successful businessman in California years later. He had always attributed his fortune to the Entablature contest. He even wanted to be laid to rest near Mount Rushmore.

Sculptor Borglum, however, did not like any of the contest entries and he forfeited on the promise to carve the winning entry onto the mountain. In 1975, bronze plaque with William Burkett's winning entry was installed on the wall of sculptor's original studio.

Enjoying the quiet of early morning in the high Coolidge's bed, I was still thinking about the Entablature and the amazing history of America. I slept in the bed of an American President! What a distance from my childhood on a different planet!

Felix woke up surprised to find me still in the bed, "You have this look, Vika; like you are on another planet."

THE GIRLFRIENDS
KIEV, UKRAINE, THE 1940S

The girls were inseparable, even though Victoria was four years younger. They all lived in the building, which before the war was a dormitory for the liquors plant's workers. The five-story brick monster still housed a few families who lived there under the Germans and occupied empty apartments of evacuees or those fighting in the war.

Only three Jewish families remained in the large building, all three of them were good friends, and all three had young girls.

Victoria met Talla for the first time when she came to the second floor apartment with her Babushka to visit her Babushka's new girlfriend, Tina. While Tina and Babushka had their weak tea in the kitchen, Tina's granddaughter Talla played a hostess to Victoria. She took her around the apartment and then showed her the piano.

Babushka drank her full glass of hot tea with a tiny piece of sugar; she broke this small piece off the large lump with a very small pincer; she held this piece of sugar between her false tees, and it would never dissolve until the very end. It took a long time for Babushka to drink her tea from the tall glass in the metal glass-holder. After she finished her tea, she went to get Victoria.

Victoria was in awe. She felt her heart beating to the sounds from this box, her eyes blinking every time she pressed the beautiful ivory and the scary black planks, and she could not possibly leave this miracle! However, smart Talla, who knew how to play the piano, promised to take Victoria to the courtyard to meet her girlfriends. That is where Victoria met Lina.

Lina lived with her Mom on the fifth floor. Lina's father died in the war, and her Mom Sofa worked at the bakery. They lived in one small room furnished with a narrow soldier's bed covered with a gray thin soldier's blanket, small wobbly table with one chair and a large wardrobe without a mirror, housing lonely one dress that belonged to Lina's Mom Sofa.

Lina was a thin, tall girl with funny pigtails that seemed to come straight out her head. She was four years older than Victoria but liked to play with her. However, Victoria always managed to get Lina into trouble.

They did not like to play in Lina's room because it had only one chair. Somebody always had to sit on the bed, but Lina's Mom was very particular that the bed, where she slept at night together with Lina, was for sleeping, not for sitting on it.

Lina was still fumbling with the key when Victoria suddenly froze. She could not take her eyes off the table.

"What is that?" she whispered. The shiny metal object hypnotized her. It reflected the sun that shined freely through the drapeless window.

"Scissors, silly," laughed Lina, not ready to admit that Mom had brought those only yesterday.

"We have to try these, now." Victoria felt she could not live another moment if she would not click these shiny "scissors" and would not see what they could do.

"Let us cut your braids off," she ventured. "It would be better for you Lina, without braids."

"My Mom would kill me," Lina was ready to sacrifice her braids, but was afraid of her Mom.

"Let us try on the blanket then," Victoria was relentless. "It is gray and thin, and we can do long ribbons!"

"We would be cold at night, Victoria," tried to reason Lina. "And Mom definitely would kill me for that!"

She tried to withstand Victoria's pressure. "Let us wait for my Mom from work; she would find something for us to cut."

"No way," thought Victoria.

When Sofa returned from work with a piece of fabric she planned to convert into her new blouse, she found crying Lina, hands over her face.

Victoria won. She cut off Lina's eyelashes.

Irina was another member of the small girlish gang. Her grandparents survived the war in Kiev, under the Germans. Her Grandfather was old and sick, and he stayed in the apartment while Irina with her parents evacuated beyond the Ural Mountains. They were not Jewish, and they were only ones who saved their apartment, their belongings, and their books. The girls loved to play on the soft carpets, to look at the books and to listen to the grandfather who loved to tell stories.

Irina was a tall, beautiful girl with large blue dreamy eyes on her perfect face. Little Vika felt proud to have such a beautiful girlfriend. She held her head high when Irina invited her over or played with her outside. Those were her best days.

Heavy green metal gates separated the courtyard from the street. During the week, when the plant was working, the security guards were at the gates. They would open the gates for the large trucks, check the documents, lets trucks with grain into the plant and then would let trucks carrying crates with bottles of vodka out.

In theory, the girls were not allowed to leave the courtyard. There were German prisoners of the war everywhere, cleaning and rebuilding the city. There were homeless, hungry people outside the gates. There were thieves and robbers, and the little girls were not permitted to wander. But nobody was watching.

High on the hills above Dnieper River, just a few blocks from their street was an old monastery that survived bombing as if God by himself had protected it. The monastery had an orchard that a few monks tended to. It was a miracle that grove survived the war and the apple trees were about to produce real apples.

On a hot summer day, so hot that asphalt started to run, and the leaves on the trees rolled into burned narrow tubes, the four girls quietly slipped behind the green gates and ran as fast as they could up the street to the hills above the river. They passed a convoy of Germans, but nobody even lifted head to look at them.

Victoria tried to keep up, but she was shorter and younger, and her girlfriends had to wait for her. They helped her to climb over the freshly painted brick wall and hold her when she jumped down on the other side. They were her real friends.

The apples were as green as the gates of the courtyard. They were small and sour, and the girls' mouths felt too small for the tongue. Nevertheless, these were the apples!

Talla, Lina, and Irina stuffed their tank tops with their booty and were ready to scram when they saw Victoria crying. She was only wearing shorts with no top; she was still a little girl, and there was nothing on her chest that needed a cover.

She could fit only three apples in her shorts and was upset seeing how many apples her girlfriend could fit into their tank tops.

Lina, whose eyelashes were growing back, took pity. "You can put a few apples in my tank top, Victoria. I still have some space".

Nobody had noticed their absence, even the watchful Babushkas, and they were very proud of their trophies. Lina's Mom, Sofa was still at work, and Victoria followed Lina to her room. Apples spilled on the floor when Lina took off her tank top. She picked up the apples and showed Victoria to the door.

"I took these back home, and now they are all mine," she announced triumphantly. "I changed my mind," she started, however at this moment Victoria jumped and locked her jaws on Lina's left breast. She was so blindly mad at Lina's betrayal that her jaw would not open and she hung from Lina's chest holding to her breast like a bulldog that would not let her pray go.

*****

"They were my first girlfriends, and I loved them all," I tried to confess to Felix. "They were my first attempt at friendship, and I am not sure, I passed."

"How did you fail?" smiled Felix. "What happened to them?"

"Talla taught me to play a piano. By the time my family moved out three years later, I could play many songs on her piano. Years later, I returned to invite the girls to my wedding, but nobody lived there anymore."

"My Dad saw Lina just before we left Kiev, and he told me about this visit. He did not elaborate on the reason she saw him. When he examined her, he noticed a scar on her left breast and asked if she had mastitis (breast inflammation) while nursing. Lina smiled broadly, 'No, doctor! Victoria bit me there when we were young. Just tell her, she was right then."

"You should tell me this story before we got married, Vika. I did not realize how dangerous you could be," joked Felix. I was happy he felt better and got his sense of humor back.

I was still running in my old shorts on the dangerous and dusty streets of the war-torn town of my childhood. I could taste green apples, see new shiny scissors and rattle the keys on the old piano. I saw Galya, beautiful half-Ukrainian-half-Dutch blond with blue eyes in a red silk coat, the envy of the whole school, welcoming me to the first grade at the new school. I thought about Dora, the beloved friend of my youth. We shared everything, and she kept all the secrets. We rehearsed the plays, which we wrote, went to the best concert without the tickets (her Mom worked at the State Concert Bureau) and had the best and the scariest times learning to date the boys.

The beautiful Ellen, straight from ancient Greece. I was so jealous of her when we were still in school, and all my friends were in love with her. Beautiful Ellen with her gorgeous shield-like straight dark hair and huge gray eyes, her waspy figure and ringing as a bell voice. We went to medical school together, laughed, studied and dated. I was always surprised how somebody could look at me when the gorgeous Ellen was at my side.

I was so lucky to have many beautiful girlfriends through all my life. I felt they were a precious gift that made me feel loved and protected, safe and not lonely.

The sun was in full blast through the veranda windows now, and we got up; I thought I could see lovely Grace Coolidge knitting there in the early sun.

We had "a jeep safari" booked for today and went downstairs for breakfast. A beautiful portrait of Grace Coolidge hung at the landing. I was surprised she was not sunburned from all that sun on her private veranda upstairs.

There was a newspaper on our table, along with the morning menu.

"How lovely," I thought. "Old habits die hard; they, probably, provided one for the President in 1927."

Casually, Felix opened the newspaper and started to read the front page. I picked up my copy and hold my breath. The newspaper was published in the mid-1870s. However, my husband was not fazed reading the stories about Lt. Colonel Custer, Lakota Indians, gold rash and local news from the Black Hills. It seemed that the Lakota tribe sued the Federal Government for the ownership of these sacred mountains for more than a century.

A young, beautiful blond women wearing sexy torn- in- all- the- right- places jeans stopped by our table. "I am Christi" she introduced herself. "Let's do some paperwork and go on a jeep safari."

Felix was on a cloud nine; we were lucky to be the only passengers in the pink jeep.

The Dakota's sky was incredibly blue, and clouds were snowy white, not ivory or gray as back East. Fantastic emerald greenery covered the Hills, and we could not fathom why they were called Black.

Christi was an expert driver. Our jeep was climbing and skidding, all while she was looking for the best views and the largest herd of bison. She loved her job, "the best job in the world," as Christi put it. "Tours are fun, but most of the days I ride state horses, hike and clean the trails or herd buffalos, not a bad way to make a living at fifty-four!" she almost bragged. Felix sighed loudly.

She moved here from Iowa after a string of unhappy marriages, brought her children with her and yesterday personally delivered her fourth grandchild (another groan from Felix).

Steven Spielberg himself filmed her when she guided his

group on tour. She took us on the impossible roads and showed us truly amazing things.

There are 1300 buffalos at Custer State Park, and I was sure I took a picture of every one of them. Twice! Mature animals, their massive heads adorned with short horns, and babies clinging to their mothers moved and rest, fought and played as our jeep stayed for what seemed an eternity in the middle of the enormous herd. Fenimore Cooper, here we come; we were in awe, felt privileged and humbled facing this living history of America.

We came back to the Lodge, and half an hour later you could find us sitting on the porch, in the chairs occupied by Mr. & Mrs. Coolidge in 1927, reading amazing stories about Custer's expedition into the Black Hills and Calamity Jane!

We had buffalo short ribs and buffalo burger for the late dinner and felt guilty for the cute buffalos on my photos. It was a great start for the Jewish New Year, although we were not sure this was a proper holiday meal.

As we watched bright stars above South Dakota, we thought about the first settlers, hot days in the wagon, Indian chiefs, and gold diggers. We slept in the same bed as the President; saw the Presidents personally at the Mountain Rushmore and faced buffalos, the living and breathing history of the country, we now proudly call our own.

Back in our room, I curled up with Felix who watched TV in bed. Next, to him, I felt safe and loved, kind of, like with my girlfriends.

DAY 10, SEPTEMBER 6
CODY, WY
CHAMBERLAIN INN, HEMINGWAY SUITE

A small antelope waved her white tail and nodded "goodbye" as she crossed the road in front of our car. She sprinted to the woods and joined her girlfriends. The Black Hills were green, and the lakes of the Badlands were reflecting upside-down trees, small red-roofed houses, and snowy white clouds.

Towns were mostly two stories with a mandatory saloon, proud American flag, and roadworks. Somebody said that the Dakotas had "the most negligible number of attractions per capita" and were the worst states for road trips, but for me, it was an exciting visit to the American past and a glimpse of the era bygone.

We were on our way to Tetons and the Yellowstone National Park, stopping for a day in Cody, Wyoming.

Mountains were growing taller and taller; Bighorn National Park was a mass of black forest and, as we climbed round and round of the narrow road through the mountains, we could see below the loops of the last few miles that we just drove. The serpentine road looked like a maze on our GPS screen. Exciting three hundred and seventy- seven-mile journey through the Big Horn Mountains brought us to elevations above eight thousand feet. The vista was more than spectacular and driving at thirty-five mile-an-hour- speed- limit presented an opportunity to take more pictures. However, no photo could convey shortness of breath and exhilaration.

Speaking of shortness of breath, not quite three months ago Felix got sick with what we thought was "a virus". He did not complain too much just got himself in the bed with a book and a sour expression on his face. After two days, the book was aside, and the fever was climbing. For some strange reason the good wife, and the doctor, still was not concerned.

I even left him alone for a short trip to babysit my sixteen-year- old grandson while his parents went on vacation. Felix was not an alarmist, but he was still sick when I returned home two days later.

In my doctor's book, any mundane virus could be fixed with hot showers, fluids, chicken soup and two Tylenols. However, even with all these, Felix did not get better.

Finally, after a week of high fever, on Monday morning I put my stethoscope to his hot chest and was appalled by his tremendously decreased breath sounds. His lungs were almost gone! A few hours later, he ended up in the Intensive Care Unit diagnosed with Legionella Pneumonia. After five days, I brought him back home with an Oxygen tube up his nose and a small "blow me" toy, to help to expand his lungs eaten up by a nasty bug.

Now he did not have enough lung capacity to withstand an eight thousand-feet elevation. He was short of breath and did not feel well. We were half-of-the-country away from our home, and he felt weak, dizzy and guilty. "I am sorry, Vika, I am sure I will feel better tomorrow."

The trip of our lives was about to end up in disaster. I clenched my teeth, swallowed my tears and started to plan our flight back home to a hospital and necessary arrangements for the car.

"Easy" was not the word to describe my life, but I smiled bravely to Felix, "Everything is easy when you live in America."

We decided to stay the night and see how Felix would feel

tomorrow. For now, he rested comfortably in the passenger seat. I kept watching him at the corner of my eye. He looked better after a nap, as we started our descent to Wyoming. He moved and opened his eyes. His breathing was fine; however, I could sense that he was still nervous. Trying to distract him, I said, "Remember, how we could not say anything on the phone? Someone was always listening. What did we call it? 'Unrelenting eye of the Party'? Adults had always whispered when conferring with each other, afraid that kids would hear something they should not hear and would repeat it at school or the friend's house. You could not tell a joke to a friend or a co-worker; people were afraid of their own shadows. A fight on the bus, a note from an unhappy neighbor or a suspicion that you were a gay could put you in prison for years; how did we survive all this?"

Felix perked up and smiled, "I was arrested so many times I thought that Korolenko fifteen was my home address."

Every "kievlyanin" (the resident of Kiev) knew the KGB quarters' address by heart. Even now, decades later, I could not shake it out of my memory.

"People were very angry and unhappy with their lives," Felix continued thoughtfully. "They always tried to take it out on somebody, preferably Jewish, and I was a perfect target."

I was happy to see him smiling. His years of fighting and getting into trouble were long gone.

"I did not look like a master in boxing, and everybody wanted to insult and beat up a skinny Jewish boy wearing glasses. I certainly looked like easy prey. In the end, they regretted it, of course, but I was sorry too. I had always ended up arrested and had spent many unpleasant nights at the KGB or Militia offices".

We left mountains painted by the sun and deeply wrinkled by the wind and arrived in quaint Cody, Wyoming. The charming Inn greeted us with an inviting sweet smell of freshly baked pastries. I took one and settled in the cozy armchair in our room.

"Smells like Easter and Babich," I said dreamily. I was back to my parents' home.

BORIS BABICH
KIEV, UKRAINE, THE 1950S

He was an aristocrat; the statement was either a compliment or a detriment, depending on whom you were talking to. Among Victoria's friends, it was a plus, of course. Tall and fit Babich was her Dad's best friend. He had rosy cheeks, straight hair, and piercing blue eyes.

Well-dressed and handsome Boris was a permanent fixture at Victoria parents' apartment. She did not remember herself "before Babich"; he had been always there.

Before the Revolution, his family had four buildings on the Major's Prospect in Saint Petersburg, and he was born in one of them into wealth and pedigree. The Revolution took away both, and in the middle of the night, his parents with his older sister ran to Paris trying to save their lives. The crying baby could compromise their run; they left a little Boris with the nanny and an expansive library.

This library was his substitute for parents, education and, sometimes, bread. He was a voracious reader and planned to be a writer, but in 1941, the Country sent him to fight in the Great War for his Motherland and his city. He was young and brave. His amputated left leg was his contribution to breaking the siege of Leningrad. During these eight hundred and seventy-two days of blockade, more than two million people died of starvation in the city surrounded by German Army.

On a cold winter day of nineteen-forty-four, Boris Babich walked familiar streets on his new crutches supporting his one-legged body. He was proud to be "a liberator," and he could not wait to get back to his old room and his books.

A gaunt man in old rags opened the door; he was hostile and rude. "What do you want? What did you forget here, soldier?" The man was so thin that Boris could almost see through him.

"This is my room with my things," started Boris and stopped. His furniture was gone; only two legs of his mother's favorite chair were on the floor next to the handmade stove. Books, his books, were everywhere, some half burned, some waiting to be burned. Sad and lonely he sat down next to the fire.

"Be careful, boy. Your cheeks are too rosy for this city," the new owner of the room whispered angrily at Boris.

Very few people were able to survive on an inhuman daily ration of hundred-and-twenty-five-grams of bread made of sawdust. The words of cannibalism were whispered on the streets.

Boris sorted out the remnants of his beloved library and moved on.

The immense Soviet Union was one country without borders and passport control. Fifteen free Socialist Republics created the Union, however, in reality, the Russian centralized dominance won, and all the nationalistic movements were suppressed. In fact, everybody lived in Russia and spoke the official Russian language.

Warm provincial Ukraine was as good a place as any, destroyed Kiev had old friends, and an exciting metropolitan past and Boris Babich severed his ties with Leningrad.

Chestnut trees were in full bloom in Kiev, and these white puffs made Boris think and dream of Paris. He had never heard from his family who had left him as a child and there was no way to know what happened to his parents and sister. He learned to love Kiev with its beautiful hills, milder than Leningrad's weather, whimsical architecture and friendly people.

In spring, he loved chestnut trees and lilac in bloom but the most of all, he loved his friends, journalists, writers, musicians and people from famous Movie Studio or "kinoshniki". They all were incredibly poor, and camaraderie was the best substitute for food.

Lenya's one room was their favorite gathering place. Here, they read their new articles, discussed politics, drank small shots of pure alcohol and ate boiled with the skin potatoes. Here, they were not afraid; they dreamed their big dreams and hoped for the better future.

Tall and handsome Boris was not interested in girls. Victoria always thought that her beautiful mother Sarra was his only true but platonic love. Her judgment was based solely on the gentle kiss Boris planted on Sarra's hand with every hello and goodbye; but after all, he was an aristocrat.

Lenya came back from the Great War with one small worn—out suitcase. At the end of the war, every Soviet officer sent home from occupied Germany luggage with the war trophies, the higher rank, the bigger the luggage.

Lenya, now Major of Medical Services, brought home back from the roads to

Berlin two things: a tin ashtray with a naked mermaid, which was somewhat a funny pick for a non-smoker, and his first play "SMERSH"(Death to the fascist spies), that won him the first place at the "Young Play writers Competition".

"This is a disgrace; you have a young daughter at home!" exclaimed his Mom and the ashtray disappeared immediately. His play was a much bigger problem; Lenya had to go to Minsk to get the substantial five hundred rubles award, but he did not have even ten rubles for the train ticket.

"Come on, guys! Turn out your pockets," Boris Babich appealed to his friends at the "vecherinka" (the evening party), passing his cap around. Their artsy friends made very little money and Lenya's friends from the medical school, mostly Jewish doctors, were unemployable in the anti-Semitic Kiev. However, eventually, Boris collected the cash for Lenya's trip. Not only they bought the ticket; there was enough left for the suit and a dashing hat.

The five hundred rubles prize money for his first play fed Lenya's family during the cold and hungry first year after the war.

Boris Babich lived in a small shack, which leaned against a destroyed five-story building. Every time somebody tried to open the door to his tiny room, somewhere inside the bombed building, a few red bricks would tumble down, and a cloud of red dust would cover the face.

"Now we know where Boris got his red cheeks," joked Lenya. His family including Babushka always counted Boris for dinner. He worked during the day and wrote endless plays, movies scenarios and librettos at night; none ever saw the light of the ramp.

The telephone woke up Victoria in the middle of the night.

"It is Boris," she heard her Dad's whisper after a few seconds.

"Patron," Boris was the only one who called Lenya "Patron'." "Sorry, it is not good news. I would like to bring some books for you to read in the morning."

In the dark room, her Father sat with his face in his hands, silent tears streaming on his cheeks.

"We cannot live in this horror," Victoria overheard her parents' conversation. "What if they would come for me?" Lenya was terrified. "What would happen to you and the girls?"

Pale as a sheet of paper Sarra was devastated, "Boris, being who he is, would never survive in jail."

"I could not explain on the phone," whispered unshaven Boris next morning with old crutches in his armpits. "They are trying to pin charge in cosmopolitanism on me." He came with two large stacks of books tied up with the worn out brown rope. It was raining hard, but he had no umbrella; he covered the piles with his only jacket trying to protect the books from the rain. His face, hair, and shirt were soaked; his tears mixed with the rain.

"Patron, I know they will arrest me. Please save the books."

There was not much space in their one small room where five people slept at night and where Lenya managed to see his private patients in the morning.

On a sad rainy day, his last day of freedom, Boris saved and hid from Militia his beloved books. He carried stacks and stacks of the beautifully published old editions by the streetcar back and forth through the city. The rubber ends of his crutches were slippery in the rain, and he had to wait for the tram for a long time again and again, but now his treasured library was stashed a few rows deep on the four built-in shelves behind Lenya's medical books.

They all lived in the nightmare. The constant fear was the backbone of their existence. They were hostages of the system, the mute and frightened slaves of it. Their lives and lives of their families depended on the whim of the Party leader or a new Party slogan, no matter how stupid or preposterous it was.

By the Party directive, an article in the Communist Party newspaper "Pravda" ("Truth") called Jewish intellectuals the "rootless cosmopolitans" and anti-patriots. That was enough to imprison hundreds of journalists, movie directors, writers and artists and to destroy their careers forever.

For the longest time, nobody slept in the family's one-room living quarters. Sarra and Lenya did not sleep in their narrow twin bed listening to every step under their first-floor window; Aunt Rose did not sleep changing Victoria's baby sister Ella's diapers, and Victoria did not sleep as well. She had a ball; under her blanket with the flashlight, she was reading the best of the French Literature: Honore de Balzac, Guy de Maupassant, Alexandre Dumas, Victor Hugo, Stendhal and Gustave Flaubert from the Boris Babich's library.

"Patron," said Boris three years later, "let's write a libretto." He was a new man after these three years in jail on the charges of cosmopolitanism, not that Victoria knew what this meant. Some of her Dad's friends disappeared for a while, some came back, but the loud and rowdy group of friends that gathered at their home now was not what it used to be.

Boris's rosy cheeks came back, his straight hair was combed to part on the side and his new prosthesis, which he wore instead of the crutches, left him with only a slight limp. He was working at the clothing factory now. Victoria had trouble remembering his title, the "confectioner."

He had an inbred good taste, which got him a job where he put together all the essential parts of a suit, fabric, buttons, and lining. At the factory, among the whole generation of young dressmakers grown up in the society that had lost eleven million soldiers in the Great War, he was the most eligible bachelor.

However, Boris was not interested in women. After prison, he had no choice and had to work; however, the writing remained his calling, and he had in mind a very patriotic libretto for the genuinely Soviet ballet.

The echoes of cosmopolitanism were still rolling, the time was dark, and even a pen name could not save a Jewish writer; Russian last name Babich was a much more acceptable name for the author.

"Patron, just imagine a group of mountain climbers ascending the cliff to erect the red flag, a symbol of the victorious communism, on the top of the mountain. They found the mountain flower edelweiss and the real love blossomed under the Soviet red flag," Boris looked like he was on the top of the mountain. "This would be the truly contemporary ballet," he boasted.

He was so convincing that Lenya agreed and with their own money, they went to the Leningrad Ballet Theater to promote their heroic libretto.

The Prima ballerina of Leningrad Ballet Olga Lepeshinsky had a different view, "We usually dance horizontally," she informed the upset friends.

They were in Leningrad of Boris's youth, and he played a graceful tour guide. Four buildings on the Prospect were still there, but his family and his left leg were gone; six days a week aristocrat Boris Babich had to choose the right buttons for the proletarian suits.

After the war, the bad luck landed young Raya at the clothing factory, the place where ninety-five percent of workers were women. Proletarian Raya who had never dated anyone in her life and aristocrat Boris who was not interested in women became good friends.

Raya was a real Communist, a party member for many years. She believed in the doctrine of communism. "Factories and land should belong to the masses, and everyone should be paid according to their ability and needs," she declared from the podium. However, she was an honest and smart woman, and now she was upset how these principles were applied in real life.

Meanwhile, the Party had found a new enemy, and the communists were instructed to find and to persecute homosexuals. Boris heard it first hand or rather from the first mouth, from the Party Secretary Raya herself.

Easter Sunday filled Lenya's new condominium with the fragrant smell of flowering chestnut trees.

"Boris, you should not," exclaimed Sarra, but she was obviously pleased. Boris was holding a tray with a very tall Easter Cake "Babka" surrounded by a ring of brightly colored Easter eggs. "Christ has risen," boomed Babich kissing everybody the required three times on both cheeks.

"Victoria, lay the table, please," commanded Sarra. The sweet smell of freshly baked pastry floated from the dining room to the rest of the large apartment competing with the smell of gorgeous white candles on chestnut trees.

Lenya bought his new condominium with the money from his success: thriving, however illegal, private practice, playwright's honorariums and teaching. Finally, they had a dining room with real dining set for six, master bedroom with two twin beds together, "The Sanctuary"- Lenya's office with an impressively thick Oriental rug and real bookcases filled with special edition books behind the glass doors. Further, along the turned hallway, was the children's room that first housed Ella and later, Victoria with her boys, little Dima and younger Dave. They had a kitchen, all to themselves and a bathroom with a water heater. One toilet served the needs of only one family; there was no waiting line and only one pocket on the wall with a cut newspaper in it. They did not have a choice of the furniture; they bought everything by "blat," the Russian word for the profitable connection.

It was important to have "blat" or people in the right place who owed you a favor. You had to have "blat' if you wanted a book, a better piece of meat, furniture or a ticket to the theater. You would not see what you were buying; everything was in closed boxes so that nobody could see it before delivery. Nevertheless, Victoria's parents were happy to get their hands on any furniture or household items for their new spacious home because the stores were empty.

"Patron," can I, please, have a word with you?" asked Boris and the adults disappeared into Lenya's office. Although Victoria was a student at the medical school and she felt very adult, she was not invited.

"Arnold," whispered Boris at the sanctuary of Lenya's private office. "Poor Arnold is dead. He hanged himself last night. He was arrested a week ago on suspicion of homosexuality."

"O, my god," gasped an eavesdropping Victoria who, in spite of her adulthood, had no idea what homosexuality was, "I thought he was in love with Mom." She was partial to young red-haired Arnold.

"They beat him up mercilessly, and nobody knows if he did it himself or they 'helped' him," continued Boris.

His blue eyes were not piercing but filled with tears and even his holiday suit looked wrinkled and shabby. "I cannot go to prison, Patron. No way! I am scared; they already started to ask questions at the factory." There was a long heavy silence in Lenya's office.

Next weekend Boris and Secretary of Communist Party Raya got married at the community marriage office; their love was born under the threat of imprisonment. Lenya was the witness, and Sarra served the wedding dinner.

*****

The sun was still warm, and Felix felt a bit better away from the high altitude. Cody, the small town of about five thousand was all about Buffalo Bill. In this particular fall, however, only tourists were interested in Buffalo Bill; the locals, strangely enough, were all about Prince Albert II of Monaco, who was coming for a visit. Tickets to the "Patrons Ball" were sold out in the first hour; it was amazing, how many people in Wyoming wanted to meet the Royals.

We had large juicy steaks at Irma's Saloon at the hotel built by Buffalo Bill, watched a small alfresco performance by dressed up folks and retired to our Hemingway Suite.

I had many reservations writing my nightly blog at the desk where Hemingway was writing in nineteen-thirty two. An old rotary phone, his books, and typewriter were still on the small desk, the old clock ticked on the bedside table and his signature in the hotel Register asserted his stay at the room number eighteen. The keys engraved with number eighteen were in my pocketbook. It was hard to believe that over eighty years passed and the bathtub kept the same legs with claws. Where was Mr. Hemingway to write about all of this?

Felix was asleep, and his breathing was quiet and not labored. I hoped we would be fine tomorrow driving to Yellowstone for more views of the mountains and our Golden Wedding Anniversary.

DAY 11, SEPTEMBER 7
YELLOWSTONE NATIONAL PARK
LAKE YELLOWSTONE HOTEL

I remember this sunny seventh of September in Kiev fifty years ago as if it were yesterday.

There was no wedding to speak off, no pictures, no limo or flowers. I had on a short ivory dress with black lace attached to wide raglan sleeves and embellished with small black beads collar. I was a widow after all. Felix wore a suit made in Romania, which cost me forty-eight rubles.

"Victoria, you can confess now! Did you buy this suit as 'a funeral special'?" Felix was in a good mood. "It had only the front and no back."

I did not want to respond; I choose this stupid striped maroon suit myself.

Felix and I, and our two witnesses, my sister Ella and Felix's friend Michael, stood in the long room scarcely decorated with a desk at the end of a shabby runner. I do not remember, which "leader's of all the people and times" portrait was prominently displayed above the desk. Finally, the clerk, a gloomy woman in a dark business suit, ordered loudly, "Approach."

Felix pushed Michael, jokingly, he nudged him forward to go to sign the Certificate of Marriage; and all four of us giggled in spite of the seriousness of the moment. Finally, we all signed the Book and walked a few blocks to Felix's apartment to pick up his Mom. We caught a taxi and went to my parents for dinner with the rest of the family.

THE GOLDEN ANNIVERSARY
KIEV, UKRAINE, THE 1960S

"Victoria," said her Mom. "I want you to come with me. Please".
"But I just came back from Moscow, Mom. I am tired, and I had planned to spend my evening with Dima."

"We promised to come to this wedding a long time ago, but Dad is in Crimea at the "Playwrights' Seminar," and I do not want to go alone. For once, Victoria, please, help me out".

Sarra's tone did not leave any room for more arguments and Victoria went to get dressed.

It was difficult and complicated to live with her parents. That horrible July day a year and a half ago had never left her. It was hovering around her like a shroud, like a fog she could not shake off. She had lost not only her husband, the father of her baby; she had lost herself.

She was in the numb haze when her parents brought her back home from the beach. Without a word, she went to the phone to call his family and friends. She did not cry or scream, but by the last call, she felt suffocated and crushed. She had never picked up the telephone again for the next three years. Her parents had notified everybody else.

She came home from the beach where she had lost him forever, took a shower and went to her parents' bed, and she could not sleep anywhere else since then. She stayed in this bed without eating or drinking for the first two days, and only the baby and the funeral got her back on her feet.

On the sweltering July 12, they brought Dmitry's body for the viewing at her parents' home. Droves of friends, relatives, neighbors, acquaintances, her Dad's patients and just curious people came to express their condolences. As the long line slowly walked by, she sat next to the coffin and nodded, but she did not hear.

She looked at her husband as she had never looked at him before, forever. She had noticed things she had never seen before, and she promised him to remember these forever.

She sat there, in the hot room next to his cold body and watched the drops of sweat appearing under the place where Dima's glasses used to be, and she bloated them out gently, as she would do that for a surgeon in the operating room.

She noticed that the fold of his left ear had never opened and that the webs between his fingers were high and his hands did not look like the hands of the good violinist that he was. She continued to study his features knowing that they will be stored in her memory forever. For their baby.

She wore her Mom's black silk blouse with white lace, black stockings and a black skirt and she did not allow her Mom to hold her when the coffin with the body started to float slowly out of their third-floor apartment on the shoulders of her Dad and Dima's friends. She followed the coffin alone; it was her husband, her catastrophe, and her heartache, forever.

She returned from the cemetery a different woman. She changed, showered, and ate her first meal in three days. She had to think about her baby now. She had no doubt it would be a boy, his father's son, and he would have to live for two. She would name him Dima, and she would never be alone again.

She went to the cemetery every day for a year. First, to find the comfort, to be close to him; then, when a little Dima was born, to tell him about his son, his namesake; and after that, to reassure him that she did not die, that she was strong, and she took care of everything; their baby and her first job at the hospital.

However, she still slept in her parents' bed. She just could not sleep alone.

Dima was a beautiful one-year-old red-haired boy when for the first time she left him with her parents and took vacations. Victoria got permission to visit Bulgaria for a New Year holiday with a group of teachers and engineers.

"Take a vacation, Victoria," said her Dad." I will pay for the trip."

"Go, darling, have some fun" chimed in her Mom. "We will take care of little Dima."

It was a long time since she was excited about anything, but this trip promised to be great.

"Mom, can you, please, do me a favor? Please, discourage Len from coming over to spend time with Dima." Victoria turned around avoiding her Mom's eyebrows raised in the silent question.

Victoria ran into old acquaintance about a month ago. Tall and handsome Len was married to Victoria's classmate from the medical school and was recently divorced. He seemed very nice but very persistent. He called all the time, visited almost daily and was eager to take care of Victoria and Dima.

"His son is a little older than Dima. He lives with Len's ex and Len, probably, just misses him," thought Victoria. She thought that attention of a handsome man would entertain her, but she felt annoyed when he started to call her "baby" and tried to advise her on Dima's upbringing. They were not even dating, and he was already too much. She was just not ready.

The trip was fabulous. First, the group stayed in the capital of Bulgaria Sofia. The city looked a lot like typical Soviet Renaissance but stores were full, and Victoria bought two bottles of Coca-Cola to bring back for Dima to taste.

They went to a ski resort for New Year. In the early morning, when the sun sparkled on fresh snow, Victoria borrowed somebody's skis and firmly planted poles in the snow. She wore her best jacket and Dima's fur hat "pirozhok," which was not a skiing hat, but looked very elegant on Victoria.

"Please, take my picture," she asked one of the friends. "I want everybody to know I was skiing in the Alps."

The trip made Victoria feel alive again; however, it infected her with a dangerous for the Soviet citizens' love of travel. The thought of traveling would always make her heart beat faster. She was jealous of everybody who was about to travel. Sometimes she envied herself when she planned a new trip.

The international train from Sofia was luxurious, each compartment with two plush beds. The attendants served Russian tea, in the glasses with metallic glass holders, and western cookies.

"Stan," introduced himself a man sitting across from Victoria. "The name is Stanislav, but Stan is easier for Russians."

He knew a lot about the Russians. He was a Deputy Secretary of Sport in Sofia, but he lived in Moscow finishing his Ph.D. at the Moscow University. He was in his thirties, a married man with a professional and political career. He had the time of his life in Moscow, where a foreigner was more than a king. They talked all night, and on this train from Sofia, Stan lost his heart to a twenty three-year-young widow.

Victoria liked him too, and she promised to come to visit him in Moscow in a few days. By the morning, they could not survive the separation longer than that.

Something happened to Victoria. Suddenly, she felt young, free, and happy again. The black constricted chain around her heart broke, and she could breathe and be herself again. She was alive, bursting with energy and laughter. Her plan to spend the rest of her vacation in Moscow did not sit well with her parents, especially with her Dad.

"Did you not miss Dima? You just came back from vacation, why do you have to leave again, Victoria. Dima needs you." Dad knew his daughter well, and he was upset.

"Dima is happy with you, and I still have a few days left on my vacation. Please,

Daddy, I will stay with Jenny. There are a lot of concerts and great theatres in Moscow during the Holidays".

Her Dad had a large family in Moscow. His Aunt Fanny, uncles and cousins all lived in Moscow. Victoria, when visiting, always stayed with the family and that appeased her Dad. He even got her two, impossible to get, tickets for a new play.

The week in Moscow flew quickly. Jenny was covering for madly in love Victoria; she liked impossibly elegant Stan. Victoria's head spun between theaters and restaurants for foreigners, Jenny who was glad to see her happy, and incredibly romantic, loving Stan. She missed Dima but did not want to leave Stan. She wanted to stay in Moscow but had to go home.

When she finally returned from Moscow, she was happy that her Dad was away. She did not need an inquisition; she just wanted to talk to her Mom. But now she had to go to this stupid wedding.

"It would be good for you to meet new people," reassured her Mom.

"I already did," muttered Victoria under her chin.

Nevertheless, it was a fabulous wedding. A cold winter moon splashed a golden glow over the white walls of the Restaurant at the Dnieper River Port.

The bride, a daughter of Lenya's medical school classmate, was beautiful. The usual long Russian table was lavish with bottles of wines and vodkas strategically placed every few inches. Most of the guests were her parents' friends rather than the promised young people, and Victoria pulled her Mom downstairs where the real band played at a different wedding, and people crowded the dance floor.

New, confident and happy Victoria looked around for a place to sit. "Let us see what is going on here."

Right next to them, two young men set on the comfortable chairs deep in the conversation.

Sarra, who looked especially stunning tonight in her new light pantsuit, turned to Vika, "The young men of today, do they know how to behave?" She had short red hair and long legs that seemed to start at her armpits. Her dramatic whisper was not a whisper at all, "How can they sit when the ladies are standing?"

"Mom, stop!" started Victoria when one of the men hurriedly got up and extended his hand to Sarra, "May I, please, have this dance?"

By the time they returned from the dance floor, they were the best friends. He called her Sarra, and she introduced him to Victoria. He was well built and clean-shaven, cute with his round glasses and a very deep voice.

His name was Felix.

*****

The morning in the historic Indian Territory of Cody, Wyoming was all about history. Impressively tall, holographic Buffalo Bill greeted us at the spectacular Buffalo Bill Center of the West. Bill's mustache and hat were imposing, his car elegant and his collection of guns … Well, Felix was in awe.

Beautiful grounds, handsome white wigwam, historical documentaries, art and Indian artifacts were more than impressive. We held our hands walking through the history of the land.

The drive through lovely hills and reservoirs toward Yellowstone was easy, and I smiled on the passenger's seat dancing my first dance with Felix.

THE GOLDEN ANNIVERSARY
KIEV, UKRAINE, THE 1960S

"Your Mom is quite a woman, Victoria, and I hope you will grow up to be just like her," smiled Felix. "By the way, she suggested I dance with you."

He was apparently not impressed with Victoria. However, he held her tightly, expertly moving her through the dance floor.

Felix was not joking when he asked, "What grade are you in?"

Surprised Victoria was lost for words; she thought she looked very elegant in her little black and green dress with cold shoulders. Mom's famous tailor Clair had made it specially for her trip abroad.

She combed her red hair up "Babette" style, and long straight bangs swiveled in front of her eyes.

She smiled thinly, ready to kill her obnoxious dance partner.

"Just for your information, I am not a school girl. I am a doctor, a widow with a one-year-old son. I agree, my Mom is a stunning woman, but she is married."

Victoria almost added, "Here you have it, you self-confident prick. "

Her Mom, however, had a ball and she liked Felix. She invited him upstairs and introduced him to her friends. During their nonstop conversations and drinking, she managed to learn everything about him. She was a real woman.

Felix lived last year in Moscow where he was briefly married and divorced amicably.

"There were no children to share, no assets to divide and only my ex-father-in-law will miss his drinking partner," he chuckled. He just returned from Moscow when his Mom asked him to accompany her to the wedding.

"What a funny coincidence," Sarra tried to involve in their conversation still irritated Victoria.

Felix was a charmer. He told jokes, he danced, he drank, he was attentive, and by the end of the night, he called the taxi and escorted the women to their home across the city.

"Please, give him the telephone number, Victoria," whispered Sarra in the taxi. She squeezed her daughter's hand, "He looks so much like Dima."

They exchanged their telephone numbers at five in the morning, and Felix promised Victoria to keep in touch.

After a cold sleepless night, Victoria was happy to jump into her parents' bed next to her Mom.

"OK, he was cute," she mumbled falling asleep.

The telephone rang at eight, and half-asleep Victoria lifted the receiver. "It is probably Dad."

"Good Morning, Victoria" the deep velvety voice in the phone was to die for. "It is Felix. Would you join me at the movie tonight? I got us two tickets for an American movie 'Apartment.' I will pick you up at seven than".

He hung up but his voice, the beautiful sexy voice, which made Victoria want more, was still reverberating in her head.

They never made it to the movie that night. It was a cold January, and Victoria invited Felix to her room, which she abandoned since Dima's death.

"Let us stop by my house," suggested Felix, after they figured out that they were almost neighbors. "I can pick up my guitar."

That sounded interesting, and Victoria offered to wait on the street, but Felix would not hear of it on a cold evening like that. "I do not want to find your frozen body here, Victoria, not yet."

He introduced Victoria to his Mom, who immediately wanted to serve hot tea and to know everything about Victoria. Eventually, Felix picked up the guitar and they left.

He bought Champagne, and he played his guitar and sang beautifully. His low voice pulled invisible strings in her heart. They both loved old Russian romances and Gypsy's songs, and they sang all night as if they rehearsed together all their lives.

They spent their childhood on the same streets and graduated from neighboring schools. They went to the same movie theaters and knew the same people. They read the same books and knew many by heart. Felix quoted famous "The twelve chairs" and "The Little Golden Calf," and Victoria recited her favorite "Black Man" by Esenin.

They were young and free. Felix traveled for work; Victoria started to work on her Ph.D. in Genetics, and little Dima stayed with her parents.

They spent days in and days out on her "recame" making love and rebuilding their shattered lives.

They lived on Champagne and cans of young peas, which were the only items available at the "Gastronom," a big grocery store across the street.

Felix's aunt was a doctor and worked with Victoria's father, and Felix's Mom liked Victoria at first sight. However, burned once, they were very noncommittal with no promises and no plans.

"I never call anybody when I am on a business trip," said Felix.

The telephone rang on the beautiful early spring day when Lenya's friends gathered in his office to hear his new play. Nobody would pick up the phone, afraid to interrupt Lenya. However, the phone rang and rang, and finally, Victoria went to the hallway to stop this nuisance.

A familiar low, velvety voice asked, "What are you doing not picking up the phone? I am on a business trip, and I miss you".

"Long live Bell, the inventor of the telephone!" she sent him a telegram the next morning.

The rule "I do not call" was soon forgotten. Each time after Felix's call, Victoria sent him a whimsical love telegram with quotes from his favorite novels. He laughed but always called back so she could just listen to his voice and remember how much she loves him.

Stan continued to call her. However, he was in Moscow, and she did not want to hurt him by telling she was seeing somebody else.

"Vika, I have a meeting in the South, and I will stop in Kiev for a day, just to see you," Stan's voice was happy with anticipation.

They did not see each other after Moscow, but he was still in love with her. He wanted to divorce his wife, to leave his family and to destroy his promising career for her.

Victoria hoped that Felix would be away on a business trip by the time Stan came.

She wanted to spare Stan's ego and to break up with him without telling him about someone else in her life.

However, Felix was right there when Stan arrived in her apartment. His overnight bag was full of early spring flowers from the South, and Victoria pulled him out to the kitchen to deliver the news. Lizzy Snisarenko pretended she was cooking when Stan unloaded the beautiful flowers on Victoria's corner table in the kitchen. Victoria's heart dropped, and blood left her face; she was sorry she did break up with him on the phone. It was not pretty, he was very upset and she felt terrible. Lizzy did not approve either.

Victoria knew Felix was the one. It was two years since Dmitry's death and her little son growing up with her parents was a year- and- a- half- old.

Felix still cherished his freedom more than a new girlfriend. A year after his divorce, he did not feel ready. However, Victoria knew better.

"We have to get married while Dima is still little so that he would get used to his new father. We can exchange my room and your Mom's room for the two-room apartment and live together as a family. Everybody knows what is going on and I would like to get married again," Victoria's logic was ironclad.

Peace was not the word to describe what was going on in her parents' apartment. Her Dad was furious. He blamed his wife who found "this boy." He cried to show how sorry he was for "the love of his life - little Dima" and he argued with Victoria all the time. He did not want a stepfather for his grandson. He was terrified to lose Dima to another man. He did not want his daughter to remarry.

"You have everything, and I mean everything. You are the doctor, you were married once, and you are working on your PhD. You have your beautiful son and your own place. What else do you need, what else?"

Apparently, the days and nights that his twenty-five-year-old daughter was spending with the man she loved were not a good enough argument.

However, Victoria was a real daughter of her father. "Felix is a great man, Dad. He is generous and kind, and he loves Dima. He is a good engineer, and he can provide for his family. And he is Jewish, what else do you want?"

"You cannot marry this boy Victoria!" her Father tried to convince her. "All he cares is the beach, and you will end up with him in the shack on the beach! Is that what you want?"

"It is a summer Dad, where do you want him to go?"

His stubborn daughter made up her mind already. She bought the suit and the rings, and they applied at the local Office of Death and Marriages. She was a little surprised with a wedding present from Dima's old friends, a ten-day-vacation at a scuba diving camp on the Black Sea.

"They hope that you would drown me too," Felix joked, but Victoria was not amused.

*****

And that was pretty much it, not counting the next fifty years, children, separation, emigration, hard work, traveling, building the house, planting a tree and Grandchildren. Yellowstone will have to wait until tomorrow.

DAY 12, SEPTEMBER 8
YELLOWSTONE NATIONAL PARK, WY
OLD FAITHFUL INN

In the soft light of sunset, I inhaled the view of mirror-smooth waters of the lake. I did not know the name, was it Yellowstone Lake or Shoshone Lake or Isa Lake? The serenity and eternal stillness did not need the name. The elegant striped silk furniture, checkered carpet and yellow walls of our suite at the grand Yellowstone Lake Hotel were a mere background for the view. We were celebrating our Golden Wedding Anniversary at the top of the continent.

Majestic sunset played out on the lake under the accompaniment of classical music by the trio of musicians, and a bottle of Champagne graced the snowy white tablecloth at the dinner. Nobody sent congratulations or E-mails and no one called; Yellowstone did not have Wi-Fi, TVs in the hotel or cell phone reception. Surprisingly, we survived with no problems.

Yesterday, we conquered the Continental Divide at the elevation of eight thousand- two hundred and- sixty- two feet and this morning in the bedroom, Felix was breathing just fine in our spacious California King bed. I felt sorry to wake him up, but we had to meet our guide for a day of touring the world's first national park. The first morning of the next fifty years promised to be as exciting as the first fifty years of our marriage.

I thought about my parents. Their marriage ended up with the death of my father after almost forty years together. They were happy, but their life, like the lives of millions of others in the Soviet Union, was a tragedy. Lies, fear and constant brainwashing were its fabric. They never knew what they were missing, what they would never see and what they would never have; the places they had never visited, the books they had never read, the clothes they had never worn and the food they had never tried. Nevertheless, they were happy, mostly.

SARRA
KIEV, UKRAINE, THE 1940S

"Tovarisch Shamis!" The note from the podium alarmed Cecily. "Where is your friend Sarra? Why is she missing important Komsomol meeting?" Cecily felt her cheeks start to match the color of red flags decorating Kiev Medical School auditorium.

She was furious because she had warned her girlfriend not to play hooky, especially when there was a Komsomol meeting, but free-spirited Sarra did not care.

"Please, be reasonable, Cecily. Would anybody in this crowd notice that I am not there? I am not feeling well, really. Maybe I got a sore throat," a mischievous smile played on Sarra's beautiful face.

This night, her parents had a ticket to the movie, and she had a plan. Her Mom just got a new hat, and Sarra was dying to try it on. She was looking forward to having an apartment all to herself. Well, to herself and her younger brother and sister, but they did not count.

They lived in the lovely apartment in the big gray building on one of the central streets in Kiev. Her father managed a big department store, and her Mom stayed home with kids.

Nineteen-year-old Sarra was in medical school, and her younger fifteen-year-old sister and eleven-year-old brother were still in school.

Before the Revolution, Sarra's grandfather Mark was a wealthy man in a small Ukrainian town where he had manufacturing plant and four daughters. The laughter of the beautiful happy girls filled the big fancy house on the Main Street. Every single man in the town was watching these girls, heirs to a big fortune. The oldest Clara was a champion ice skater.

The town ice rink was flooded with lights and music. "I love winter," Clara's cheeks were pink as she waltzed with Efim on her new skates. She was tall and thin with long legs. She wore her hair up, and she skated divinely.

"Clara, darling, can I, please, have your permission to talk to your father?" Efim was a manager at the plant and four years younger than his date. They were fond of each other, went on a few dates and ice-skated together. He was very handsome, and Clara liked him, but he was just the junior manager, and she was not sure if her father would approve.

Lately, Efim grew more impatient; he was worried that somebody else would steal elegant Clara. He did not plan for the Revolution and the Civil war.

The devastating war raged over Ukraine. Makhno and Petlura, reds and whites, Army and Cossacks fought their bloody battles on the wide Ukrainian steps and in the small villages.

In the town, they lodged in the big house on the Main Street. The manufacturing plant went up in flames, Mark was arrested and executed, and his four beautiful daughters were hiding at the friends' house.

Clara's doubts about young Efim went up in a smoke of the plant's fire and the sounds of the firing squad. She had nothing to inherit; they married quietly and moved to Kiev.

He was managing the department store in the suburbs, they had three children, and she did not ice skate anymore.

The Komsomol Meeting was long and loud.

"Would anybody notice I am not there?" Cecily whispered wistfully, mimicking Sarra's rhetorical question. She was a stylish young girl, smart and confident, always doing the right thing. Young Cecily was not nearly as lightheaded as was her best girlfriend Sarra.

"Lenya, Komsomol Secretary would notice." His signature was right there on the note.

"I am sorry, Sarra, but I have to do this," Cecily smiled as she scribbled Sarra's home address on the message.

She touched the shoulder of the student in front of her, "Please, pass it to Komsomol's Secretary Lenya on the stage."

She thought she was very smart by cooperating with the authority; for a year now, Sarra was dying to get the attention of the tall and handsome Lenya.

Cecily and Sarra were the best friends since the third grade when Sarra's family moved to the same building where prominent Kiev gynecologist, Professor Shamis, lived with his wife and their only daughter.

The girls sat at the same desk at school, did their homework at the same table at each other's apartments and played the same games outside.

"I am going to be a doctor like my Daddy," Cecily always knew. "I am going to medical school."

"You cannot go without me," reasoned an upset Sarra. "I would die."

She contemplated for a few moments, "I am going to be a doctor too, like your Daddy," and then she had a second thought, "I hate math though." "Would I have to take math at the medical school?" She was thrilled with the negative answer, and the problem of the girls' future was solved right there.

This fateful Komsomol meeting was the only thing Cecily attended alone, without her girlfriend.

Clara and Efim finally left for the movie theater, and Sarra got out of the bed where she played hooky. She stood in front of the hallway mirror in the long-sleeved cotton nightgown and her Mother's elegant new hat when the bell rang at their door on the fifth floor.

"O, my God! It could be somebody from the school," Sarra panicked. "Cecily was right; it was so stupid of me to skip the Komsomol meeting."

Nothing could delight her younger brother Zack more than to see his older sister so scared. He ran to the door and opened it, in spite of his parents' constant coaching never to open the door without asking who was behind it.

A tall young man in a hat and a long coat was at the door. Sarra, still with her mother's new hat perched on her head jumped on her bed and pulled a blanket up to her chin.

"Tovarisch Sarra, my name is Lenya, and I am here to check why did you miss the important Komsomol meeting," the tall man could hardly hold a laugh.

"I have a sore throat," Sarra whispered inaudibly. She forgot all about the hat however, she felt terrible in her ugly long nightgown under the blanket.

"I see you are very ill," continued Secretary of Komsomol with all somberness he could master. "Is there anything I can do for you?" he gently took her Mom's hat off her head and put it on a bedside table.

Sarra did not even look at him; her eyes fixed on the tapestry hanging on the wall above her bed. Two deer were running through the snowy forest. Their heads were thrown back, long legs buried in snow, exactly how she felt caught in this stupid bed! She was heartbroken, "He is here, and I look like an idiot!" she wanted to scream.

Clara and Efim noticed long black coat on the hook in the hallway and tiptoed to their bedroom. In Sarra's room, soft man's voice was reading poetry.

They were married in April; Lenya had another year, and Sarra had three years to finish medical school.

At the Office of Registration of Death and Marriages, they looked like brother and sister, both tall and thin, dark eyes and full lips. Just like their parents, they planned their lives, careers, and children. They did not plan for the World War.

Their first wedding anniversary flew by and in June, under the deafening sound of the first German bombs, Lenya graduated from Medical School.

Lenya's class was called to active military duty right after Graduation. There were no festivities, just the goodbyes. At the Railroad Station, the class of the newly minted doctors embarked into two large trucks destined for the front line.

"Tovarisch Secretary, Lenya!" his classmates called urgently. "Somebody has to go to the Military Office to tell them we are doctors, not just soldiers."

"You are right, comrades," everyone waited for Komsomol Secretary's decision. He jumped off the truck and accompanied by two of his best friends went to "voenkomat" (the Military Office).

"We are doctors," Lenya held his new diploma high in his hand, and he sounded calm and collected. "We will protect and serve our Motherland by providing medical care."

It was not easy to convince a very busy Colonel to sign their new orders, but eloquent Lenya would not give up. In all that chaos and confusion, he got permission to delay departure. Pleased with the decision, they rushed back to the trucks; proud Lenya could not wait to tell his friends.

The Railroad Station was covered with smoke. An early morning attack by German aviation reached the center of the city, and a bomb hit one of the trucks. The smoking crater was all that was left. Lucky survivors sorted out the wounded from the dead.

Half of the graduating Class of Kiev Medical School perished in the first week of the war.

Lenya cried all night. Nevertheless, in the morning, he was back to the Military Office, this time with his wife. His Motherland was calling, and they were ready.

The summer day was like all summer days; sunny at first, the low dark clouds gathering later, roaring thunder indistinguishable from the sounds of bombardment. The Colonel was brief, "Here are your orders, Captain of Medical Service. You will accept command of the front hospital and your wife would be your chief surgeon."

Sarra was shocked, "I have finished only three years, Comrade Colonel; I just watched some surgeries as a student." She had never held a scalpel in her hand.

"It is wartime, doctor, and this is your order; what part of it you did not understand?"

"Sarra, you better behave; I am your commander now!" Lenya laughed.

The Colonel was serious, "You studied anatomy. There is no time for your fancy diplomas! Carry out, Lieutenant!"

Lenya pulled her out of the office, and they held their hands all the way to the Railroad Station. They did not have time to say goodbye to their parents.

Railroad Station "Vokzal" was a center of life and chaos.

"Kievlyane", as people who lived in Kiev called themselves, were trying to leave the town, to evacuate. Every available railroad coach- and even freight cars- were full of people heading east, old and frail, babies and families, sitting and standing, heading to remote areas of Middle Asia, away from the Germans.

Lenya was looking for the train going west; he could not wait to meet an enemy eye to eye. Finally, they found a large railway truck attached to the train going west. It was jam-packed with sitting soldiers who made room for two more.

Endless Ukrainian fields were pregnant with bread; fat cows were full of milk and chickens were laying eggs; however, there was no hope anywhere. The German Army was pushing ahead with their warplanes and tanks.

Heavy clouds covered the sun and sprinkled a warm rain. Soldiers huddled under canvas and started to sing quietly. In spite of the rain, the mood on the platform was almost celebratory. Soldiers sang patriotic songs, shared bread and offered water to strangers. They were untouchable, protected from the enemy's wrath and fury by their youth and high spirits.

They did not notice a tunnel ahead. Suddenly the thick black smoke covered the railway lorry. The train siren blasted as the train speed up through the tunnel. Tap-dance of the train tires reverberated from the tunnel's walls.

"Bomb, bomb" screamed panicky people. "We are on fire!"

"Jump!" yelled Lenya. He caught Sarra's hand, his only possession, and pulled her to the edge of the truck. "Jump, we have to jump, Sarra."

"No" cried terrified Sarra, "I cannot!"

At full speed through the long tunnel, soldiers were jumping from the moving flatbed truck and horrendous sounds of falling bodies added to the terror and confusion.

"Sarra, jump, please" begged Lenya.

"No!" bowled hysterical Sarra "No!"

Covered with soot, deafened by the noise of the siren, her lung full of smoke, she cried "No, no!" and kept holding on, when suddenly, at full speed the train emerged from the tunnel to a sunny summer day.

There was no fire, just the ash from the locomotive, train siren and long tunnel, fear and the panic.

The train did not stop to pick up the dead.

*****

The park reminded me of the Great War. Geysers were regularly erupting and blasting, the water mist reminding the smoke of the war. Hot springs, steaming mud pots, steam spewing caverns and active geysers were everywhere. All ten thousand of them, more than in the rest of the whole world together. They were covered only by the fragile earth's crust, thinner than anywhere else; just one mile thick compare to the average five. Six hundred thousand years of geothermal activity bottled up under a thin plate of the caldera.

We checked into our Hotel appropriately called Old Faithful Inn. One of the most significant log buildings in the world, built in 1904, the Inn was right next to the Old Faithful Geyser erupting every seventy-five minutes.

In the impressive atrium with the log-lined ceiling, hundreds of candelabras, stone fireplace and massive clock, we met our guide John, the country boy from Montana as he called himself. The history was lurking from every corner and hiding behind every column of the old hotel.

We drove in the park for eight hours and the day's images still thrill me. No photos or words could describe the feeling of facing nature at her best.

Hundreds of graceful bison grazing in the valleys, the majesty of mountains and canyons, exuberance of geysers and waterfalls, cliffs painted with the most beautiful pastels and vivid greens of the grass made the park heavenly and sacred. Our guide turned out to be a talented and celebrated photographer of Yellowstone with many coffee table books to his credit.

There was no coffee table in our somewhat rustic room.

There was no TV or Wi-Fi, and after a splendid and appropriately rustic dinner at the restaurant with the incredibly high ceiling, we went to our separate beds. Old Faithful Inn was true and authentic; they did not know about king beds back then in 1904. King size beds came only in the 1940s, and I felt sad and lonely alone in my bed.

EFIM
KIEV, UKRAINE, THE 1940S

Everybody who could run ran. As Germans were approaching, civilians were leaving the city. They could not bring the luggage, only what was on their backs and in early September, that was not much, Kiev was a southern city blessed with warm Septembers that did not require warm clothes.

"Clara, please, get ready, I am taking you to the Railroad Station," hurried Efim.

"Darling, why do not you leave with us?" Clara's eyes were red from crying. "I am afraid you will never find us."

"Clara, I have to close the store. I do not want my store to be looted or robbed while I am responsible for it. Please, do not worry; I will join you in a few days."

The store director and his family left the town three days ago.

Clara and kids were ready. By the Russian custom, they set down "for the road." Efim loved this "for the road" tradition when after all the rush and fluster of the last minute preparations everybody sat down quietly, collected their thoughts and thought about their future. An eerie silence hung in the room for a few minutes. Then everybody hugged each other, said their goodbyes, kissed their kisses and left their home. Forever.

The Railroad station could not possibly fit the crowd of this size. Efim in his elegant three-piece-suit was almost lost; still, he managed to squeeze through the mass of people to the edge of the platform, closer to the train. He saw crying people sitting and standing between the seats. He did not see his kids; they were not tall enough to stand out in the crowd. Only his tall wife was waving her beautiful long-fingered hand from behind somebody's back.

They would never see each other again; their marriage died forever on this crowded Railroad Station in Kiev.

The empty city was holding its breath before the occupation. Efim went to secure the store and returned home. The furniture was still there. His wife's dresses and orphaned hats were in her large wardrobe and deer were running through the snowy woods on the old tapestry in Sarra's room.

As Germans occupied the city, there were no more trains out.

The flyer called on "All Jews of Kiev and suburbs." They had to report the next morning "with documents and valuables." The flyer also mentioned "warm clothes" so most of the people believed that, Germans would "deport" the Jews. The note further threatened, "Those who will not obey will be shot when found".

Efim remembered the crowd at the train station; he thought everybody had left, but him. He was alone and scared. He did not believe in Germans' goodwill; he did not think they would deport Jews because they spoke a very similar language and he knew he could not stay in his apartment.

At night, he quietly knocked on the door of their Ukrainian neighbors. The families were friends for years; they often went to see movies and had dinners together.

"Efim", Maria throw up her hands in surprise. "What are you doing here?"

"Clara with the kids had left and I, unfortunately, got delayed." He was handsome and tall, and his suit looked good on him. "Is it anyway I can stay with you for a few days till the deportation would be over?"

Efim Nelkin, Killed in Baby Yar

She was short and plump with a thick blonde braid ringed like a snake on the top of her head. Her blue eyes angrily narrowed when her husband came to the door saying "Efim, come in, friend."

He was hot and cramped inside her wardrobe where he slept that night. The first narrow ray of the sun made its way through the crack in the door and woke him up. "Morning," he said to himself. "What am I going to do now?"

The closet door flung open as sudden sunshine flooded and blinded Efim. He heard Maria's whisper, "There, in the closet," and he saw the gun barrel aimed at him.

On the outskirts of the city, next to the deep ravine called Baby Yar (The Old Woman Ravine), the crowd moved slowly. It was forced into a narrow corridor formed by the rows of German soldiers who were hitting the Jews with the whips trying to hurry slow moving people. Frightened elders and children, beaten up women, singles, and families, young and old slowly reached the clearing on the edge of the deep ravine. They were ordered to undress. In the depth of the ravine was the sea of bodies, shoot in cold blood. They all, almost a hundred thousand of them, died here in the Baby Yar. The early autumn leaves shrouded their bodies.

*****

Felix was snoring softly. He did not remember his father.

"Your Dad was mobilized before the Germans occupied Kiev. His battalion was ordered to blow up "Dneproges," the power Station on the Dnieper River. You were only three-month-old baby. They all died there in the summer of 1941," his mom told him. I guess she was not as good as my dad in telling the stories.

DAY 13, SEPTEMBER 9
JACKSON HOLE, WY
SPRING CREEK RANCH

W e were off to the hole, Jackson Hole, and the morning greeted us with the myriads of geysers shooting steam and water up to the sky very pregnant with heavy clouds. Bypassing a long line of antique cars curving around the entrance to "The Old Faithful" we left steaming grounds of Yellowstone. A gauzy curtain of light rain hanged behind us. In my driver's mirror, steam from the geysers was rising like smoke, like an echo of the War.

SARRA
KUYBYSHEV, RUSSIA, THE 1940S

I t was a hospital in name only, but they did their best; they were a great team. Lenya did everything: organized staff, got food and medications, surgical instruments and beds. At night, he reviewed with Sarra wound care and sutures. General surgery was not his strong point; however, he taught his wife everything he had learned and remembered from the medical school.

After the war, he would tell great jokes about her misdiagnosis, fear of scalpel and less than stellar cooking skills. However, in the midst of war, Sarra took care of the wounded, operated as much as she could and saved many lives. After two years of war, she realized that she was pregnant.

Clara with her two younger children Magda and Zack had never reached the warm Asian republic. They settled in Samara, then Kuybyshev, one of the large industrial centers of Russia. The city planned to be an alternative capital of Russia in case Moscow would fall to the invading Germans; all the Government organizations, diplomatic missions and cultural companies had already moved to this town on the Volga River. In the unthinkable case of the defeat, Stalin had prepared a bunker specially built for him.

Large military plants made aircrafts and supplied the front with firearms and civilian hospitals became military medical facilities.

Clara and seventeen-year-old Magda worked at the military plant.

"Kuybyshev is a relatively safe place to deliver the baby," Lenya was thinking ahead. "And your Mom and Magda would be happy to help you for the first few weeks."

"Do not even try this, Lenya; I am going right back with you and the baby." Pregnant Sarra looked funny in her military uniform, but she was not one to argue with. She was an excellent surgeon, and the hospital would never be the same without her.

"It is a boy, Major!" The chief Army Gynecologist sat behind the massive desk. "I assure you, it is a boy. Look, I even wrote it in my famous 'predictions' book right here 'a boy'". He pointed at the thick leather-bound notebook on the desk.

Kuibyshev Delivery Clinic, now Central Military Hospital, stood on the cliff above the vast Volga River.

At the office of the Chief Doctor, Lenya paced the whole length of the room from the door to the window. Sunny day in early May was full of promise and expectation.

"Look at all these people carrying water from the river uphill," he suddenly panicked; Sarra was in the delivery room, and he was afraid of complications. "Do not you have water in the city?"

"Relax Major; it is beer. There is a beer factory near the river and people are buying the cheap beer there. You do not think Comrade Stalin is about to move to the city with no water."

The telephone interrupted their conversation.

"It is a girl? Wonderful, just as I predicted," the doctor was smiling as he put down the receiver.

"Congratulations, Major! You have a new daughter!"

Stunned Lenya could not believe it, "You said 'a boy'." He immediately understood how ridiculous he sounded.

"Did I? Let us see what I wrote here," the Chief Gynecologist was smiling. He opened his "Predictions" book, "The last entry clearly said 'A girl'".

"My dear young friend, here is a trick for you. If you ever predict 'a girl', you would write 'a boy'. If it were a girl, nobody would question you, but if it were a boy, parents would not hesitate to show you how wrong you were. Then you'll show them a book, and here it is; you are always right!"

The next day the military daily newspaper "On the Guard of the Motherland" published Lenya's poem dedicated to his newborn daughter.

On the warm May night,
Light breeze lullabies the water.
Your Father could hear far away, on the front,
The first cry of his precious daughter.
This cry is calling us on to fight;
The road to Berlin had begun.
We all are dreaming of ending the night
To return to daughter or son.
The soldiers are slipping, after hostile
Days of bombing when the world is rattled;
I see, my daughter, your lovely smile,
I can feel it ahead of the battle.
I see little hands and your lovely face,
Blond curls on your neck little wrenched.
Remember, that many like her, in disgrace
Nazis had burned in the trenches.
Many were killed; it would never change.
Tore tanks our children to bits.
Burn in my heart, the sacred revenge,
And lead us to righteous deeds.

She was Victoria for the victory, she was named after her grandfather Volf, and she was the girl who would be her Dad's first-born son.

After only a few months, Sarra brought Victoria back to the front hospital, back to their daily routine of taking care of the sick and wounded soldiers. They were moving westward now, behind the front lines, pursuing retreating German Armies. As they liberated towns and villages, the hospital would confiscate empty houses to treat wounded, but they stayed in the dugouts.

During the bombings or heavy firefights, Sarra would put Victoria on the steps. "If we would be hit, they dig out steps first," she reasoned. Baby Victoria spent her first year, on the steps of their underground mud huts swiveled in the soldiers' uniforms or hospital shirts.

*****

Curvy and pleasant John D Rockefeller Jr Parkway brought us to the Grand Teton National Park. The mountains were all around us. I lost my count of the names a long time ago, the Black Hills to Tetons and everything in between.

We crisscrossed the Continental Divide many times and drove hundreds of miles on fantastic, beautiful and terrifying mountains roads. Coming to quaint Hole was a breeze, and the road was easy.

SARRA
KIEV, UKRAINE, THE 1940S

The war was almost over when they returned to their hometown tired but happy to be alive. Victoria was nearly two, and Lenya was looking forward to settling his family and becoming a civilian.

He tried to open the door to his former apartment, but the key did not fit. His whole family, with their scarce belongings, crowded the stair landing behind him. The door finally opened, just to slam right back into his face. He recognized the familiar face of their Ukrainian neighbor. "You had left, and the apartment is ours now! We have an order!"

"Did Nazis issue it?" yelled Lenya. He was furious; he fought for these people while they stole and prospered under the Germans. It was too late; they were tired with no roof above their heads.

The door to Sarra parents' apartment opened. Behind it was her Mom's friend Maria. She was not happy to see them.

"The apartment is ours now," she explained to Sarra. "We lived here for the last four years after your parents had abandoned it." She turned around showing her thick blonde braid on the top of her head and closed the door. Sarra stole the glimpse of the deer still running on the wall in her old room.

The war was over, but many men did not return home, and Clara with young Magda stayed in Kuybyshev working at the military plant. Magda was a beautiful twenty-one with no chance to find her love at the city, where most of its male population was resting in peace in the fields of Eastern Europe. However, Clara would not return to Kiev after Baby Yar. Magda never got married. Only Sarra's brother Zach came from Kuybyshev to study.

Candelabras on the chestnut trees were in full bloom, but Kiev's main Kreshchatyc Street looked like a thousand- year- old ruins. The city was bombed mercilessly at the very beginning of the war. No one knew and would never believe that before the Germans moved in, receding Red Army wired the city to destroy it.

Lenya walked into the office of the chief medical bureaucrat of the city. Short dark-haired woman with small eyes sat at the desk.

"If eyes are the reflection of the soul," thought Lenya "this woman has none." However, he was looking for work, and she held the keys. After a very brief conversation, it became clear to him that no Jewish doctor would ever find a job in this city, with this woman at the helm. During the occupation, Kiev citizens had learned too well how to deal with the Jews.

"Major, there is plenty of work somewhere else," she said. "There are no positions for your people here." His rage built up inside him as he quietly picked up a red inkwell sitting in front of her on the desk and slowly showered her hair and suit with red ink. "You will never work in Kiev," she shrieked to his exiting back.

She was right! The Major of Medical Services, the veteran of the war and recent Head of the large military hospital could not find a job in Kiev. And he was not alone; his friends, doctors returning home after the war, could not find any paying medical positions in this city.

They laughed, "We are beating our swords and stethoscopes to plowshares." Four of Lenya's close friends since medical school formed an Association of Unemployed Doctors and shared what little they had. They went to cover roofs; they worked in constructions, and occasionally moonlighted in clinics and Emergency rooms.

Jack was a tall, handsome urologist, always laughing, always with a new joke. He and his musician brother Igor lived with their mother who was the only source of income and food for the family. Elegant woman with flawless skin, she was a well-known beautician, and her clients wanted to be beautiful even in the hard times. Every Sunday, Jack faithfully delivered a half a cup of semolina, a gift from his Mother, to make sure that Victoria would have her breakfasts.

Monya, a big, tall, kind and smiley dermatologist, had survived the German occupation in a remote Ukrainian village and just returned home with his sixteen-year-old wife. They brought from the village a sack of potatoes for the winter. On a cold and gloomy first Christmas after the war, on Lenya's birthday, Monya brought a great present: two boiled potatoes and half-a-cup of pure medical alcohol. There was no end to joy in a tiny room on the third floor. They sat on the wooden trunk serving as Victoria's bed at night, on the narrow single bed ideally suited for very thin Sarra and Lenya and on two wobbly chairs of unknown origin. They wished prosperity to the birthday boy, although it was difficult to imagine this wish granted. Nevertheless, they were happy.

With the hope for the future employment, Lenya secured a volunteer teaching position at the medical school.

Winter was unusually cold and around four that afternoon, the day went dark. The patient could not breathe. He was a young man. The ambulance left him half dead at the Emergency Room where Lenya was moonlighting. Time was of the essence and Lenya did not wait for an X-ray. He placed a long needle into the boy's chest to drain fluid constricting his lung. He watched his young patient all night; they both were lucky.

The crisp winter morning found both men sleeping. The patient's breathing was nice and quiet, and his cheeks were rosy. Next to his bed in the chair, his tired doctor slept with his knees under his chin. Neither doctor nor the patient woke up when the patient's father walked in the room. He worked at the bakery across the street, and he brought freshly baked heavenly sweet-smelling real challah. That smell woke up the doctor; he had not smelled anything so beautiful for the longest time.

"Doctor, I just baked it; this is for you. You saved my son; I wish I had a better present for you."

The whole family gathered around a small table with the priceless challah at the center. Babushka was a practical woman, "It is not enough for everybody. We have to sell it and buy dark bread".

Mila, Lenya's younger sister and a student at The Dental School swallowed hard, but had to agree," Somebody needs to go to the Farmers' Market right now."

There were not enough places for all six of them at the dining table and Victoria, sitting on Zack's knee, started to cry; she had never tried challah in her life. She dreamed, when she grew up, to be saleswoman at the small bakery so that she could try challah.

Sarra was finishing her studies at the medical school, and Market was on her way. She volunteered. She had never sold anything in her life, but she took the challah.

She hid the challah under her coat. It was an outdoor market and Sarra was shivering; her black winter coat was too short and too thin in the freezing cold. She was afraid to take the challah out for the fear that the militia would arrest her for speculation.

Suddenly she became hot and sweaty, and she tried to catch slowly falling snowflakes with her mouth. She did not feel well. A beautiful aroma rose to her nostrils, and her empty stomach growled loudly. She became dizzy and disoriented.

She fainted, clutching the soft challah to her chest. Fresh winter snow covered her black winter coat. She did not hear a siren of the ambulance. She woke up in Emergency Room, and there was no challah under her coat. She was hungrier than ever.

*****

Every one of them was dead by now. Jack died before he turned fifty after three heart attacks and two small strokes. He was young and full of life. His younger brother Igor Shamo, who played accordion at Mila's wedding, became a famous Ukrainian composer, a celebrity; he lived longer, but still not to ripe old age.

What is the notorious old age anyway? Who established criteria and what does it mean? My Dad and his friends endured the war, lived in constant fear under threats and abuse of Russian existence and they all died young. They were lucky if they lived to see their kids grow or knew their grandchildren. There were no golden anniversaries; people just did not live that long. I had never expected to live in the twenty-first century! Somewhere about the 1950s, I calculated, "I would be over sixty!" Surprised I sighed, "But that would be impossible."

"Victoria I am starving!" Felix interrupted my sad train of thoughts. "Do you think we can stop somewhere to grab a bite or should we wait until our hotel?" He suddenly screamed as if the best five- star French restaurant was in front of him, "Victoria, look, it is a family of elk, in front of you on the right."

It was only a beautiful sculpture, of course; however, I turned the car and drove up a short winding road to an impressive structure built from the local unfinished boulders. Full-size sculptures of the National Museum of Wildlife were amazing, more so, they were almost alive.

It was an unusual and an extraordinary museum. No matter how many pictures we took, it was not enough. The exposition, the sculptures, the artifacts and even the gift shop were no less impressive than a bison walking the highway yesterday.

We turned the corner out of the Museum and found ourselves in Jackson, Wyoming, Incorporated 1914 and Elevation 6209. Where was the proverbial hole in Jackson Hole?

We settled in our very rustic and very comfortable three-story condominium with the most amazing views. We did not waste time for unpacking and walked to The Granary restaurant. On our way, we saw a celebrity actor, Indian wigwam, stop sign that said "Whoa" and endless ski trails. The Granary was a quaint restaurant with the view that seemed to stretch from Wyoming to Massachusetts. And the food was outstanding.

Nevertheless, on the way back we stopped at the next-door Hotel Amangani to make a reservation for dinner tomorrow. There are only two Aman Resorts in the United States and, as we were booked to stay in one of them later on, we decided to try the dinner at one in Jackson Hole.

We walked back home passing by endless mountain ski trails, Indian wigwam and "whoa" stop sign. There were no celebrities in sight.

I took the stairs to inspect children bedroom, for which we had no need, of course, and found a fantastic huge stuffed bear on each bed.

I was so sorry for myself thinking about every bed I had slept in my childhood that did not have this incredibly soft and plush bear. I was deceived and deprived of so much happiness on every cot, every mattress, every folding bed, even on the orange "recome." I was very sorry for Ella who had to share the sofa bed with me instead of a plush teddy bear, and I was sad for my cold feet in the winter, which I tried to warm up touching her warm sleepy legs.

I could see my Dad and hear his voice reading The Three

Bears tale to me, improvising every sound and every gesture, playing the Bear family as only a great actor could.

I set on the bed, hugged the bear and cried. I cried for my childhood, my parents and the war; I cried for our horrible and at the same time beautiful and sweet life back under Socialism long time ago.

"Victoria, are you crying?" Felix was rushing upstairs. "What happened? Did you hurt yourself? Is something wrong? Did I say something to upset you?"

He was surprised and concerned because usually, I am not the crying type. We were far away from home, two very ambitious but "over the hill" people with no family or friends nearby to come to the rescue if needed. Our lifelines, telephone, and computer were fragile and unpredictable. We relied on each other for everything, and this was a very long and challenging trip. We both had to be in a great shape to finish what we started. There was no U-turn around and go back, no place or time for physical or psychological meltdowns and even no way for the car trouble.

I smiled and got up from the bed. I had just realized that we operated under these conditions for the last fifty years.

DAY 14, SEPTEMBER 10
JACKSON HOLE, WY
SPRING CREEK RANCH

E arly morning in Wyoming was crisp and bright. We could not resist and, wrapped in our bed covers, stayed on the balcony inhaling small pearls of mountains dew.

The tall cold mountains were all around us; front, back, and sideways. Their peaks did not look friendly. I would have loved this view a month ago, but after driving in the mountains for two weeks, I did not appreciate the heights.

A couple of small miracles happened that day in the glorious town of Jackson Hole. First, we did not have to pack and to drag our luggage back to the car. Instead, we got dressed and went for a fabulous breakfast at the restaurant.

Only in Wyoming, you could have your sunny side up eggs served over a trout that was still swimming in the Spring Creek this morning. Thinking about a beautiful silvery trout sparkling in the morning sun, I was glad I did not order the fish. Yogurt and berries were fine with me.

Two tall log piles were guarding the entrance to our condominium; ski trails were hosting horseback riding group and the day was glorious. I was working my camera non-stop.

Then, I stepped on a pebble and fell. I fell so very slowly trying to catch my balance, to break the fall and to protect my camera. My poor husband stood frozen in horror. I still fell managing to endure only minor abrasions and a couple of strained muscles; however, my camera suffered a terrible concussion with injured zoom and a screen that turned bright pink. My quick diagnoses was a hemorrhaging stroke. I clicked camera on and off, turned it upside down but my first aid was not able to resuscitate it.

I was heartbroken; as organized as I am, I did not find time to upload or to backup my photos for the last two weeks. The pictures of the family wedding in Kansas, the herd of bison at the Custer State Park, the Presidents on Mount Rushmore and all the beautiful geysers and Sapphire Pools at Yellowstone were not backed up and lost, together with the damaged camera. We had nothing to show for all these hundreds of traveled miles.

Sad and achy, we took a hotel shuttle to town and went to a camera store. The lovely lady by the name Sue confirmed my suspicion about the hopeless state of my camera. I was devastated.

What happened next, I could attribute only to the divine intervention; while helpless Sue turned the camera this way and that way, suddenly it started to function again. It remembered all the photos I had taken for the last three weeks and some more of the beautiful town of Jackson Hole.

We marveled at the flyer, offering five-hundred-dollar-reward for the arrest and conviction of Jesse James and had a few drinks at the "Million Dollar Cowboy Bar" sitting on the bar stools, imitating and shaking like the rattling saddles. The old painting "The Battle of Pierre's Hole" circa 1832 and a bronze cash Register of a similar age created the anachronistic ambiance in the bar.

Enjoying our restored camera, Felix took a picture of me with a huge but friendly bear that was a perfect work of taxidermist. We even set under an arch made entirely of elks' antlers. A white and intricate arch was donated by the twenty- five- thousand- acre National Elk Refuge that provided a winter shelter for several thousand elks.

"Maybe we should buy a couple as a souvenir," Felix suggested trying to hide a smile. "We'll hang them above our bed back at home." I just took a picture with my newly revived camera.

AUNT ROSE
KIEV, UKRAINE, THE 1950S

"It was great fun," announced Victoria. She burst into the room like a small tornado; two big bows in her braids, school uniform is twirling around her knees. Apparently, every school day at her first grade was fun.

"I have a great news Victoria," said Lenya. "I got a new job, and we are moving." "They gave us a new room, just for the three of us."

He kneeled next to Victoria and whispered as if telling a big secret, "Well, it is, actually, four of us, girl. Soon you are going to have a little brother".

The smile disappeared from her face, "I do not want to move, Daddy. I do not want to leave my school, and I do not want any brother, little or big!" Her Dad, her favorite man in the whole world, smiled and shook his head in disbelief.

She woke up in the middle of the night because her Mom was crying.

"Good," Victoria rubbed her eyes. "She also does not want to move, and she also does not want me to have a brother."

"Lenya, we have to take Aunt Rose in," cried Sarra softly, "Lazar beats her up! She, practically, brought me up" added Sarra, "and she would help us with the baby."

Aunt Rose came to live with the family on a rainy late fall day. She was short and thin; kerchief covered her graying short-cropped hair.

She was Sarra's aunt, one of the four beautiful, carefree girls, heirs of the fortune lost to Revolution over thirty years ago. Rose lived with Clara and Efim helping her older sister when Sarra was born. Later, when they moved to Kiev, there was no place for Rose in their city apartment. Another sister- Zina got married, and Rose and the youngest sister Bella moved in with her to help her with the children.

Zina married a stocky owner of the farm outside of the city. Short red-haired Lazar was a ruthless "enemy of the state," "kulak" maintaining his lands and cattle. He hoped to escape horrors of "collectivization" and "dekulakization" by having his family working on the farm.

Stalin ordered to exterminate kulaks, as a class, by sending them to "Gulag." The party planned to resettle them to distant parts of Siberia and to "appropriate" their farms and cattle for the newly established collective farms.

To have a hired help could mean execution, however, to have his wife's two sisters living with them was no crime and Lazar needed help with his farm.

The air was fresh, and bread and milk were always on the table. Zina and Lazar had two small daughters, and all three sisters were busy living under one roof, taking care of the family and working on the farm.

During the war, the farm was destroyed, the cattle were lost, and the sisters grew older. In spite of his wife's protests, Lazar became more and more abusive with his sisters-in-law, but Rose and Bella had no place to go to.

Sarra, who loved her aunts, was distraught and as always, Lenya came up with the solution, "Rose is going to live with us, and Mila will take Bella."

His sister Mila was married to the dentist; they just moved back to Kiev and had a new son so that Bella would be a great help.

"Somebody will need to look after Victoria," Babushka tried not to show how unhappy she was with the prospect of two new women in her son's and her daughter's families, in her own domain.

"It is Victoria's first year at the school and with a new place, a new school and a new woman at home it will not be easy for the girl."

Lenya did not get his son. The new beautiful daughter Ella with wide open dark eyes joined her much older sister and the family moved. Their one room had a big window above the coal pit.

The five-story corner building took the whole city block and used coal for heating. Large trucks delivered coal every week and dumped it to the pit under the window of Lenya's new room. After every delivery, as the dust settled Aunt Rose washed the window.

The building had five entrance halls and a vast rectangular yard. There were rows and rows of small, dilapidated sheds built mostly with plywood, corrugated metal, and cardboard. The adults stored inside everything that had no value and would not attract a thief; but for the kids, the sheds were the favorite place to play hide and seek or to jump from one wobbly roof to the next.

There was a pitiful sandbox for younger children, right next to the sheds; but it was more suited to the needs of stray cats than for the kids.

Aunt Rose loved taking care of Ella, especially when she walked on the street with her pride and joy "co-o-o-ing" quietly in her royal blue carriage with real Plexiglass windows. People turned and stared at the beautiful stroller and the baby, the first generation after the war.

Ever since they moved, Victoria begged her Dad for a bike, and she could not be happier when one night he came home with a shiny new bike.

One beautiful Sunday morning, the whole family lined up in the inner yard to watch Victoria riding her new bike for the first time. She smiled and got on the bike. It looked so easy when her friends rode their bikes, but this one was stubborn and did not listen to her. She tried to turn, but somehow she drove her new shiny bike right into the coal pit under their window. Her dirty face and clothes did not make Aunt Rose happy. Her Dad, however, was not upset with the broken bicycle; he could not believe his daughter could fail so miserably.

"Victoria, you are late for school, hurry up!" It was Aunt Rose's task to send Victoria to school every morning. Victoria tried to lace up her ankle-high winter shoes while reading a book opened on the floor. Her half-eaten breakfast was waiting its turn on the table.

"Lenya," complained Rose, "she is reading those books again."

From the very beginning, Rose did not get along with the headstrong seven-year-old.

"You had told her that she is too young to read Balzac, but she is only interested in reading the books that Boris left here," she complained to Lenya. "And yesterday she was running on the sheds' roofs again. I don't know how many times you told her not to". Aunt Rose always had a long list of things wrong about Victoria.

"She is not doing her homework; she did not open a textbook even once last night."

"Daddy, but I have all 'excellent,' and I don't understand why she is always complaining," fenced Victoria.

"And she stole Sarra's olives," started Rose again. That was the last straw; Victoria could not let her Dad hear this story. This was her worst downfall, even worse than riding the bike to the coal pit.

Last month, Galya, Victoria's best girlfriend, organized a potluck dinner on the windowsill between the second and the third floors. Every invited girl agreed to bring some food and Victoria volunteered for dessert; she saw her Mom brought home plums, an incredible rarity in the winter.

Galya had a beautiful blond hair and sky blue eyes inherited from her Dutch mother. Her Ukrainian father died a few years ago from war wounds. Victoria and Galya shared the desk in the same class and lived in the same building; they were inseparable. Last Sunday, Galya's grandmother even took Victoria to the church where she sent her up the aisle to kiss the priest's hand.

"If only Aunt Rose knew that," thought Victoria with secret revenge.

To her party, Galya brought three boiled potatoes, and other girls pitched in bread and two pieces of meat from somebody's stew. Everybody wanted to try the plums promised by Victoria. The guests could not wait but Galya, as a hostess, was the first one to try.

The plums were rotten; they were very wrinkled and salty. Galya spat out the first one. The rest of the plums shared the same fate. Her girlfriends were angry with Victoria and Galya threw her out of the party.

"Take your rotten dessert with you," Galya ordered to crying Victoria. Victoria hated olives ever since.

Lenya swept the book from the floor and nudged Victoria to the door, "Run, Vika, you are late for school. We will talk later about those sheds".

"Thank god, she did not see me yesterday in the church," smiled Victoria.

The street they lived on was not a big street, not a main drag, for sure, just the side street with some traffic. There were not many cars on Kiev's roads, mostly one or two horses pulling big wooden carts. At their leisure, horses relieved themselves on the fresh snow right on the street. If you were not careful crossing the street, an occasional truck would splash horses' urine thawing in dirty snow all over you. However, by night, everything would freeze, and kids waited for the trucks or wagons with great anticipation; they hooked their wire hooks to the back of the trucks and ice-skated on the yellowish ice back and force all evening.

"I did not fall even once last night on my new "snegurochki" skates," Victoria informed Galya proudly next morning. The misfortune with olives was long forgotten, and they were the best girlfriends again.

Victoria could not wait to share another important piece of news with her friend. "I am going with my Mom to see a 'televisor' tonight," she bragged during the recess.

"What is that?" Galya was doubtful. She did not trust her girlfriend after "plums." "I know about a telephone, but did you say 'televisor'?"

"It is like a movie at home, just much smaller."

They knew all about the movies. Everybody used to stay hours in line for the tickets to see the trophy movies from Germany at the local cinema; the girls even saw a few Tarzan's films at the nearby Club of Food Workers.

"Do you need a ticket?" questioned Galya with suspicion.

"No," Victoria was thrilled to be in Galya's favor again. "Mom's girlfriend Aunt

Cecily has a box at home, and we are going to see it tonight. I will tell you all about it tomorrow".

She came home right after school and changed her uniform. She put a holiday 's white apron instead of everyday' s black on the top of her brown dress with white lace on the color and cuffs, and she knotted big white bows into her thin braids.

"Mom will be home soon, and wc will go to see a 'television' at Aunt Cecily's," she explained proudly in the face of an interrogatory look of Aunt Rose.

Sarra and Cecily worked together at the local clinic. They still were the best of friends. They were both happily married with three daughters between them. They came together, and Victoria could hear their laughter behind the door.

"Victoria, what kind of a holiday is today?" inquired Cecily from the threshold. "What are the white apron and bows for?"

"I am going with Mom to see televisor, your box with the movie," boasted Victoria. She really could not wait anymore.

Cecily turned to Sarra, "Are you insane? Did you plan to take Victoria to see 'Anna Karenina' tonight?"

Sarra did not hesitate; she looked at her stunned daughter, smiled and ordered, "Victoria you will stay home with Aunt Rose. Please, change; you will not need those big bows". With that, two women left without a second thought.

Victoria could not even cry; she was ready to kill them both, and, especially, smiling "I told you so!" Aunt Rose.

She moved the chair to the phone on the wall. She knew Aunt Cecily's phone by heart; she often called there when her Mom was visiting Cecily. And Baba Sonya, Cecily's Mom, was Victoria's good friend. When they returned from the war and had no place to stay, Victoria even slept with Baba Sonya on the cot on the floor in Aunt Cecily's room. Her fingers trembled as she dialed three-fifty one-forty eight number.

"Allo," Cecily's Mom Sonya answered softly.

"I wish your Cecily would be dead!" wailed Victoria into the phone and slammed the receiver.

Crying Sonya was standing on the marble landing with the door to the apartment open while Cecily and Sarra climbed the wide marble staircase.

"Cecily, somebody just called you with the death threat!" The older woman was very upset and frightened. Sarra and Cecily looked at each other and laughed. "It is Victoria, we are sure" was the unanimous verdict.

*****

We took a hotel shuttle back to the hotel and went for dinner. The menu book had a gorgeous brushed copper cover. It reminded me of a beautiful art book of Tretyakov Gallery in Moscow. Cecily gave this book to me for my sweet sixteenth birthday. The inscription read "To Victoria with love from Aunty Cecily who did not die."

At the dinner, I ordered a martini with three olives and tried to psychoanalyze myself. I loved olives. "How did my childhood misadventures affect my life?" I asked Felix. "We flew plenty since my unfortunate flying experience of my childhood. We even flew in a helicopter and a two-sitter-plane very similar to the old 'cornhusker,' above South Africa."

"We went scuba diving in Tahiti!" Felix was very proud of me. Go figure! However, seventy years later, I am still deathly afraid of wasps.

DAY 15, SEPTEMBER 11
JACKSON HOLE, WY
SPRING CREEK RANCH

It was a perfect family: Dad, Mom, and two kids. They wandered inside the camp of Recreational Vehicles and, despite a big circle of spectators and photographers whispering in awe, enjoyed their stay close to the river and the "facilities."

They were the tallest in the crowd of the tall inhabitants, at least six feet up to the neck. The Papa moose (o, yes!) was mostly scratching his antlers on the trees, while the family fed on a scant grass of the RVs' park not paying any attention to my bright red vest.

The air was pregnant with anticipation of the family's every move. People were moving aside giving way and staying a respectable distance. We took plenty of photos and, led by our guide, drove off, to seek more opportunities.

We saw homes and barns of the first Homesteaders, the cheapskates who got this land for nothing. All they needed to do was to make at least hundred dollars' worth improvement to the property every year. Well, hundred dollars then was much more than today.

The Teton National Park was pastoral and picturesque. We saw Pronghorns, which is a gracious antelope, a black bear who was lunching on berries and the dams built by the beavers. The running herd of bison shook the ground and came straight from the Fenimore Cooper's novel. Countless beautiful aspens looked exactly like the beloved birches back in Russia. After the sunset, we retired to civilization to give a reprieve to our greatly overwhelmed senses.

We sat on our balcony, drinking eighteen years old Macallan Scotch and thought about the first Homesteaders. Where they as scared and naïve as we were when we came to this country almost forty years ago? Did they feel that the land was theirs by right because they fought for it and spoke the language?

The early evening was descending slowly, covering mountains with the silver see-through veil. There was no sound, just the wind playing an incredible organ on the giant trees high up on the summits.

"Felix, do you remember our journey to America?" I asked quietly. "We were 'the settlers', and now we have four American- born grandchildren."

Felix just nodded in agreement. "It was a long time ago, Victoria; we are the Americans."

I did not hear him; I was far away, on the last train from Russia.

KIEV, UKRAINE, THE 1970S
THE LAST TRAIN FROM RUSSIA

She was not interested. She was not interested at all in these flat fields of young wheat, bridges over small rivers, blue skies and occasional grouping of picturesque huts under straw roofs rolling outside the window. Victoria told the kids to look at the scenery to remember the country they were leaving forever, but she did not feel the magnitude of this farewell, she just wanted out.

She wished for the proverbial tornado to take them, and their luggage, and the whole train to their new home, somewhere far away. A few hours ago, she said goodbyes to her parents, and she still felt her father's tears on her face. Her Dad, big and handsome in a three-piece suit with a stylish tie, ran after the moving train that was taking away his daughter and his grandchildren. He ran until the last car disappeared into Ukrainian fields. He will die not quite a year later; at age sixty-four, from the sorrow.

Victoria desperately wanted this June day to be done with. She wanted to see Felix, who should be waiting for them at the border railroad station. They would go through customs, board the only train to the west and would leave Russia. It was not a small feat for a summer day.

She checked her luggage, two large suitcases mostly filled with Russian souvenirs, a few bottles of vodka, a few jars of caviar and new clothes for the children and her two precious large bags. She packed the black bag with the unique expensive photo equipment that would be easy to sell or to exchange for food. The blue bag had two hand-sewn sacks and snacks for the road.

She counted the money again, the ninety dollars per person allowed by the government to take out of Russia, not much for the long journey to the unknown.

The letters from the people who left earlier described that Russian customs operated only thirty minutes before departure of the night train. The Customs did not care; they intentionally wanted to make it as hard as possible for those lucky enough to leave. They usually emptied the suitcases on the luggage belt, and the large sacks were the only way to gather things back before the train leaves.

She packed thirty-six years of her life in that luggage and, by the Customs' rules, it had to weigh no more than thirty-five kilos, about a kilo for each year of her life.

She did not worry terribly; there were rumors that Customs took bribes from the refugees and were not very strict with allotted weight limits. That is why Felix left earlier, staying at this border town for the last three days. He was on the committee, a small group of Jewish refugees that organized daily payoffs, simply bribes, to the customs officers in exchange for minor favors with the luggage. Felix called yesterday sounding a bit funny. He had hung up on her when she asked about the Committee.

In her bag, Victoria had four tickets for a private compartment on the night train from Kiev to Vienna. These tickets were impossible to get, and they cost them a small fortune, however now, they made her feel secure. They would board the night train to Vienna and then this day would be done with.

She mastered a shadow of a smile, but her reflection in the train's window looked pale and worried. The train slowly rolled into the gray terminal. The rails, more rails, and empty cars were everywhere. It seemed that the whole town of Chop was one big grim terminal.

Felix was not among the anxious people waiting for the train. She looked at her sister Ella: "Do you see him? Where the hell is he?"

Ella and her husband Alex were seeing Victoria and the kids to the Russian border to make sure they would leave the country safely.

Suddenly Victoria saw him.

"Felix! Dad!" screamed Ella and the children in one voice.

"Look, he is running," shouted kids happily. Felix looked beat up and tired; his shirt was crumpled, and his face wore a three-day-old stubble.

After all the stress of the day, Victoria was appalled, "Why are you late Felix? What happened to your clothes? Did not you have a fresh shirt or a new sweater? Where did you stay?"

They unloaded luggage as fast as they could, and Felix took them inside the crowded terminal.

"Victoria, please listen to me." He pulled her aside, away from the kids. "You have to shut up if you want us to go to the West. Otherwise, they might send us all to the Far East instead. We do not want this to happen."

She listened to him, and the horror was rising in her chest.

"I spent the last three days under arrest in the Terminal Basement; I escaped through the bathroom window fifteen minutes ago to meet you. I have to get back now! They would be looking for me in a few minutes. The KGB arrested the full Committee three days ago on the charges of bribing the Customs Officers. They questioned me; that is why I hung up the phone when you asked me about the Committee; the KGB was listening. I told them nothing, denied everything and the KGB Officer, the Captain, somehow believed me; but they took my Visa and Passport, and I have no idea what would happen next. They promised to decide by the departure of the night train".

It was a disaster. "The Code," thought Victoria. "It is like running The Code Blue." The Code was the extreme emergency signal in the hospital when a patient stopped breathing, or the heart stopped beating. The doctor in charge ran The Code. Other doctors, nurses, everybody had to follow the orders.

During her Residency, after graduating from medical school, Victoria saw a female Resident running The Code. The girl was extremely anxious, almost in tears; her lips and voice trembled as she was giving the orders. It felt like a contagious disease; the other doctors and nurses became nervous and shaky, questioning the leading doctor's orders.

It was then, in the crowded room with the dying patient, that Victoria swore she would never allow fear to overcome her. As she ran the Code, she was confident and trustworthy, always firmly in charge of her emotions.

Now, in the busy terminal where her dreams of leaving Russia were about to shatter, when her family was in jeopardy, she stood calm and strong.

"What should we do?" she asked Felix.

"Repack luggage for the exact weight, feed kids and wait for me in the line for the Customs. The Captain might let me go at the last minute before the train leaves. Do not go through the Customs and do not get on the train if they would not let me go. Please."

He was already running back to the Terminal basement, where the KGB held arrested members of the Committee in an improvised for the occasion cells.

The line for the Customs was long. Tired and anxious people stood in this line for hours with one thought and one desire to leave this country. People from the different Soviet Republics, families large and small, young and old stayed in this line at the only border train station in the western Soviet Union.

Under the pressure of KGB, Officers searched for valuables or any reason to hold, delay and prohibit exit from the country. Maybe they hated and wanted to punish all those "traitors of the Motherland," or perhaps they were just envious because they had to stay.

All their lives the people in the line were treated as third-class citizens; they were collectively hated and statewide-denied access to higher education and decent jobs. Now, they had a privilege; Russian Jews were permitted to leave the country with a meager ninety dollars and thirty kilos of Russian junk. They could leave after denouncing their Russian citizenship and paying two thousand rubles for the opportunity to give up their passports.

"Passports," suddenly remembered Victoria. "We would have to leave our Passports here. Where is Felix with his Passport and Visa?" She swallowed the tears.

"And what to do with the suitcases; they have to be exactly thirty-five kilos." She forgot about the tears and started to repack feverishly.

Most of the souvenirs, everything non-vital had to go. Ella and Alex helped her to stuff all these now useless things into the terminal's safety deposit boxes.

Victoria asked her boys to change in the new clothes and threw away the old ones. Dima, the shy older boy, tried to resist; there was no way he would take his pants off at the crowded Terminal. His Mom's look convinced him without a word; both boys stripped, changed, and got back into the line.

Suddenly, four loud men with four large suitcases and a few bags cut in the line in front of Victoria.

"Sorry," Victoria raised her voice, "but you were not here before." She was almost crying. "You cannot barge in the middle of the line like that." They did not pay any attention. In addition to suitcases, they brought into the line a stout older woman and started to say their goodbyes.

Victoria decided to deal with the intruders later; she had her kids and her luggage to take care of.

A few minutes later, a short military man with glasses came to Victoria and whispered that Felix would be out soon; she could not even say a word as he magically disappeared.

"Do you need to use a ladies' room?" Victoria turned to Ella innocently. "Come with me please." Downstairs at the bathroom, she waved Ella in and locked the door. "Help me, Ella," she tried to tie a long string of a beautiful coral to her bra straps.

The blood came off Ella's face, "They will arrest you at the Customs Victoria! You will never make it," she whispered.

"I have to take care of my kids," mouthed Victoria with clenched teeth and put another small string of coral, a gift from her mother, around her neck for anybody to see. Ella's hands shook as she closed the small golden lock.

Everyone knew from the earlier refugees that semiprecious coral was the only valuable thing you could sell in Italy. It was the holy stone of the year and an easy sell. People could not live on ninety dollars for long, and Victoria was prepared.

According to the letters, the refugees stayed in Vienna for about two weeks; then, those who wanted to go to America were transferred to Italy to wait for the "grant" from the relatives or the community.

Victoria was still in her running the code mode when she took place in the roped off line next to her kids with her much lightened up and significantly slimmed down suitcases. Ella passed two heavy bags to Victoria under the rope, one with photo equipment and one with food, but the female Custom officer saw the move.

"No food allowed," yelled the woman and pushed heavy bags behind the rope away from Victoria's luggage.

With all the problems, Victoria did not notice that night fell behind the Terminal's windows. It was almost ten o'clock, and the train was leaving at midnight. The people in line were anxious, some changed places allowing elderly to rest, some argued and yelled, somebody was repacking right on the floor, as Victoria did a few hours before.

"Diversions are good," thought Victoria and quietly moved her bags back under the rope.

"No food allowed," said the woman in uniform and moved the bags behind the rope. Victoria was so preoccupied with the bags that she did not see Felix escorted by the KGB Captain who was holding Felix's Passport and Visa. The female officer was busy checking Felix's documents supplied by the Captain.

"My children would never go hungry," silently repeated Victoria and moved her bags back under the rope for the third time.

Finally, the line started to move. Three–four-person-wide crowd, like a slowly moving python, swallowed Victoria, kids, luggage, and Felix who was trying to keep up with them.

There were no goodbyes, no kisses, just the long mute exchange of glances with Ella crying quietly behind the ropes. Then the wide wooden doors of Customs closed behind them.

With a shudder, Victoria saw as some passengers were pulled out of the line to the small rooms for personal searches behind the closed doors. The old woman in front of Victoria, the one who got in the line ahead of her, at the last moment was escorted for a personal search.

"Why do I feel sorry for her?" wondered Victoria.

The slow-moving belt held everything they had, the pitiful disarray of souvenirs, which survived the repacking, Victoria's only black dress, a few cans of sardines, mascara, lipstick and a big shiny camera.

"Coral," shouted the young Officer. "Show me your coral." Apparently, they had their sources among refugees.

"Here is all I have, the allowed three ounces of coral," Victoria opened her blue polyester jacket and touched her neck where her Mom's small coral string was on prominent display.

In her peripheral visual field, she saw the blinding eye of the arriving train. She felt Felix's warm hand holding her sweaty palm.

"You can go," finally said the officer. He took his time to check their Passports and Visas while their things were scattered all over the luggage belt.

With one wide sweep, Felix and Victoria got their belongings in the large sacks and ran with their boys through the door into the night where the last train from Russia whistled and started to move.

They ran and passed their children to the sea of hands of the people standing on the steps of the car, they tossed their bags in, and Felix pushed Victoria in and got on the steps as the train was gathering speed. They were on their way to freedom!

Their tickets worked, and their compartment was empty as they got Dima and Dave up on two narrow upper beds. The boys were tired and scared. Felix and Victoria hugged in celebration, but they knew the day was not done yet; they had to repack for a short stay in Vienna.

A loud knock on the door woke up the children.

"Vodka, davai vodka, and caviar!" The Czech staff that served the international train Moscow-Kiev-Chop-Vienna did not intend to pass on a piece of refugees' pie.

"Give me vodka and caviar or else; I would throw your family off the train!"

Terrified, used to threats, people opened the doors and offered their last possessions in exchange for the ride to freedom.

They packed and repacked all night and with the first rays of the sun, Felix and Victoria woke up their boys to look at the new free world.

They could not take their eyes off the manicured fields, dollhouses and beautiful blue summer sky of Austria. The train slowly rolled to Vienna Terminal. There were no greetings or welcomes, only the rows of soldiers with machine guns.

Felix put his hands on his boys' shoulders, "They are here to protect us."

"Do not worry, somebody is going to meet us," Victoria tried to reassure children.

She looked at the slow approaching Vienna, the sun reflected on the guns protecting their freedom, she looked at her family alive and together and finally, the day when they took the last train from Russia was over.

And she sobbed uncontrollably.

*****

I swallowed the last of my Macallan watered down by ice and looked into the night. The nightmare we lived through forty years ago was like a poisonous snake, tamed and safely stored in my memory, yet always alive. I could never think about this last day without my heart skipping a beat, my voice quivering and my eyes welling up with tears.

I will never forget and will never forgive the Soviets the horror of these twenty-four hours; my Dad running after the leaving train, disheveled Felix on the platform, the string of coral attached to my bra, the last goodbye look at Ella, jumping on the moving midnight train, the demands and threats and, finally, the sun sparkling on the guns in Vienna. But we were free.

DAY 16, SEPTEMBER 12
JACKSON HOLE, WY
SPRING CREEK RANCH

I t was supposed to be our rest day, the day we rightfully deserved after two weeks of constant driving and moving. We needed a rest from the days, when we woke up every morning in a different bed and when in the evening the floor was shaking under our feet as if we were still in a moving car. We needed a rest from the days when the lifeline to our family and friends, our computer, was still in the different time zone, and we were not sure, when to celebrate the important Holiday, today or, maybe, tomorrow.

I could not sleep last night, tossing and turning in our comfortable bed. I tried to remember funny or cute facts about coming to a new country with two kids, two suitcases and ninety dollars in my pocket and there were not many of these. Yes, that June day when we left the Soviet Union on the last train was over, but life was not easy.

EMIGRATION
VIENNA, AUSTRIA, THE1970S

F elix got a hero welcomed when Sohnut, the Jewish Agency that organized the Russian Aliyah to Israel, met them in Vienna. The Agency already knew about the arrests at the Chop Railroad Station; they knew he did not name the names or disclosed a purpose of the Committee; they knew he managed to persuade the KGB there were no organized bribes and to let him go. As a payoff, Sohnut settled them at the private home instead of a suburban dormitory for refugees.

The large living room was crowded with five opened folding beds. At the far corner, a short man wearing thick glasses set on one of them.

"He looks familiar," thought Victoria.

"Pavel, how did you get here?" Felix was hugging and slapping the stranger.

"Vika, meet Pavel; this is the guy I was telling you about. We had shared the cell at the railroad basement. He was also on the committee. Do you remember he was the one who talked to you before they let me go"?

Victoria wanted to ask Pavel what he was doing in their room when a stern looking woman in the bright apron opened the door. Straight from the threshold, she started to talk in a curious mixture of German, or maybe Yiddish, and very broken Russian.

"Frau Krause," she hit herself at the ample chest. "Your boys, nicht! Stove, refrigerator, TV no work, nicht! You understand?"

Felix tried to translate, "Nothing works and the boys are not allowed in the kitchen". Dima and Dave already huddled next to Victoria's knees wondering if they did something wrong.

Just like KGB had decided that Felix and Pavel had to share the prison cell in Chop, Sohnut decided that Felix's family would share with him the room at the "pension" for the next two weeks. There was no one to appeal or complain, so they combined their daily allowances, four parts from the family and one from Pavel, and Victoria did a small grocery shopping and cooked simple meals on the stove. Frau Krause decided that her young boarders were well behaved, and magically the next morning all the appliances started to work.

All five of them lived out of suitcases, slept in the same room and shared meals. There was no privacy and no secrets; they became a family of five.

Dima was the fussiest eater in the family. His grandfather would create the most elaborate stories to make the boy eat anything besides bread and water. In Vienna, Dima suddenly acquired a craving for orange juice.

Pavel planned to save on the food to buy new clothes, and he tried to create the rules. "We do not need fruits or juices; the kids could drink water after the dinner."

"There would be no soup for the next few days, Pavel," Victoria informed him quietly, "You can drink water before the dinner."

She won the battle and kids got their favorite juice.

It was the best day when they took boys to Prater. With only a few spare coins in their possession, they managed to have a ball in warm and welcoming Vienna.

The next day Felix smiled, coming back from shopping. "Russian pig, he called me a Russian pig," he laughed.

"What did you do?" worried Victoria.

"I chose three beautiful apples at the small store around the corner, but when owner weighed them, I realized that I did not have enough money."

"He called me Russian pig, Victoria! This is the first time somebody called me 'Russian,' not 'dirty Jew' or 'kike,' but Russian!"

Victoria did not find it funny; she was still upset about the interview at the Sohnut office yesterday. It was awful.

"You would never get your license in America! In Israel you would be a doctor without any exams," the Representative almost yelled at her after learning that she was a doctor. "I practically can assure you that you would commit suicide in the USA," he promised.

Earlier, twelve-year-old Dima was happy to read his poem about Israel and proudly discussed his grandfather's Zionist ideas.

Now, the Sohnut worker turned to Dima; he was stern and somber,

"You do not have to go with your parents to America." The Representative sounded very convincing. "You are almost thirteen, and you can go to Israel on your own; Israel needs smart and talented boys like you."

The sunny, warm room suddenly became cold and dark. Victoria could see Dima's frightened eyes brimmed with tears. At this point, Felix had had enough. He got up and embraced his family, "We are grateful for your help, sir, and will consider your advice. However, I prefer to go to the United States and my family, my wife and my children, will come with me." He tried to console crying Victoria all the way back to the apartment.

Despite Lenya and Sohnut's advice, they could not take their family to Israel. All their lives were built on memories of the war. Victoria did not sleep a single night in Vienna listening to people speaking German under their window. She would never dare to bring three young men in her family to a country with a military draft.

Their two weeks in Vienna were up, and they had to move on.

"There will be a special train to Rome on Tuesday," explained a cold, distant woman from Sohnut. The Agency already settled the refugees going to Israel and now had to deal with those who were going to the United States. The woman was beautiful in the white starched blouse and dark skirt, and she spoke perfect Russian.

"We have a few hundred Russian Jews here, and all of you will be on the train tonight in your cars with no other people." She continued with instructions, "You will travel together carrying your suitcases. Please, take all your belongings with you."

"People leaving for Israel are flying direct today; those leaving for America and Canada will stay in Italy, where HIAS will process your documents."

The train packed with refugees left Vienna late in the evening. In the eerie silence, people loaded their families and luggage with the remnants of their Soviet life into the railroad cars. Their suitcases were full of an incredible array of junk that people planned to sell in Italy to subsidize small stipends from the resettling agencies.

"Sitting room only," announced chief conductor. He looked in bewilderment at six or seven people of all ages sitting shoulder to shoulder on the benches designed for four. Piles and piles of old suitcases, bags, bundles, and boxes were on the floor at their knees. They did as they were told getting ready for the long night on the train. There was no announced schedule, but everybody knew it would take the train all night to travel to Rome.

Warm July night settled behind dark windows, and people started to doze off resting their tired heads on their neighbors' shoulders.

The train stopped so abruptly that people facing forward were thrown from their seats, landing on the top of the luggage scattered on the floor.

Outside was an absolute blackness, no lights from the station or other trains. A few men speaking loud broken Russian entered the car. They opened the windows and started to unload the luggage. "Quick, quick, "bistro," get out, get out!" they yelled, stirring sleeping people.

Startled and frightened refugees held onto each other and resisted with all their strength; they tried to save whatever little they had.

"Kids, let's start with the kids," heard Victoria and in a sheer panic, she held onto her boys. One of the men got Dave and passed him over the open window to somebody's' hands outside.

Nothing could stop her now; she screamed at the top of her lungs, "Dave!" She got Dima's hand and ran. She ran over legs and climbed over suitcases scattered on the floor; with a sob in her throat, pulling Dima behind her, she ran to save her boy.

Buses were waiting outside. In the darkness of the night, in the middle of nowhere, American Agency HIAS, afraid of actions against Israel and Russian Jews, took them off the train before it would arrive in Rome in the morning.

Now, the real refugees, in the night lighted up by busses' headlights, they held their kids, looked for their luggage and boarded unmarked buses. They were going to Rome. On the bus, Victoria still could not let her boys' hands go.

*****

I tried to sleep in the middle of the day. Usually, I could never do this, especially, when we traveled. When I drive, Felix usually takes a nap on the passenger seat, or maybe he just keeps his eyes closed from fear, even though I am a careful driver. However, when he or anybody else drives, I can never fall asleep. I have to watch, navigate and advise. That is just me.

After the dinner, we watched TV for prescribed R&R, and I wrote Emails to my boys. I still love to hold their hands.

DAY 17, SEPTEMBER 13
PARK CITY, UT
MONTAGE
VISTA VIEW SUITE

I t was a driving day. We started with a sumptuous breakfast in the mildly overcast Jackson Hole and drove through the rest of Wyoming, which could be compared only to unrivaled Switzerland. The green mountains, turquoise rivers, and the endless meadows were spectacular.

Then came Idaho with its towns, populations 166 or less, endless Bear Lake and severely overcast sky that finally delivered a wholly blinding and deafening downpour of a rain on an utterly abandoned one-lane road. After that, sunny Utah was salvation with its beautiful Park City and a fabulous Montage on the top of the mountain.

The beauty and comfort of our suite with promised fireplace and vista view were only secondary to impeccable service everywhere in the hotel. Tired and hungry we changed quickly and headed downstairs for dinner at the restaurant.

The restaurant had a soaring ceiling and traditional lantern lights emanating a warm golden glow that reminded us of the approaching High Holidays. We did not expect anything but food, and we did not plan to meet Benjamin, the restaurant manager.

We liked each other instantaneously when he paid just a courtesy visit to our table, and within minutes, we had a very lively conversation about our backgrounds. Benjamin, the French from Nice, the descendant of Moroccan and Egyptian Jews, came to Park City about a year ago with his family; his wife was expecting their second child.

He was so professionally concerned about our dinner, so warm and friendly, that our conversation spread well beyond the boundaries of the table talk. We covered history, culture, emigration and, of course, High Holidays. We exchanged our families' photos and E-mails; we had surprisingly common views, beliefs, and traditions.

At this pre-Holidays evening, we felt close to Jewish people everywhere in the world, thinking the same thoughts, singing the same songs and eating the same food. We taught our children the same rules and traditions and told them the same stories.

He was one of us: my person, my family! It was hard to leave Benjamin, as it was hard to leave so many kind, warm and helpful people we had met during our travel. However, it was a bit more, than that; we knew we would be thinking of him and his family, as we will be thinking of our own family and friends, driving across Nevada to Reno on Saturday.

We opened the door to our suite and saw an elegant plate of chocolate covered strawberries with Hag Sameach written in the Pastry Chef's handwriting. There was also a beautiful card from Benjamin.

My Dad used to say, "Ex Nostres - our own people."

EMIGRATION
ROME, ITALY, THE 1970S

The people, who exited the bus with Victoria and her family in front of the narrow tall building in Rome, were also "our people".

They spoke good Russian and explained to the newcomers that Hotel "Colibri" was on the seventh floor.

Dusk settled on the streets of Rome; however, Felix and the boys wanted to walk around and explore, they were in Rome after all. They just needed to bring the luggage to their room and deal with Victoria who was worried that banks or exchange booths were already closed this late on Friday. "We do not have any Italian money, how am I going to feed the kids?"

They felt very "under-luggage", when they saw a refugee family from Uzbekistan, arriving from Vienna with about forty suitcases now scattered on the street. Happy with their small load they took one piece of luggage each and walked in. The elevator did not work.

The tiny room on the seventh floor had a tall window facing the deep and narrow well.

They saw Italian wells like this many times before, in every Italian movie. A small table for two was under the window. Sizeable European wardrobe with a mirror door was on the left. Two twin beds with thin gray blankets completed the interior.

"How are four of us going to sleep in these two beds?" wondered Victoria.

She opened the wardrobe door, which suddenly separated and fell on Victoria, mirror first, but luckily did not break.

That was as much as she could endure now; she sat on the bed and cried.

A loud knock on the door made her jump.

"Cameras, lenses, do you have anything to sell?" The man at the door looked like a savior to her. She pulled out the bag full of photo equipment saved from the Chop customs and invited the man to look.

"Victoria, do not do this," urged her Felix. " His prices are meager, and the money will not last."

"Do you have a better solution? " She was tired and angry, and she just needed the money to feed her kids.

She did not argue with the man, who paid with Italian mille-liras, which sounded like a lot of money. They shook hands and man disappeared with the bag and their hopes for money to support them for a while.

As the door closed, they heard a loud voice from the well, "Eat, Russos come to the dining room on the second floor! Food! Food on the second floor, per favore!"

They all ran downstairs almost knocking off the southern family still dragging their suitcases up to the seventh floor.

Their room in Rome in July was sweltering like a frying pan, and within a few days, they developed a solid routine. Early in the morning, all four of them went to the Round Market, a flea market where Russian refugees were selling Russian junk. Like other refugees, they tried to sell whatever Russian souvenirs they had. In the afternoon, they went for free sightseeing and returned to "Colibri" for a pasta dinner at night.

Their stay in the hotel was booked only for ten nights, and Felix was looking for a cheap room in the suburbs, away from sizzling Rome, where they could wait for their visas. He was busy shuttling by the train between the suburbs and HIAS, the agency that they hoped would find a community in America who would sponsor them.

"Doctor, the woman needs a doctor," somebody knocked on the door. Victoria rushed outside.

In the very end of a long hallway, people were gathering at the open door to a small room. In a hot room right next to the brightly tiled bathroom, one for the whole floor, an older woman was sitting on the unmade bed panting and moaning. She was in obvious distress. Her gray hair uncombed, the woman was struggling for air. Her lips looked like a distorted blue flower on a pale, pasty face. Her legs were planted solidly on the floor like marble columns that Victoria admired recently in Rome museums.

Victoria ran for her medical bag. "Just from her looks it is pulmonary edema," she whispered to Felix who joined the crowd. " Please, ask people to leave; she needs more air." "We will call an ambulance if needed," added Victoria bravely. Neither she nor anybody in the crowd would know how to call an ambulance in Italy; she was afraid Russian zero-one would not work here.

She took her stethoscope, the one she loved and trusted for many years, and listen to the woman's chest. She was lucky to have in her bag not only the first aid kit but also a small pharmacy for every occasion; they left forever, and she was still a doctor.

With a beautifully crafted German syringe, a present from her Dad, she injected Lasix and Strophanthin into woman's vein. Diuretic and cardiac glycoside were apparently the right choices; they would stimulate aging heart to work stronger; they would push fluid that suffocated woman's lungs, to her kidneys, instead.

"Maria," the woman was able to whisper after a few minutes. "My name is Maria." She looked at her savior with love and tears in her eyes. Only now, Victoria recognized a pushy woman from the Chop customs' line.

It was a very early morning at the Round Flea Market, and Felix was organizing his family's stand. "Dima, please, fasten your pins to this cloth and stand here."

Dima had an extensive collection of Russian cities' pins, which he insisted on taking with him to America because he could not live without them. However, seeing his family trying to sell everything at the Round Market, he decided to sell his coveted collection. Dave agreed to help him for a fraction of the profit. The kids were quick studies how to be real capitalists.

"Victoria, here is the last jar of caviar," instructed Felix. "Please, stay here and ask in Italian 'Would you like caviale?' It means caviar. I have to step aside and will be right back".

Within minutes, a small but very loud crowd of men gathered around Victoria. She was holding a small jar of caviar and could not understand why all these men were so interested in it and why they were laughing and slapping each other encouragingly.

Terrified, red-faced Felix cut through the crowd, "No, no more, she has no more caviale!" he screamed on the top of his lungs.

"Victoria, not chiavare, you idiot! Caviale! You were offering them 'to fuck, to screw', not caviar!"

"Italian is definitely not my language," thought upset Victoria as the crowd started to disperse. "I am not very good at selling," she added dejectedly.

However, she was a good doctor and Maria, her grateful patient, was doing much better with Victoria's help and medications.

Maria was traveling alone to her daughter who lived in New York now. She wanted to see and to live with her children and grandchildren, but she waited for the visa for a long time, and she got older and sicker. Now she worried her family would not accept her.

"Felix," Maria caught him in a hallway when he returned from his almost daily hunt for an apartment in the suburb. "Felix, please take me with you. I would pay my part of the rent and will help Victoria with the kids. Please, Felix, I cannot look for an apartment or afford it anyway".

"If this is any indication," said Victoria when Felix told her about Maria's plight, "it seems we will always share our room with strangers, first in Vienna and now in Italy. I just wonder who is going to live with us in America." However, she did not mind keeping an eye on her patient.

Felix finally rented a one-room apartment about an hour from Rome by a cheap and frequent train. It was close to the center of town and even more close to the beach. An excited Victoria started to pack.

She was ready to leave; she hated this hotel and this room and their beds where the only way they could fit was to sleep "tops to tails."

Dave suffered the most, Dima was much taller, and his feet were right at Dave's face; Dima was fine, Dave's shorter feet were at his chest.

Their parents had a very different problem; they did not sleep together for almost seven years. They were still married; however, their decision to leave the country together was a contract. Their verbal agreement did not have a clause on personal life and did not include a paragraph about sex.

In Kiev, they continued to live in their separate apartments, and the folding cot in Vienna was okay; however, here they slept on the narrow single bed.

*****

Felix fell asleep watching TV on the sofa with his bare feet up on the armrest.

"How come he still has these beautiful feet?" I was jealous. "Where is the justice? Why does he not have hammer toes, bunions, and calluses?"

I remembered these perfect feet; I would recognize them anywhere. I faced them every morning in Rome, waking up in our narrow bed. A small ray of sun sneaked into our room in "Colibri," our so-called hotel straight out of Italian Neorealism movie, I lay quietly trying not to touch these feet. I did not want to wake up their owner. We did not think or discuss our relationship; we just tried to keep our family together. It was not a time to start the fire that would rekindle our love. We had to survive first.

I shut off the TV and woke up Felix. It was time to go to bed. Not only we survived, but for many years, the fire of our love was hot and bright; now it was warm and comfortable, just like our plush and spacious king-size bed.

DAY 18, SEPTEMBER 14
ELKO, NV
HILTON GARDEN INN

When we woke up, thick fog rested on the top of the mountains like the frosting on the cake. It incased our hotel and the balcony and was slowly advancing to our bedroom. Fog was so thick it seemed you could slice it with a knife. Our balcony was open, and our bed looked like a milk bath floating on the cloud. We waited until afternoon for the fog to disappear. Layer after layer dissipated slowly only to have more and more layers rising from the valley as if a gigantic can-can dancer was lifting her lacy skirt upon yet another underskirt. However, on the eve of Yom Kippur, we had two hundred and sixty-two miles to drive; we had to go.

We entered Nevada expecting the desert, sand, and cacti when an overcast and threatening sky won over. It was the wrath of the Gods, a downpour of biblical proportion. On the mostly empty road - only occasional truck- our windshield was a waterfall with zero visibility. We were afraid to stop and risk being hit by a truck unable to see us, and we could drive only when there was an occasional tail light to follow. Between the fog and the rain, we almost expected a snowstorm next. Indeed, the day before the Day of Atonement was a trying and exciting day.

Flooded by rain, the desert was fantastic but hard to fathom. Shallow waters looked like small silver lakes reflecting dreamy low clouds; fields of vaporizing mineral deposits resembled melted snow and wild sage, mile after mile, was powdered by sand.

The time changed, we had lost another hour, it was an eve of Yom Kippur, the most solemn Jewish holiday, and we were spending the night in a town with five brothels, numerous casinos, and no temple. So why did we expect the God to smile upon us?

EMIGRATION
ROME, ITALY, THE 1970S

God did not smile upon us on our last day in Rome. It was a routinely hot day, and Victoria planned obligatory sightseeing.

"Mommy, please, one cup of coffee," begged Dima. He was twelve, all grown up, and to confirm his adulthood he drank coffee in the morning. Victoria did not approve, but Felix stood by Dima purely out of male solidarity.

"Dima," Victoria tried again "why do you want to drink hot coffee in this heat? Please leave this water heater alone. I do not like you to use this electrical coil; you know you have two hands and both of them are left. And, please, do not use all the sugar again, the way you drink coffee you can pour it in a sugar bowl."

The whole family loved the electrical coil they brought from Russia. It served them coffee and tea, and on more than one occasion was handy to make an instant soup for dinner.

Suddenly, there was a scream.

In all her years being a doctor, assisting during the surgeries, providing first aid and working in an Emergency Room, Victoria had never heard a scream like that. The shriek started at the table and spread to the stone well outside; it hung along the hallway and descended stairs, it pulled people out of their rooms, and it stopped Victoria's heart as she saw a full cup of boiling sugary coffee spilling into Dima's lap.

"The Code!" In the millisecond, she carried her boy to the bed and pulled down his shorts.

Maria was already at the door, and she held out the towel, "Victoria, pee on this!" In Russia, the old women's' tales considered sterile urine a remedy for the fresh burn.

"Pee, please," ordered the old, short of breath woman, but Victoria was in shock. Maria took charge; she produced a piece of harsh dark brown Russian laundry soap and smeared it on the towel, "Do not waste the time Victoria; apply it to the burn all the time!"

The time stopped, the noise died, Victoria could not think, she felt like a terrible failure. She was responsible for her boy, her father trusted her to take care of Dima, and only three weeks later, she failed.

They faced the disaster together; Victoria sitting on the bed, holding Dima's hand, changing cold soapy cloth, administering Tylenol and fluids; Felix standing right next to her, his hand on her shoulder, ready to help with anything, and Dave, the hand in his Father's hand, crying silently with his brother and Mom.

The thoughts she thought that night, the silent prayers she prayed, and the tears she cried tore her heart apart; she begged late Dmitry, and her Dad and God to save her son, not to scar or handicap him and to let them all get to America alive.

The first ray of sun danced on Dima's face and woke up Victoria. She was afraid to take the cloth off and to look at the burn; however, she was a doctor. Her hands shook when she slowly lifted the cover.

She could not understand, there was no medical explanation for it, yet she could see it with her own eyes. There was only a small first-degree burn on Dima's right thigh where yesterday was a terrifying extensive burn.

She was ecstatic and speechless, and her boy woke up and smiled at her as if nothing ever happened.

Victoria put aside a piece of harsh dark brown Russian laundry soap, exactly like one, with which Babushka washed her at the banya, and smiled.

God was smiling upon them and the next day all five of them, including Maria, moved to a small town with the ocean breeze.

*****

Elko, Nevada was a small town with a large and smoky casino. In our room at the hotel, we ate our simple Yom Kippur Eve dinner bought at the Supermarket, and I drank my last glass of water for the next twenty-four hours.

Felix was dying to check out the casino, not quite a fateful and solemn beginning of the holiday.

All seats at the Blackjack table were taken. Felix tried to

follow the game while I looked at the players. It was a curious group, for sure. Even sitting, they all were taller than Felix standing; they smoked fat stinky cigars and wore cowboys' hats, just to add to the height and an insult to injury. Felix tried to clarify the rules of the game, but nobody could understand his question or his English. We did not stay; both of us had plenty to apologize for tomorrow. We did not need a problem with the God. We returned to our hotel. We did not pray; we just wished for a better day and an easy fast tomorrow.

DAY 19, SEPTEMBER 15
RENO, NV
PEPPERMILL RESORT AND CASINO

The sandy hills of Nevada created a perfect background for our Yom Kippur drive. Hungry and thirsty, we drove through deserted ancient land while I counted how many times in my life I fasted on Yom Kippur. The number, close to sixty, was impressive.

"No, you cannot fast Victoria. Little girls are not allowed to fast," in spite of my nudging and begging, Babushka was strict with her rules. I was dying to fast on Yom Kippur, as did every adult in my family.

I was already in a high school when she finally said I could join the club.

"No cheating; you can brush your teeth and rinse your mouth, but do not swallow," she said, and I had never cheated. I had to go to school as usually, but it was still a sacred day, not that I prayed or did something different.

There were no official religious holidays in the Soviet Union; only New Year Day, May Day and the Day of the Great October Revolution were considered the holidays and were work free.

I never told my Ukrainian friends about the holiday or fast when I worked on Yom Kippur. It was my day, and it belonged to me. The wrinkly hills of Nevada eroded by the wind were a perfect place and a good beginning for the New Year; we were still on the road, still chasing our adventurous dream.

EMIGRATION
LADISPOLI, ITALY, THE 1970S

Ladispoli was a Mecca for Russian emigrants and Victoria, and Felix's old friends were all there. Cecily with her family and Victoria's favorite Baba Sonya were there always happy to see them. Volodya, who left Kiev only a week before Victoria, was always ready to drive them to the market in his new car. They made new friends with a couple who was going to New York; they also had two children. The husband's brother was already an American doctor, and Victoria collected the bits and pieces of information about her unknown professional future.

After Victoria's fiasco with selling caviar at the flea market, Felix did not trust her to sell. Today, he promised to take kids to the beach, but then he remembered it was Saturday, the busy day when Italian vacationers shopped at "the Russian market."

Victoria could not take kids to the beach either; she was useless there without Felix. She did not like the water, and she would never let her sons swim alone. She preferred to sweat at the market trying to sell whatever little they still had, a few matryoshka dolls, embroidered towels, screws and some extra photo lenses.

The rumors about value of coral in Italy turned out to be true, and during their first week in Rome, Victoria sold her Mom's beautiful string of coral for nine hundred dollars. She wrapped this money in the paper and hid it deep down in her purse along with their Visas and Russian Driver Licenses. For her, these money were sacred, her parents' untouchable money that will secure her parents coming to America.

Long alley led to a square in the center of a picturesque Italian resort town. The summer season was in full swing and vacationers were looking for entertainment.

On weekends at dusk, the tree-lined alley became an improvised "Russian market," where refugees sold souvenirs, bed linen, workers' tools and whatever was left of the Russian Vodka, caviar, amber, and coral.

It was not easy to accept the paradoxes of their life. Two refugees with a doctor and engineer's diplomas and their two boys were selling Russian souvenirs at the Italian flea market.

The hot August sun was gentler and kinder outside of Rome, and they were lucky to find a small one-room apartment between the Main Street and the beach.

There were four folding beds in their living room and a table with four chairs. Maria had a small windowless room with a cot all to herself; it was probably a walk-in closet, but they had never seen one before. The living room was the dining room when they were eating at the small round table and the bedroom at night. They had a small kitchen and a bathroom, and they were comfortable. In the letter to her worrying parents, Victoria described the apartment as "two-room with a kitchen."

Every morning, Victoria and Felix went to buy food at the local market. They tasted fresh, straight out of the sea oysters, bought chicken and fruits, milk and bread and occasionally splurged on espresso at the outside café. They reinforced their small HIAS stipend with the money from the sale of the photo camera, and the souvenirs and Maria helped with the rent; they were frugal and counted their money, and Felix always managed to buy a few flowers for Victoria.

"They have money," hissed old Russian women shopping at the market. "He always buys her flowers!"

Maria felt much better and helped Victoria with the kids and in the kitchen. She was under Victoria's constant care, on the diet and medications. They were counting every lira and tried to sell whatever little of Russian junk they still had.

When a dark Italian with long curly hair and blue eyes stopped to look at her stuff, Victoria knew she was in trouble. Her Italian was limited to remnants of Latin from medical school, but his looks did not need the language. "Lillo," he introduced himself.

Their mornings were busy with house chores and cooking, and they usually would take kids to the beach afterward. They spent the evenings with friends and fellow-refugees on the Central Square, while the kids stayed home with Maria.

The Russian community lived by its own rules and rumors. People whispered the new stories every day, and nobody knew what and whom to believe.

"My friend's family stayed in Italy for four months because HIAS could not find a sponsor," complained the old man in the driving cap and everybody would get upset and frightened; no one wanted to stay in the suspended unreal life of a refugee, even in heavenly Italy.

A stout woman in the fashionable diamond coma-shaped earrings had a better story, "My cousin's family went to America and the community had a house and a car waiting for them."

Every refugee wanted to believe in a miracle, and every refugee worried, worried, worried.

Every week Felix went to Rome to check with HIAS, if any community in the USA would sponsor his family and the answer always was the same: "We will let you know, it takes about two month."

In Kiev, while waiting for a Visa, Victoria met her childhood girlfriend Alla; her family had relatives in America, and they were leaving for Chicago.

"I will help you with the warrant for Chicago," offered Alla. "I have close relatives there, and they would help."

Victoria was thrilled with the opportunity, "I also have some relatives in Chicago."

She always knew her grandfather Volf's older brother immigrated to Chicago during the WWI and family rumors were that he was one of the founders of the Jewish Community there. However, all the connections were lost after the Revolution. Only a few years before, her Dad's cousin went to Chicago and found the family. He gave Victoria the address, but she did not want to ask the distant cousins for any favors.

By now, Alla was already in Chicago, and Victoria planned to take her up on her promise. The problem was that Italian International Telephone System was not equipped with Russian speaking operators and, truth to be told, Victoria did not have money to call Chicago. Her friends suggested to call collect, but Victoria did not want her friend to pay for the call. She planned to save money for a few weeks to call Chicago more close to their departure.

It was hot August and waiting was boring. Lillo became a friend. He taught Felix and Victoria Italian and frequently invited them to the disco at night. They loved the place where they could forget about their misery, responsibilities and unknown future and they loved to dance together again.

They returned home late, but Maria was waiting for them; she got permission and a ticket for New York; her daughter wanted her to live with the family. She cried hugging Victoria.

"Let's take a tour of Italy while we are waiting," Felix came up with an idea. "It is a cheap trip on the bus with Russian-speaking guide. They usually depart from the Central Square".

Victoria understood. Felix was tired of Lillo Italian language lessons and his lingering around Victoria; he did not care that Volodya drove them to the better market with less competition. He did not need anyone's help to deal with their problems, and he did not see any benefits in Victoria's significantly improved Italian. Felix had had enough of that. He had his family, and he could manage on his own.

Next morning they took kids on a grand tour of Italy.

*****

I was not sure if I was still dreaming of Italy or if the view from the suite at the posh Reno resort just reminded me of it.

Our dinner after the twenty-four-hour fast was well deserved and I surprised our waiter ordering tea and white roll with honey to start. That is how my Babushka always started her meal after Yom Kippur fast.

Felix ordered a beautiful bottle of California wine by the number on the wine list, and an elegant array of the dishes crowded our table for two.

The check came as a big surprise; it was about three hundred dollars more than we expected. After some rolled eyes and soul-searching, we figured out that Felix mixed up numbers on the wine list and by mistake had ordered an expensive bottle. However, a good bottle of wine only helped our festive mood, and we headed to the exciting Casino where Felix played poker at the high- rollers room.

It was a tiresome day, and I returned to our suite; we had a long and winding drive to Yosemite tomorrow. I warned Felix that we would need to wake up early, but he was still playing. I did not worry; I won six dollars on the slots machines to save our budget.

I left a bedside light on, and the room became dark and mysterious. The Italian style street lamps were shining brightly above red pool umbrellas, and I was still in Italy forty years ago.

EMIGRATION
LADISPOLI, ITALY, THE 1970S

The big bus was loaded with Russian Jews, which meant loud conversations and children on the parents' knees. They all were here for the kids to see Italy, but nobody could afford a separate seat for a child.

They drove North, admiring the leaning Tower of Pisa and standing in awe under

Juliet's balcony in Verona. Victoria and Felix were surprised and proud when in Sienna, they could not understand the lively discussion in the mixture of English and Italian between Dima and the priest in the Casa di Sancta Caterina, the house of the patron saint of Italy. They inhaled the views of a divine country; they copied to their memory majestic landscapes, palazzos and cathedrals and they were in awe of the ancient history and beauty. Victoria tried to memorize every stone; they did not have even a simple camera to take the pictures!

Even in the overcrowded bus, she felt like she was on a flying carpet. Acquired long time ago, the virus of the traveling bliss was at work, and she was happy.

She made fast friends with the fellow travelers, and in Florence, she promised the kids and her new friends to treat them to ice cream on one of the old city piazzas.

"Ice cream for everybody," she ordered with a grand flourish when their loud group of seven took the table. O, what fun the small splurge was after a few weeks of constant wait for the allowance from HIAS, selling on the market and counting every lira.

The magical twilight settled over Ponte Vecchio, where their small group pretended they were regular tourists enjoying the evening, not countryless and penniless well-educated refugees with an uncertain future.

They sat in the outside café and enjoyed gelato.

The impression on Victoria's face said it all when she got the check. Felix thought she was going to faint, the kids stopped laughing, and her new friends thanked her and left quickly.

She was in shock; ice cream back in Kiev cost twenty-two kopeks out of her hundred and fifty rubles doctor's monthly salary, a bit more than 0.1%. Her generous offer of ice cream in Florence was about to bite off more than a week of HIAS allowance for their family of four.

Felix bravely counted the cash; they knew nothing about banks, checkbooks and credit cards.

On the way to South of Italy, they met Victoria's family friends. Three generations of the same family were moving to Canada to reunite with their grandmother.

"I have known them since childhood," whispered Victoria to Felix on the bus. "The grandparents are Bella and Igor. I think Igor was in love with my Mom and my Dad was attracted to Bella. Bella's parents were Dad's patients, and that is how they met.

Bella was a petite dentist with a beautiful voice. She always sang at the parties accompanying herself on accordion. Doctors and dentist earned so little that she had a part-time job as a musician at workers' club.

Her tall dark and handsome husband was an engineer, and they had a little daughter Lila. Bella's father was a well to do executive, director of a small factory, and his stately elegant wife always invited my parents for fancy dinners.

Once my parents took me with them. I was about thirteen, and for the first time in my life, my Mom gave me her nylon stockings to wear. They were very thin and expensive, and Mom warned me not to rip them.

I remember this evening as if it was yesterday; beautiful furniture, thick carpets and cute Bella with her accordion singing a duet with my father after the dinner. That is when I noticed a broken string with a tiny hole in my stocking. I was terrified that I managed to tear this beautiful see-through stocking. Trying to conceal the hole, I pulled the string, and at this horrible moment, half of the stocking dropped to my ankle. I thought my heart went with the stocking too!

At home, Mom gave me great advice, 'In the future, Victoria, try to buy two pairs, so if you tear one, you still can use another one.' I took her advice to heart, and in my first year of medical school in the long line at the shoe store, I bought two identical pairs of black Italian shoes!"

They both laughed softly afraid to wake up sleeping passengers.

"Bella's father," continued Victoria "was an entrepreneur and when first plastic bags arrived from abroad, he started to produce these at his factory, as a side business, and made a lot of money.

Unfortunately, somebody noticed and wrote the letter to KGB. Promptly, he went to jail; the government did not like free enterprise. He died in prison.

Turned out, that he had a brother in Canada who was looking for him and after a few years, Bella's mother got permission for a short visit. She went to Edmonton to meet her brother-in-law, they fell in love, and she had never come back. It took years for Bella and her children to get permission to leave Russia."

"Amazing," whispered Felix falling asleep as the bus was rolling to Naples "how do you always remember all these stories."

They toured Pompeii and proceeded to Sorrento where tourists bought cheap, well-packed small Italian table-bars. Victoria and Felix shared cappuccino and cognac at the open-air cafe, while Bella watched four boys, hers and Lenya's grandchildren who became fast friends. Bella was still a beautiful petite woman. Always smiling, with her perfect teeth she could be great advertising for her dental practice.

"What does she think?" thought Victoria. "They were all so young; she and Mom, and Dad. Does she feel old now, looking at their grandchildren? Does she feel sorry, they are not as young and beautiful anymore? What will happen to us when we get old?"

She turned to Felix. "When I am old, I do not want to be sorry that I had missed something; did not do everything I wanted to do, did not kiss somebody I wanted to kiss, did not travel the places I wanted to see or did not buy something I wanted to buy!"

Felix looked at her suspiciously, "What are you talking about, Victoria? Is this about us or somebody I do not know?"

"It is definitely about us; I want you to be there for me when I am old and ugly," smiled Victoria. "And I want you to bring me flowers. Always."

The group took a small boat to Capri; the sea was rough, and Victoria and the kids were seasick. Bella was gently tending to them, and Victoria could understand her Dad's attraction to this beautiful and kind woman so many years ago.

She felt better at the Capo del Mondo factory, where despite her ice cream fiasco, she managed to buy a cheap porcelain souvenir for their new home in America. Shopping always made her feel better.

They returned home late at night, and the next morning happy Bella waved in her hand permission and tickets for Canada. "We are going; we are going!" The document arrived while they were traveling on the bus.

Felix took a train to Rome to HIAS where he was told that they were going to Haverhill, Massachusetts; they had the coveted warrant.

They did not celebrate; instead of feeling relieved, Victoria panicked. "Please Felix, go back and tell them we are not going!" she cried.

This night she complained to their new friend, "I would rather go to New York." Felix just sighed.

"You do not want to go to New York, Victoria, trust me," Slava was very convincing. "You would not want to get your mattress from the garbage or to live in the slums. There would be no one to help you and your family, I know!"

They all went to the local library and read about the place called ha-ver-hil. "What am I going to do in the village of forty-five thousand?" Victoria was heartbroken.

"Mom, it is not too bad," reasoned Dima. "It will be easier to learn English."

"With whom am I going to talk there? A nurse and a teacher? And all those dirt roads?" Victoria was desperate.

"Mom, stop, please," her men were trying to calm her down.

Everybody they knew was leaving. Cecily went to New York, and Volodya moved with his family to Kansas City. They needed to make a decision.

"Mom, it would be easier to learn how to drive in a small town," Dima became a real politician. When it was about his Mom, he knew exactly which buttons to push.

"I am going to call Alla in Chicago now," announced Victoria, "and then we would decide."

They all squeezed into the telephone booth at the small Post office.

"Victoria, why didn't you call earlier?" Alla was upset. "I was waiting for you, but you did not call, and I already sent a warrant to my neighbor. I am sorry, but I thought you had changed your mind. I cannot invite another family now."

"Thank you," the life was gone from Victoria's voice. Next day they went to Rome for more interviews and medical exams. They were going to Haverhill.

At the Central Square, they said goodbyes to their old and new friends. People were leaving and coming as if a giant food processor was grinding the total Jewish population of the USSR and its Republics. A friend, who enjoyed ice cream in Florence with them, bought a pizza for the whole family, the first one in their lives.

They had no money to go to any of the lighted up restaurants in the town, they bought only one dress for Victoria at the flea market, and they had no photos to show for their incredible tour of Italy. From the enormous black bag with photo equipment they dragged from Russia, they could not spare a camera for themselves. They packed their two light suitcases, counted their money, ninety dollars in total, took their sons by hands and boarded the plane. They were going home to America.

*****

I woke up when Felix opened the door, "Did you lose?" I knew, of course, that he did. He was a habitual looser at any casino.

"A little," said Felix.

"Please, do not worry Felix; we still have more than when we came to this country."

"Definitely!" laughed Felix and we both fell asleep at no time. We were home in America.

DAY 20, SEPTEMBER 16
YOSEMITE NATIONAL PARK, CA
AHWAHNEE HOTEL

O, the roads we choose … First, we went eighty- east instead of eighty- west. We were thrilled where the next turn around was only five miles away instead of fifty-nine, which would be typical for Nevada.

Later, we drove three times up and down an unmarked mountain road because we could not believe that the unpaved and dangerously curvy bicycle road was the highway marked on our map. Nevertheless, we had managed to reach California.

We knew right away that we were in California:

1) When we encounter traffic on the mountain road to Sacramento,
2) When we saw cypresses and palms for the first time,
3) When gas price rise over four dollars.

After about twenty-one turns, we entered the Yosemite National Park from the side of the recent forest fire, where still warm and smoldering grounds filled our car with smoke and smell of war. As after every war, it was a terrible picture of pain and devastation. Only later, we had learned that these relatively small fires were good for the park. The personnel would even set up the measured fires occasionally to control underbrush.

Our car was hiking on its all four tired tires higher and higher, and by the Old Priest Grade, the incline became so steep that I wanted to inform Caroline, our travel agent, who mapped our trip that we were in the car not in the elevator.

The posted speed limit was fifteen miles an hour, and the cliffs around us were magnificent, some clothed in full-length emerald gowns of the trees and some sexy and glorious in their naked beauty.

Whatever we saw of Yosemite today was hard to describe; we had never seen anything like this, although Felix informed me, "We had not been to the Himalayas."

The first thing we heard at the incredible Ahwahnee Hotel was, "Beware of the bears!" The horror stories about bears ripping off the entire car doors because of the empty lunch containers were left in the car, made us clean up everything out of our vehicle, even the souvenir soaps.

The Ahwahnee, an impressive octogenarian hotel built from the local stones and boulders, was squeezed between two massive mountain ridges, a few feet on either side of our window in the "preferred view" room.

We had a dinner reservation in the main dining room, and I was about to get dressed when Felix said, "Can I wear jeans? There is a resort casual dress code at the restaurant."

I laughed, "Do you remember how we arrived in America? You wore jeans, the only pants you had, and your only shirt. You did not have a change of clothes in our suitcase."

"Not true," Felix replied indignantly, "We bought a second-hand black trench on a flea market in Rome."

AMERICANA
HAVERHILL, MA, USA, THE 1970S

Everybody was exhausted. They had traveled over twenty-four hours since they left their apartment in Italy at four o'clock in the morning. They waited for hours at the Rome airport and flew a crowded chartered plane full of refugees. When the plane finally landed early in the evening in New York Kennedy Airport, Victoria and Felix could not wait to look at America. They left Dima and Dave to watch the family's small pile of luggage and slipped outside to meet their new Motherland.

"Felix, look at all these huge cars; these are the limousines." Victoria saw those on a picture in a glossy magazine. "Only millionaires can afford these," she added assertively.

"The drivers are mostly black," doubted Felix. "I did not expect to see so many black millionaires." He had read enough books about racism in America.

"Mom, Dad, come back! She is waiting for you!" Dave called from the door.

The young Representative from HIAS collected them for a transfer to La Guardia for a flight to Boston.

"Here are the blue HIAS stars," she explained. "Please, do not forget to put them on your sleeves, when you land in Boston. That is how your sponsors would recognize you."

A small plane was already waiting; they thanked the girl and said good-bye. Then, at the last minute, Victoria panicked, "Who is going to meet us? What is his name?"

"Of course, I almost forgot!" The HIAS girl tore a corner from her list with the names of refugees and scribbled something. There was no time to read; it became dark, and Victoria just held the piece of paper in her fist.

It was a short flight, and they were about to land in Boston.

There was the sea of lights below the landing plane, and Victoria swallowed hard; maybe someday there would be her family's light down there.

"No way!" Felix confirmed his intentions by stretching both his hands in front of him and pushing HIAS blue star back into her hands. "I am not going to wear this!"

"They forgot to color these in yellow!" He looked very chic in his black Italian trench. "Yellow would look better on black."

Victoria could not understand how he managed to joke in this situation. They were standing at the wall in the airport with their two kids and two suitcases and nobody to meet them. First, the blue HIAS stars remained in her bag, next to their Visas, then Victoria tried to pin those on the boys, but they were just as adamant as was Felix.

"Bad examples are contagious," Victoria quoted a popular Russian proverb. She looked at her closed fist where she still had a piece of paper from the HIAS girl. By now, Victoria knew the content by heart "Tara Silverman 617-479-8964 ". She closed the fist.

"Let's wait for a few minutes," suggested reasonable Dima. "She might be just late."

However, after a half an hour of a gut-wrenching wait, Victoria was worried, "Why did we buy this cognac on the plane on our last Italian money? We might need to pay for a taxi!"

She marched to the Information booth and opened her fist. With the impossible mixture of Russian, English and recently acquired Italian, she tried to explain and showed the piece of paper. Surprisingly, a sweet woman in the window understood her, and suddenly Victoria heard over the loudspeaker the familiar name. "Ms. Tara Silverman, please come to the information kiosk."

They were still standing there with the blue stars now prominently displayed on their sleeves when they saw a man and two women with flowers running down an escalator.

"Here they are," Victoria whispered not taking her eyes off the group.

"Yes, but wait, now they are going to roll out a red carpet for you!" always doubted sarcastic Felix.

The group did not even stop at the information booth; they ran straight to them, they were smiling and saying something Victoria did not understand. They hugged and kissed, lifted the boys, cried and laughed, and hugged and kissed again.

"Never was anybody so happy to see my family and me," Victoria cried softly.

Tara, whose name was on the note from the HIAS, brought her large station wagon to load their small luggage.

"Did you see her limousine?" Victoria whispered to Felix. "She is a millionaire!"

All her life Victoria studied English; first in school, then at the Medical School, then at the three-year course, preparing for her post-doctorate degree, which required an English exam. Both boys went to the Special English School where they studied English from the first grade, and Felix took two months of private lessons after they got permission to leave. They all realized that they could not speak or understand English during their ride to Haverhill in the spacious station wagon.

When the newcomers were settled in the best suite at a downtown hotel, Tara tried to explain that they would come back tomorrow to take the family out for lunch (Victoria saw the word in books, but had no idea what 'lunch' meant).

They did understand "Goodbye"; however, Felix was not ready.

On the chartered plane to America, they spent their last Italian lira on the bottle of a duty-free cognac, and now, their first evening on American soil, his Russian soul wanted to celebrate. He rushed to the bathroom where he found four plastic glasses, (there were five adults in the room), opened the bottle and topped the glasses with cognac.

"To success," said the Russians. "Na zdrovie," said the Americans. They clinked the plastic cups, and the Americans moistened their lips with cognac; Felix took a large swallow from the bottle. Victoria saw surprise and almost fear in the widened eyes of their sponsors, and she heard Tara saying something she understood, "Aid a shiker?"

Her Babushka did not teach her Yiddish, but both, she and Felix, understood the question perfectly well, "A Jew - the drunkard?"

After an awkward pause, three Americans bravely took a sip each, while Victoria emptied her cup and Felix took yet another large swallow from the bottle. Finally, the Americans left after making sure a small fridge had milk and cookies for kids.

It was late; only the streetlights were on behind large window. Dima and Dave were asleep in the bedroom.

In the dark living room, Victoria and Felix sat down on the bed to watch a small black and white TV. A tall and handsome comedian was obviously funny as the audience laughed.

"I know this guy," Victoria was happy to see a familiar face. "It is Frank Sinatra."

"You know nothing Victoria, I recognized him right away; it is Burt Lancaster."

The late show with Johnny Carson was playing on.

*****

Almost four decades later, we entered a spectacular dining room of Ahwahnee Hotel emblazoned with hundreds of electric candles in iron candelabras and sconces under incredibly high vaulted ceiling fit for King Kong. The lone candlestick on our table was over three feet tall. The setting of massive local stones, old American- made wooden furniture and native Art could dwarf any food. In the hallway, the large wooden box had a cover decorated with an Indian motif; it held Guest Ice.

We were thousands miles and years, struggles and tears, victories and losses, soaring achievements, gray hair and wrinkles away from that first night at the American hotel in front of a small black and white TV.

DAY 21, SEPTEMBER 17
YOSEMITE NATIONAL PARK, CA
AHWAHNEE HOTEL

We woke up with a minute sliver of light in our large window. It sneaked between the six-story-high stonewall of Ahwahnee Hotel on the left, an incredibly tall clean-shaven cliff in the front and a giant dark emerald tree on the right. Only a narrow strip on the top was bright with a blue sky.

After a quick breakfast, we met our guide Michael and went to explore Yosemite, God's drawing room. Soaring cliffs, sweet-smelling meadows, vividly green waters reflecting soft white clouds, polished boulders and waterfalls, all were painted with a majestic brush of genius. I was in awe; I wanted to cry and laugh, and store all this beauty in my soul forever.

Michael told us the old stories of the Ahwahneechee, who lived here for generations. At the smooth cliffs, the grinding boulder was polished for millions of years. We saw a large metallic horizontal barrel with a latch and small round holes, a bear trap. When we returned to the hotel for lunch, he told us about the glorious Annual Bracebridge Dinner, an old tradition of Christmas at Yosemite with seven- course-four-hour dinner, singers and centuries' old court characters.

He drove us to see the soaring Half Dome and the impressive El Capitan up and close. The long spectacular day went to the tune of four hundred dollars, not including the lunch and gratuity; and it was worth every dime!

AMERICANA
HAVERHILL, MA, THE 1970S

"Lunch, what is the lunch and when is it?" asked concerned Victoria. Not that she had a choice of clothes or the time, or any choice at all.

They spent all morning spellbound in front of the hotel window. It was Sunday, and a small New England town's Central Square was sleepy and deserted. Old trees and large professional buildings lined up the streets, which led to a small fountain in the center. Soft September sun reflected in clean windows and occasional cars.

Victoria and Felix stayed at the window looking at their new life, and Victoria said quietly, "Finally, I am home."

She had left the family she adored, the country where she was born, the language she knew and the profession she loved. She had left her friends and her past, she had left everybody and everything and she came to an unknown place with two kids, two suitcases and ninety dollars in her pocket.

Victoria looked at the strange town where strange people spoke a strange language, and she knew in her heart, that she had reached her destination in life; she was finally home.

She was traveling for so long; she was so tired, there was nowhere else to go, and just the look of a quiet New England town gave her enough comfort and understanding that she had finally arrived. She was home.

Lunch turned out to be only slightly earlier than a Russian dinner. The same two women who met them at the airport, Tara and Molly, picked them up and took them to the restaurant. By the time everybody settled at the big table, they were hungry; they did not know where or how to get breakfast, so the kids drank milk and ate cookies.

The walls were dark oak, the tablecloth was gleaming white, and the waitress was smiling. The menu was scary, it was written in the unknown language, and they could not understand a word in it.

Victoria, who sat next to Tara, found the solution immediately; after Tara ordered, Victoria just whispered "same." Dima had no trouble, he had always read the menu from right to left, he pointed at the most expensive dish, and Dave copied his brother.

Felix had a problem; he ordered "hamburger," the only familiar word on the menu. He got upset when the waitress unexpectedly returned with coffee.

"We did not eat yet!" he almost screamed at Victoria in Russian but calmed down when the Americans were served coffee as well.

Tara was a beautiful Israeli with a mane of dark curly hair and kind gray eyes. Her Polish husband learned some Russian when he was a child during the War. Not that it helped or prevented all the funny things that happened to the newly minted Americans, but it was comforting for them to know that somebody else could confirm there was a country, the language and the culture they came from, that they did not just drop from the outer space.

The whole community was throbbing with excitement; people were surprised by how "modern" "the Russians" looked compare to a poster at the Temple, depicting them based on a recent production of "Fiddler on the Roof."

"The Russians" were stunned when three days later, they saw their new fully furnished apartment full of presents and Dr. Milden even brought a new bottle of cognac after the report of the Welcoming Committee. Everybody in the community was kind and charitable although the word "charity" was not present yet in the newcomers' limited vocabulary.

A few days later, at the end of the Rosh Hashanah service, the family stood next to the Rabbi, welcomed and greeted by the whole Jewish Community. Victoria was wearing her black dress, the only dress she had brought from Russia, and she cried black tears from ruined Russian-made mascara while her heart was filled with joy and gratitude.

They were invited to dinners and birthdays, driven to all the appointments (social security, doctors, and schools) and were taken to movies, shopping, and endless lunches. The kids started the new school, and Victoria and Felix signed up for the "English Idioms Course" at the local college.

They were dazzled, overwhelmed and over saturated with English and everything American when after the lecture at the college they met a Russian couple from the neighboring town. The couple was already two years in the United States, and Victoria and Felix desperately needed the explanations and advice in Russian, not English.

Victoria started with the most important thing, the money." How do you pay for everything, the groceries, the rent, the college?"

Not that she needed to know it right away; so far the grant from HIAS and the Jewish Community paid for everything, but just in case, for the future.

"You should write a check," the man told her smiling.

"What is it? Where would I get a check? And how do you 'write it'?" asked Victoria.

"In the bank, of course," it was apparent that her ignorance and stupidity irritated the man.

"We do not have a bank; we are not millionaires!" Victoria almost cried when the man doubled over from laughing and had to sit down on the steps. He did not expect to give these green newcomers a lecture on the American financial system. He did not learn yet how to be kind to strangers.

The college was the place for learning, for sure, because that was where Victoria had learned for the first time that she was Russian.

She smiled at a Chinese girl sitting next to her in the class, and the girl asked her what her nationality was.

"Jewish," firmly answered Victoria happy that she could understand the question.

"No, I had asked what nationality?"

"Sure, I understood, I am Jewish."

"No, you do not understand," the girl started to lose her patience. "I am asking about your nationality, not your religion!"

Victoria was over thirty years old, and for all these years, she was sure she was Jewish; even in her passport on the fifth line after her last name, the first name, the father's name and the birthday was clearly written "Jewish". And now this girl was screaming at her "No."

It would be funny if this short word on the fifth line in their passports did not destroy so many dreams of education and good jobs, hopes, and dreams of a world without Holocaust and antisemitism, dreams of freedom and the future.

She knew she was Jewish when her father told her it was not enough to be just good at anything. "You have to be the best," he said.

She knew she was Jewish when she could not even attempt to get into Kiev Medical School and had to try somewhere else, not in the capital city.

She knew she was Jewish when during the first minute of the English exam the Medical School professor told her she spoke English with "a funny accent".

She knew she was Jewish when the first time Victoria wore her new fur coat, her classmate in medical school told her she was dressed in the Jewish national costume.

She knew she was Jewish, when after graduation, unlike some of her girlfriends, she could not work in Kiev.

She knew she was Jewish, when at the intersection, which she was about to cross holding her two little sons by hands, a car stopped, its passengers screaming through the open windows, "You, kike, get out of here together with your kids! Go to Israel, dirty Jew!"

She knew she was Jewish because she looked like one in the sea of Slavic faces, among the people who just a few short decades earlier collaborated with Nazis and witnessed Baby Yar.

She knew she was Jewish when after she announced at the meeting at work that, if drafted, she would never serve in the war against Israel, she spent a sleepless night afraid that her colleagues report her and she would be arrested.

She knew she was Jewish, when the patient, whose life she saved, was not grateful but genuinely surprised and asked her "Why? Why did you stay with me for three days to save my life? Are not you Jewish?"

She could not count all the fights that Felix fought when somebody called him zhid or dirty Jew, and how many nights he had spent behind bars for fighting back.

She remembered how Dima could not participate in the annual concert in the kindergarten; he was not allowed to read a poem about Ukraine because he did not look the part.

She turned to the Chinese girl and repeated proudly, "I am a Jew!"

"What country you were born in?" her classmate wanted to get to the bottom of the problem. Victoria lost the thread of the conversation and could not understand where this was going.

"I was born In Russia."

"So you are Russian!" celebrated the girl, "Russian, stupid, Russian." She was ecstatic with her victory and looked triumphantly at stunned Victoria.

The discoveries large and small were plenty every day. Their lives slowly started to fall into some routine although in reality, everything was for the first time.

Dima and Dave were doing great in school and tried to help with the home choirs. Older Dima even got a paper route, and his tips were a great help.

"They are real Americans," Victoria thought proudly. She was surprised when the neighbor stopped by the next day.

"Is it your boy, who delivers newspapers to the nursing home at the end of the street? The conditions there are not great," continued the concerned neighbor. "Your boy hides around the corner and vomits every day after he leaves the nursing home. It is not a good paper route for him".

That put an end to Dima's carrier as a paperboy. Dave continued to do laundry and helped with the cooking. Eventually, he picked up a paper route too.

Tara and Molly in turns took Victoria to the supermarket, taught her how to shop and paid the bills. They made sure that milk, bread, juice, fruits, and vegetables were in the cart.

Victoria shopped the "Russian style," no cut up or half-prepared products. A whole chicken was easy to cut, and she utilized everything. She skinned the bird with surgical precision and cooked a chicken soup from the bones, stew from the thighs and legs, chicken cutlets from the breast meat, chicken pate from the liver and stuffed and sutured chicken skin.

Both, Felix and Victoria went to CITA program. It was a newly established program for immigrants to learn English and to acquire some working skills. CITA had never dealt with a doctor or engineer before, so they sent Victoria to the hospital library to learn medical terminology. She chatted with the friendly librarian, however; she could not read American textbooks, even after all these years studying English.

Nevertheless, one day, she discovered it was easy to read the American newspaper.

"Last week I read this whole paper," Victoria bragged to Tara proudly picking up a copy of National Enquirer at the checkout at the supermarket. "It is a wonderful, interesting paper and easy to read, it helps me to learn English," Victoria was ecstatic, and Tara just smiled. She still remembered her own first years in the United States.

Smoking Felix with his dark skin and curly hair fit right in with Puerto Ricans and Mexicans at the CITA Program.

His English was still marginal when he got an interview at the big defense company, and Tara's Polish husband Yanek volunteered to translate.

Back from the disastrous interview, Felix could not stop laughing when he told Victoria that Yanek knew only one phrase in Russian, "I speak Russian."

After this interview, CITA supervisor realized that Felix was a real engineer; he invited Felix to his office and advised him to leave the program. There was a chance that with Felix's dark looks and Spanish accent, which he picked up together with his English, no prospective employer would ever believe him that he is a highly qualified electrical engineer from Russia.

Molly, Tara and their friends in the community were always available to drive, but the family needed a car. There was a money problem, of course.

"We have your parents' money Victoria." An easygoing, generous Felix was never one to count the money; he never knew how much money they had. It surprised Victoria that he remembered about this money at all. "The money we got for Mom's coral, remember?"

"We cannot take this money, Felix, it is not ours." Victoria was getting angry. "I would never spend a dime of this money, car or no car."

Fast study of the American system, Felix came up with the solution, "We will not take the money Victoria, we would just borrow it. By the time your parents will be here we will have the money to pay them back".

Their first shiny car was huge, and Felix proudly announced, "It cost only nine hundred dollars," so it was a perfect match.

The car lasted all of five days until Felix totaled it but, thankfully, Felix was all right. Neither Molly nor Tara could understand Victoria's despair.

"You have insurance, and you will buy a new car," Molly tried to console Victoria. It was hard for her to understand that in Russia a car was like a family member, one and only, one for your whole life.

*****

"The car is OK, and there are no bears in sight," Felix went to check on our car before tomorrow's drive. Moon stuck in the right top corner of our window between the cliff and the tree. The majestic night fell on Yosemite.

I smiled thinking about our cars' troubles in the first years; Felix never liked those stories and did not find them funny. The Insurance agent, who became a friend, invented a nickname "Felix –crash" and, after yet another string of minor accidents, told Felix, that he should have brought T-24 tank from Russia.

I had learned everything about car insurance, worried for my husband and had never cried about the car again.

DAY 22, SEPTEMBER 18
CARMEL, CA
CARMEL VALLEY RANCH

I t was an anniversary of a sort and the morning could not be more picturesque.

We had done three weeks of traveling the behemoth of travel, the Cross- Country drive. The drive when every day was not just another day of driving, but an incredible adventure; when your brain swelled with images, your lungs breathed the air of excitement, your eyes were reflecting a kaleidoscope of magical landscapes and another day lead you to yet another magnificent place.

I took a farewell look at Ahwahnee, which loosely meant, "the valley shaped like a big mouth" referencing the shape of the Yosemite Valley; the building was a happy marriage of logs and boulders, green shutters and carved wood. I took the last photo of deer playing on the lawn with magnificent background of immense cliffs and conifers standing at the guard.

We drove a little over hundred miles repeating bend after bend of Merced, the vivacious mountain river with clear green waters reflecting all the abundant greenery around, born in deep of Sierra and comfortably resting on the bed of small rocks it carried from its birthplace.

We parted with the river and descended on the endless Californian orchards of pistachios trees, ripe cotton, and cactus flowers; we drove through vividly yellow hills, wind tunnels and cypresses until we got a glimpse of the Great Pacific somewhere around Monterey.

We started a slow six-day- long U-turn on the Pacific Highway through Carmel, Santa Barbara, and Santa Monica; we planned to rest, to see our family and to start traveling eastward the next week. We checked in the Hilltop Suite at the Ranch outside of Carmel. At sunset, we settled on the large balcony warmed up by the heat waves from the fireplace in our bedroom. Tired after a long drive, Felix closed his eyes and napped. He did not look like a cool dark guy in a black Italian trench almost forty years ago.

AMERICANA
HAVERHILL, MA, THE 1970S

Her Babushka was the keeper of the Jewish calendar, so they did not realize that the Rosh Hashanah, the Jewish New Year, was coming, when two days after their arrival, Tara said she would pick them up to go to the Temple.

They had never been to the Temple before. Victoria was the only one who had ever been to a house of worship when in the first grade she went to church with her girlfriend Galya and Galya's grandmother. She still remembered the grand church, the strange "portraits" in the heavy silver frames and the faint sweet smell of the priest's hand, which she kissed. She had never told anybody about this, afraid that her Babushka would not approve.

Today, this visit to the old Ukrainian Church in Kiev decades ago, gave her some authority with her family.

"Please, get dressed in your best clothes," she told the boys, not that they had a choice.

Three months ago, at the Chop Railroad Station, Dima and Dave had to throw their old clothes in the trash and change into the new, bought for the trip, pants, and shirts right in the middle of the crowded hall.

"We are lucky they each have one shirt for the Holiday," thought Victoria. She did not worry about herself; her whole wardrobe consisted of an elegant short black dress and a sporty jeans pantsuit that she brought from Kiev. Made of polyester, not wrinkled and comfortable to wear, the dress and the pantsuit provided her with a choice and diversity for the last few months. She had lost over thirty pounds somewhere between Ukraine and the United States, but the little black dress still fitted her.

During the service, they sat between Tara and Molly and Victoria had no idea what she should do with the prayers books In equally unknown to her Hebrew and English.

Before they left Ukraine, Felix found his grandfather's Prayer book, but Customs did not allow taking it out of the country.

"Just as well," Felix thought then; he could not read Yiddish texts, and to the chagrin of his deeply religious grandfather, he was a proud atheist brought up by a Communist Mom and Soviet propaganda.

Victoria's grandmother also had a Prayer book, but she kept it to herself, never wanting to jeopardize her son or granddaughter's future by "her old tales and beliefs."

At the end of the service, after the Rabbi wished the happy holiday to the congregation, he invited Felix, Victoria, and the kids to stay next to him to meet the community.

"Why does he want us there?" Felix felt confused. He remembered dinner last night at Tara's home. It was the first American house they ever saw, and it was beautiful.

The two-story house had a separate bedroom for each kid and a guests' bathroom that Victoria was convinced she would be happy to live in. It had a lovely garden in the front, woods at the back and the incredible real bar downstairs.

The Rabbi with his wife and another couple stopped by to meet "the Russians." The rabbi was tall handsome and young, and his wife was pretty and smiley.

"He looks like an American movie star," whispered a surprised Victoria to Felix in Russian. "I had never thought rabbi could look like that."

Everything was new and confusing to them, the house, the drinks and the menu of the dinner. They were less than two days in the country. Victoria at least could pretend that she understood English. However, Felix had a difficult time following, and he was happy when it was time to leave.

All of them were shocked when the guests kissed Tara and each other saying goodbye.

In their old world, expressions of love and gratitude were very different; no one had kissed the friends or acquaintances. Now, they realized that they would have to learn new traditions and customs, just like learning a new language. They remembered many Russian proverbs for the occasion.

"When you live with wolves, you should howl like a wolf," quietly whispered Felix in

Russian under his breath. He smiled and kissed Tara first and then proceeded to kiss everybody else, including the Rabbi. When they were heading to the door, he noticed a surprised look on Tara's face and saw her trying to hide the smile.

In the car, Molly could not stop laughing. "The Rabbi! What a surprise for him! Men do not kiss each other," she tried to explain. "Especially, not the Rabbi!"

"Please, do not get upset," she tried to console dismayed Felix.

"I enjoyed kissing the handsome rabbi," volunteered Victoria. Dave and Dima exchanged conspirators' glances and tried to suppress the laughter. Still upset Felix finally gave in and smiled.

Felix was still upset about the previous night when at the Temple he stood next to the Rabbi who introduced "new Russian family" to the congregation. Everybody came over to shake hands, to hug, to kiss and to welcome. Victoria could not even see. Overwhelmed by the kindness of the strangers, she was sobbing uncontrollably; the Russian mascara running down her face matched her black dress.

She saw Molly and was very happy to see a familiar face.

"We would like you to come for Peter's fiftieth birthday party tomorrow," smiled Molly.

It was the first real party they were invited to, and it was terrific, just like everything else in their new life.

It seemed like every American house had a bar in the basement, but this one was crowded with many people and had a black bartender.

Before this evening, Victoria knew only one black man. Dave's music teacher Lyudmila lived in the same building as Victoria. Her husband came to Russia to study at the Moscow University of Patrice Lumumba. They met at the concert in Moscow and married after his graduation. They were a happy and quiet couple.

The building was the high-rise built by the Kiev TV studio for their creative employees, mostly writers, composers, actors, and producers. Strangely, "the cultural" residents of the building, people who admired Paul Robson and Louis Armstrong, frown upon this perfect union, boycotted and refused to acknowledge the couple. Victoria occasionally set through Dave's music lesson and after that had a cup of tea with lovely Lyudmila and her husband.

Now, she sat at the bar and tried to converse with the bartender. He, however, preferred to watch Felix who was demonstrating to the crowd how the Russians drank their vodka. Felix could not speak English, but he definitely knew how to drink.

*****

I was thinking about our first days in Massachusetts. We were like newborn babies, not understanding language, traditions, and customs. We did not know how to dress and shop, how to drive and where to go, how to earn and where to keep the money. Never before, were we in the bank or at the Temple and if not for our inner compasses and guidance by our new friends, we would not know how to navigate in this new life. Brought up on Soviet propaganda, we were not sure if having a black "help" at Peter's birthday party could qualify as racism, but we were sure that he and Molly were the most kind and decent people in the world. Maybe we were not that naïve, but we tried to understand the relationships, mortgages, houses, to figure out "the salary" and "the benefits." We had never had a car, insurance or private schools, we had no clue what any abbreviation meant, and I certainly had no idea about any of the medicines at the pharmacy.

AMERICANA
HAVERHILL, MA, THE 1970S

A few days after coming to America, Felix went to buy cigarettes in a small variety store at the end of the street. It was rainy, and he put on a cap and lifted up the collar of his black trench; his English was non-existent. He got the cigarettes and put them on the counter; his hands in his pockets, he nodded at the package.

"It is free," said the jittery storeowner. "It is free for you!"

He was about to bring his both hands up when Felix, already spoiled by welcoming and generous community, mistook the gesture, shook his hands, thanked him profusely and left the store.

Tara and Molly went hysterical when two weeks later they learned how Felix was getting his free cigarettes.

The ladies were her mentors, chauffeurs, governesses, friends, and confidants. They taught Victoria how to make up beds, what to buy in the store, how to order at the restaurant and what to wear. They neglected their families, husbands, and kids, while they guided and took care of Victoria and her family with endless patience and understanding.

Back in Kiev, when her boys did not know something or did not understand the word, Victoria's Dad would suggest they should look it up in the dictionary, but Dima and Dave knew a better and shorter way, "Let us ask Mom, she knows everything."

Suddenly the boys lost their confidence; their parents knew nothing and were no authorities anymore. The parents asked the children; they were the ones who knew everything now.

However, they could not help Victoria with what to serve for Dave's approaching birthday. Dave already invited all the kids from the school and the street, and Victoria was not sure if they would like her Russian menu.

"Nothing easier," laughed Tara. "We will order pizza for kids." The concept of "to order" was unknown to Victoria; however, Tara fixed that too.

For Dave's birthday, their first party, the apartment was spotless. In spite of Tara's advice, Victoria cooked up a storm. "Just for adults," she said.

In the bedroom, she took off the hanger her new Italian dress that came from the same flea market as Felix's trench. It was white and elegant buttoned down with tan buttons; it had two chest pockets with cute tan shoelaces ties and another two pockets below the belt.

"Looking good, Mom," said Dave; he was proud of his Mom, and he looked not bad himself in his new shirt.

Victoria glanced in the mirror; she loved her dress, and she was ready.

Tara and Molly arrived first, to make sure everything was okay. Victoria opened the door; she wanted her friends to see how well prepared she was, to notice her new dress and Dave's shirt.

Funny looks on their faces puzzled Victoria, but she went back to the kitchen where she was still cooking for the party.

The party was a great success; kids loved pizza and adults loved Victoria's Russian dishes. Molly and Tara with their husbands stayed almost until morning while Victoria in her improved English tried to tell them about their last day in Russia and the last train out. They all cried, hugged and felt like a long lost family. "The only thing," Tara was leaving, but she just had to ask.

"Why did you wear a nurse's uniform for your son's birthday?"

*****

The sun finally descended into the ocean somewhere in the west. We were three thousand miles away from home, and I remembered when I saw the ocean for the first time. Strange, I did not remember when for the first time I saw the Great Pacific Ocean, but I never forgot the sunny autumn day on the East Coast.

Molly and Peter had a beautiful condominium on the beach; it was all glass and chrome and spectacular three- story- ocean view. I loved the place, its simple elegance, and airiness.

"I just need to get my license back to have one just like that," a cocky thought flashed in my mind. We crossed the road and stood on the beach as the wind picked up and blew my hair and my skirt. I dipped my hand in the unwelcoming dark, cold water; I wanted to bow to the majesty of Atlantic. It was awesome, exhilarating and somehow liberating to see the Ocean and to feel its breath for the first time in my life. I needed no license for that.

DAY 23, SEPTEMBER 19
CARMEL, CA
CARMEL VALLEY RANCH

I woke up around three-thirty in the morning; the mattress under me was vibrating slightly, just like the floor in my car. "Earthquake, earthquake in California!" I thought first. Then, when the soft vibrating continued, I realized with surprise, "O, my god! I have car legs, not sea legs".

I tried to fall back to sleep, but I knew too well the routine of my occasional sleepless nights.

The bright computer screen behind my tightly closed eyes was slowly opening and lighting up the various icons: my life, children, retirement, memories, travel, childhood, future, old age, my patients, and the spirit that had brought us here. Not in this particular order. I wrote without a paper, talked without a voice, made up schedules and planned our days. All with only one thought, really, "Get back to sleep Victoria; you would have to get up early in the morning."

Funny, I did not have to wake up early; I retired. Nevertheless, there were always things to do, luggage to pack and Felix to wake up.

I got up, opened my suitcase and picked up my favorite Burberry T-shirt for a drive to the town.

AMERICANA
HAVERHILL, MA, THE 1970S

Victoria always liked polka dots. Somehow, it reminded her of her childhood, although she did not remember if she wore anything with polka dots then. Today, Molly took her to a beautiful store and there, to the right of the entrance, was a stand with these tops; they were conservative navy with small white dots, all sizes and they cost only $2.99.

Victoria quickly did the math: if she would buy not the gallon of juice, but the smaller container, and if she would not buy this and save on that, she could buy this beautiful short sleeve blouse. She looked for Molly to consult with her and suddenly her eyes hit another rack with sexy red polka dots tops. Right next to it, hung elegant white and black, and o, so sublime, beige and white, and black with white polka dots tops. $2.99, $ 5.98 or even $8.97; she could count, but it would be an unbelievable splurge and a huge hole in her budget.

Victoria could not decide which color to buy. She felt hot and lightheaded; she was so sweaty she would not be able even to try it on. Panicky and dizzy, she, probably, would end up on the floor of the cheap department store, if she would not hold on to Molly, who walk her out of the store and sat her down outside, breathing in and out fresh air. After a few minutes, still calculating Victoria felt better and got back to the store where she bought her first American piece of cloth, the most elegant black with the white polka dots blouse for $2.99.

A few days after they settled in their apartment, they were surprised to get a call from somebody who explained that they should expect a visit from the FBI. They did not worry and did not pay too much attention, but Victoria baked cookies, just in case.

A week later, however, in the early evening, a cute young man showed up. First, he wanted to know why the boy playing on the street with the friends knew that he was from FBI. That was easy.

"Dave knew we were expecting you," answered Victoria; with her improving English, she was now the spokeswoman for the family.

"No, it was an American boy with perfect English," said the astute stranger. He looked at Felix and laughed noticing an unmistakable resemblance to the "American boy." Victoria wondered if he would next ask how they managed human cloning.

The FBI wanted to know how they got their education, positions and the post-graduation Doctorate for Victoria in anti-Semitic Ukraine. It wanted to know why Victoria was allowed to travel to Bulgaria and Poland to visit friends and why Felix was arrested at the railroad station before they left Russia. It seemed the stranger knew everything about them. Victoria and Felix discussed their answers with each other in Russian trying to give the friendly blond visitor all the information he wanted.

They talked and laughed about their limited English and promised to learn it better for the next interview. Only when the time came for a traditional Russian tea and homemade cookies did they realize that the Agent's Russian was much better than their combined English.

Felix was looking for a job; the kids were in school and Victoria spent her time in the hospital library and with her new friends. Molly and Tara took her out for lunches and shopping and introduced her to everybody in the town. She and the family were celebrities of a sort, their pictures were in the local newspaper, and they were invited to dinners and parties.

Victoria was even asked to speak at the Rotary Club dinner meeting; her vocabulary expanded; she could understand and answer the questions. While serving her salad, the waiter asked her about dressing.

"Dressing," Victoria thought surprised. "What could be wrong with my dress?" She uncomfortably pulled down her sweater. There was nothing wrong with it, at least, she did not see any problem, and she answered defiantly, "No, thank you."

She heard some people at the table said "Italian," and when a few minutes later a delicious aroma of garlic and vinegar floated above the table, she was sorry for her mistake. "I will never make it again," silently promised Victoria to herself chewing on her dry salad.

The next week, on a perfect day to play hooky, Victoria skipped her CITA program and went with Tara to Boston instead. Tara promised to treat Victoria to lunch at the famous crape cafe on Newbury Street.

They both saw right away Lee Remick having lunch in the far corner. Victoria was so excited to see a famous movie star that she heard only "salad" part of Tara's order but, as usual, she said "the same."

"Would you like a dressing?" asked the pretty waitress.

This time Victoria was sure there was nothing wrong with her dress, and she knew exactly what she wanted. "Italian, please."

The puzzled waitress looked at Victoria. "Yes, Italian, please," Victoria tended to raise her voice when she felt somebody did not understand her accent.

Ten minutes later the waitress brought lunches. Tara had ordered fruit salad with honey yogurt dressing, and sweet crepes and Victoria's plate was bursting with an aroma of garlic and vinegar.

*****

A shrewd Carmelite monk named Carmel in 1607. It took another hundred and sixty years to found a Spanish Mission at the place where now laid a beautiful old quaint town by the sea, a community of artists and intellectuals. We walked, shopped, ate and enjoyed the eighty degrees weather. I found an elegant marine boutique selling beautiful serving pieces adorned with blue glass fishes and bought all of them. Felix was a Pisces.

Back in Russia, I did not know anything about the signs of the Zodiac. I read and vaguely remembered that one of the Chekov's heroines, who was born in May, had mentioned that she was a Taurus and her birthday stone was an emerald.

I loved my May birthday arriving with new greenery and flowers. Lilies-of-the-Valley was my favorite, and on this day, Felix had always brought me the whole basket of gentle white bells. I loved emeralds too, of course; not that Felix could afford any to buy.

My first strange encounter with the signs of the Zodiac happened at work. Along with a new cardiologist, I was the first female physician invited to join a private group practice of three male internists. The schedule for the doctors was prepared three months in advance and only one doctor a time could be on vacation, so not to burden the rest of us with frequent nights on call.

The open door of my office loudly hit the wall when a triage nurse, responsible for our schedule, flew in. "You cannot possibly take off this day in May," she almost yelled, "I already have four requests for the May vacations!"

"But this is my birthday, and I would prefer not to work on my birthday," I was not ready to give up.

"May is also a birthday month of three other internists, the cardiologist and, as a matter of fact, mine as well!" We looked at each other in sheer disbelieve and finally laughed.

For the next thirty years, all five doctors got along perfectly well in spite of May being the most terrible month for scheduling. We all were true Tauruses, dependable, loyal and patient if a bit stubborn and materialistic.

It was not even funny to see how much Felix and I matched our signs descriptions when neither of us ever believed in this nonsense. In my shopping bag, happily clanked salad and cheese serving pieces with beautiful blue glassfish handles; a painting of four zaftig women carrying a huge fish on the beach, my birthday present to Felix, hung in his office, and on my desk prominently displayed was a strong and stubborn bull.

DAY 24, SEPTEMBER 20
CARMEL, CA
CARMEL VALLEY RANCH

O ur travel muse Caroline firmly believed in our ability to follow her instructions and, not to disappoint, on her advice, we started the morning with a famous Seventeen-mile Drive. We paid a required toll and dutifully stopped at every point to take a picture. On our GPS, the route looked like a very curly S repeating itself in the narrow loops.

The slow ride allowed us to appreciate every detail of the day. Trees with canopies extending across the narrow road, their branches in passionate embrace overhead, the Lone Cypress Tree and spectacular glass mansions overlooking the ocean were magnificent.

There was nothing pacific about this ocean. The vigor and wrath of the waves, the intensity of the color, and the rough stones of the coast, all were an impressive exhibition of the pure energy and scary strength.

We were happy to be back to Carmel-by-the-Sea Village, its narrow streets and quirky cottages, hidden passages and secluded courtyards were something between the bustling beach town and an artsy seaside village.

AMERICANA
HAVERHILL, MA, THE 1980S

"I got it! I got it!" announced Felix. "I got the job!"

"You already told us that last night," Victoria raised her eyebrow. She knew Felix was disappointed that the position was for a technician, but they did not have a choice; CITA was done and they were five months in America.

"You do not understand, Vika! They just called me from that place where I had an interview last week and offered me a job, the real engineering position. And their offer is eight thousand dollars more!"

"Now," thought Victoria "we will be real Americans. And I will be able to send a parcel to my parents."

They were getting letters from home almost every day, and Mom managed to send a few packages with candies and chocolate for the kids and some Russian souvenirs for Victoria's new friends.

Her Dad was desperate; he missed them, he felt he made an unforgiving mistake not leaving with them. Now, only a few months later, the door slammed shut, and there was not even a crack to go through. He was happy for them, but still worried about Victoria's license, the kids' school, and their future.

Well, the boys were not very happy with their future at the moment; they were scheduled for day surgery at the local hospital.

THE KIDS
KIEV, UKRAINE, THE 1960S

Although not forbidden, religious celebrations were frowned upon at the Soviet Union and religious rituals like bris were allowed only by medical indications. No doctor would risk his license performing bris secretly.

When Dima was born, Victoria's parents came to the hospital to take her and the baby home. Victoria stepped over the threshold to their apartment with her first-born son in her hands alone and heartbroken all over again. She would never trust anybody else to touch her baby.

When Dave was born, Felix was under her Hospital window every day; he could not wait to take them home. A friend invited him to celebrate and let him borrow the book, a new American novel that Felix could not wait to read. This morning, he was reading the book and holding flowers when the nurse finally wheeled out Victoria with their new son in her lap to the hallway. Felix was nervous and excited but he got his wife and son into the waiting taxi, and they drove home. He helped Victoria out of the car and suddenly opened his hands in despair, "I forgot my book with all the baby's documents in it on the hospital window, in the hallway where I was waiting for you."

They both knew that nobody would be interested in the documents, but the latest novel by American writer would be snatched in a minute.

"I am sorry Victoria, you have the keys and I will be right back," he got back in the taxi and drove away.

Victoria swallowed her tears as she stepped over the threshold to their apartment with her newborn son in her hands alone, again.

They had a week to consider a bris but Felix's beloved zeide Gedale, for whom they named Dave and who would insist on bris, was long gone. Felix's Mom passed away not quite a year ago, and she would never suggest a bris for her grandson. Again, Victoria would never trust anybody, but the doctor, to touch her baby.

AMERICANA
HAVERHILL, MA, THE 1980S

The boys were twelve and ten now; they were going to the Temple and Sunday school, wore yarmulkes and celebrated Shabbat. The best surgeon in the town donated his services for two "Russian boys" to become Jewish again. They were brave, and it was not a big deal.

On his first birthday in America, Felix went to work. He returned home elated. "It is a beautiful place, people were smiling and happy, and the food was everywhere. Three of my new friends even invited me to a local bar after work." He could not stop, "I do not understand why many people were wearing green but it was not a uniform. I would ask tomorrow if it is a company's policy."

On a small TV in the kitchen, a News Channel reported about the St. Patrick's Day parade in New York.

In Kiev, the beautiful chestnut trees opened their snowy- white candelabras, the fragrant branches of yellow mimosas were in full bloom and Lenya was sick. He got ill soon after Victoria left and, when the best hospitals in Kiev could not make the diagnosis, everybody decided it was a broken heart. With terrible difficulties, Sarra and Ella managed to transfer him to the Moscow Clinic where he was finally diagnosed with a rare and poorly understood blood cancer.

"Maybe the Americans would know how to treat it," Victoria thought in anguish. She went to Boston with Molly and Tara; she was going from one Massachusetts Senator's Office to another, frantic to get a guest visa for her sick father; however, nobody on this side of the ocean could solve the problem; the Russians would not let him out.

Dad wrote regularly to Victoria and the family; his letters were coming almost every day, although he was so sick he had to dictate them to Sarra. He wanted to talk to them, to give the last advice, to make sure Dima would continue to play chess and to write poetry, Dave would study hard, and Felix and Victoria would stay together, rekindle their love and support each other.

"I fulfilled my promise," Victoria overheard Felix's last conversation with her Dad. "Victoria passed her exams and got her license. Your daughter is an American doctor now!"

Sarra had never left his side; for weeks, she slept in the chair next to his hospital bed. Ella was pregnant and delivered a baby girl eleven days before Lenya passed away. To Lenya's letter to Victoria, which he dictated from his hospital bed, Sarra added one sentence on the third page, "Ella had a new daughter." The time stopped, and nothing was important anymore.

He died in June, not even a year since Victoria left Russia; he was sixty-five. At the very end of his last letter to Victoria, he wrote with his own shaky hand, "Yours, until my last breath".

*****

Last year on the hot summer days, I read and reread the old letters from my parents. Our beautiful backyard was lushly green, and water played lazy notes on a small fountain. "Dacha" our Russian friends called it, "the mansion" complimented Americans, but for me, it was my home, my American dream.

Travel always was my passion, but to me, it made sense only when you had a place to return to, your private place to curve comfortably in the chair, the place where even walls were helpful.

There is the "Society 100", the group of people who have traveled to over hundred countries. A few years ago, we were on the cruise ship, and the Society held its meeting there. I was curious and decided to attend, even though by then we had traveled only to about ninety countries. At the meeting, the members introduced themselves and reported how many countries they visited and which one was their favorite. I was in awe as I heard "hundred and fifty-seven countries" or "Antarctica is my favorite place."

Suddenly, it was my turn, and I did not have to think twice. "I am from Massachusetts, we traveled only to ninety-two countries but plan to visit more and my favorite place on earth is my backyard." Every one of the seasoned travelers understood and approved by applause.

The letters from my parents were on the table, rustling under the light wind. The thin stack was from my Dad; he got the shortest stick in the game called life, a few letters from Ella and a tall pile from my Mom, for all the eight years we were apart; a long eight years after Dad's death, she and Ella stayed behind. I cried for days reading these letters, I could not forgive myself for not understanding them right then, almost forty years ago and not appreciating what they were saying.

Then, I was young and defensive; we were with two kids in the new country with the language we did not speak, without money, without a license. We had to survive the best we could, and yes, I wrote very happy and confident letters, but the future was foggy, and the life was not a walk in the park.

My parents, my family stayed in their beautiful condominium with plenty of money; they had a car and garage, and they spoke perfect Russian. With all the shortcomings of the life in the Soviet Union, they did not have to build a new life, to start from the scratch, to prove who they were. I had no regrets, my father wanted to stay, and I wanted to leave, it was their decision, and they should have known better. I felt so righteous with arrogant and futile arguments, while my Dad was agonizing on his deathbed, because of the deadly mistake he made by not leaving with us, worrying about us, missing us and counting his last days. Even then, already in America, I did not understand freedom!

Now I understood, cried for days and was belatedly sorry for my family, the ugly country we had lived in and my Dad's sorrow that killed him. I walked around my backyard, looked at the flowers and the river and touched the bark on the birch tree, his favorite tree. I wanted to put my hand on my left chest and sing "God, bless America." My eyes were still wet from all the crying. Those were sad, heartbreaking tears for my Dad, but they were also happy and proud tears for my country, the "land that I love" and "my home, sweet home."

DAY 25, SEPT 21
SANTA BARBARA, CA
HOTEL FOUR SEASON BILTMORE

We knew the name of the road, and for the longest time, we were looking forward to driving it. Our travel agent, our sons, and friends praised the beauty and warned us of the dangers of the Pacific Coast Highway. However, this morning our GPS led us inland. After almost two hours of testing our communication skills- "O, my God! Why the hell did you take this turn?" - we got back to the Pacific Coast Highway that we longed for so long.

It was breathtakingly beautiful and easy, with deer running amok and no bear in sight. We did not see much of the Ocean as a thick fog greeted us after every sharp turn. We were driving south toward Los Angeles for the first time since we left home twenty-five days ago.

ZOYA
KIEV, UKRAINE, THE 1950S

Lenya called Zoya "his favorite niece." Of course, by Russian family tree, she was his "niece", even though she was a daughter of his first cousin.

Victoria was seven years younger than Zoya, and she had always known that her older cousin was "a girl who had never had a good day in her life."

Victoria's grandmother Asya, and Zoya's grandmother Manya were sisters, and their granddaughters grew up together in the after-war Kiev. Their family too returned to a leveled to ashes Kiev and found their Ukrainian neighbors living in their pre-war apartment.

Zoya's father was lost in the war, and the family was not sure if he was still alive. They settled in a small summer shack attached to their old building. The structure had all the conveniences of what it was – "the summer shack." The toilet was a wooden booth outside in the backyard, and right behind the door to their only room, was a store's crate with a primus. On the wall above small sink, a metal cylinder, when filled with water, grudgingly dispensed it through a shaky nipple.

Zoya's Mom, Lisa, hoped that "if" and "when" her husband return from the war, he would be able to find a better place for them to stay.

Manya was a heavyset widow with a kind, smiley face and a permanent apron around her round hips. She cooked, cleaned, and took care of her daughter and granddaughter. She was a fantastic cook, and a small table was always set, especially, when her older sister Asya visited with her granddaughter.

"Zoin'ka, honey, please, sing for Auntie," Lisa would call her daughter with her diminutive name. Zoya had a great voice and was happy to sing Babushka's favorite songs. It was a sweet treat, and Victoria applauded loudly.

Very nearsighted quiet Lisa inherited her mother's shy smile. Her round glasses were so thick that they completely hid her blue eyes. She was an accountant at the grocery store and the family always had bread and some bones for soup. They finally learned that Lisa's husband was killed in the war, but by then, they all got used to their little shack with all its "inconveniences."

It was a cold rainy day, and Victoria knew right away that something terrible happened when she saw Zoya in her wet school uniform alone on their threshold.

"Auntie" whispered pale Zoya, "it is my Babushka." She hugged Asya, and they both cried leaning on each other in the mournful embrace.

"I found her on the floor and neighbors called the ambulance. Mom is in the hospital with her, and I came by tram to tell you".

Silent tears were streaming on Asya's wrinkled cheeks; Manya was the youngest and the only one of her large family of seven siblings who lived in Kiev.

Manya survived the stroke; heavy and unable to smile, she lay in her bed for years, mute and paralyzed. Lisa was working more than ever, and after school, Zoya had to change her Babushka's bed, wash soiled linens in a small sink without running water and hang them on the ropes in the yard to dry. Zoya was only fourteen, but she cooked, cleaned, and took care of her sick Babushka and busy Mom. She was not singing anymore; nobody sings on a bad day.

Asya visited her sister often; she lived alone now, and she always was ready to help Zoya. Manya passed away slowly and quietly after a few years of struggle.

After graduation, Zoya decided to be an accountant like her Mom. In college, at the students' party, she met tall, handsome Ian and a few months later the whole family danced at the wedding.

Kiev was licking war's wounds, and the new buildings were sprouting everywhere. Zoya and her husband got a new apartment in one of the green neighborhoods and a new daughter. Lisa moved in with them. The summer shack was demolished and forgotten; the years spent there was more the nightmare than reality.

Their new quarters were merely a dollhouse, two tiny rooms with a kitchen, toilet, running water and even a small balcony. Zoya was an accountant at the Bureau that managed the city's restaurants. The pay was poor; however, she had access to something called "deficit."

"Deficit" was a product of the Soviet reality, meaning everything that was not available in the stores. The stores' windows displayed shrouded in the red fabric portraits of the leaders and posters calling to march forward to the world's victory of the communism.

Big supermarkets, called "Gastronom" were mostly empty. Poisonously blue cans with seaweed were the main attraction. On a rare occasion, around ten in the morning, when stores just opened, one could get lucky to find pale mortadella or a lonely head of cheese. Juices were sold by the glass and alcohol by the bottles.

On a cold rainy day, excited Zoya stopped by Lenya's apartment; she got an incredible "deficit" for her cousin and his family. The Party planned a big meeting at the city restaurant with a banquet to follow. The Bureau got a special shipment of caviar and lox and Zoya got some of these rarities for her family. The weather was terrible and wet and cold Zoya reasoned it would be better waiting inside with Aunty Rose for a company than to wait for Lenya and Sarra under the rain.

Thirteen-year-old Victoria opened the door. She was home alone with her school girlfriends. There was a distinct panic and smoke in a small living room as the girls tried to hide a pack of cigarettes.

"Come over, Zoya" Victoria played it cool. She was trying to disperse heavy smoke in the room with her both hands. "Mom and Dad will be home soon. Would you like a cigarette?" She tried to copy the heroine of a trophy film she had recently seen with her parents.

"I do not smoke," Zoya was stern. She opened the window, cleaned the room from smoke and Victoria's girlfriends and did not say anything to Victoria's parents when they came home.

Next morning at breakfast, Lenya was livid, "Your behavior, Victoria, is unspeakable!" In spite of her innocent face, he grounded her for two weeks.

Zoya was not among Victoria's favorite relatives anymore.

ZOYA
KIEV, UKRAINE, THE 1960S

Zoya was working more and more, her tall and handsome husband spent less and less time home, and one sunny spring day he had disappeared altogether. Little Maya, Zoya's daughter, was a cute and smart girl and everybody in the family adored her.

Zoya's voice on the phone was trembling, "Lenya, something is wrong with Maya's spine; she brought a note from the school doctor saying that she needs a special treatment."

Victoria saw how upset her dad was with the news. "I will make a few calls," he promised.

The long years that Maya had spent in the Clinic were not easy for Zoya. She was Maya's Mom, her nurse, her schoolteacher and her Ambassador to the doctors. She knew everybody and provided everything for her girl, who was the only light in her life, her only hope, and her sole purpose. The life had no meaning without Maya; nothing was relevant anymore, divorce, job, or even her aging mother. She did not rest or read; she did not sleep or eat; her whole life was Maya's bed in the Clinic. She did not have a good day in all these years.

"I want Maya to be happy," said Zoya in her beautiful high pitch singing voice. "I do not want her to have the life I have!"

The years in the spine Clinic and the last ruble for the doctors and Physical Therapy paid off when Maya, an energetic teenager with a beautiful smile and perfect body, returned home. She was tall, slim and fit with a flawlessly straight spine.

ZOYA
KIEV, UKRAINE, THE 1970S

Victoria met Zoya in the park, engulfed in the red, orange, and maroon fire of falling leaves. Even air smelled like fall. Dima and Dave ran around, while the cousins conspired how to break the news to Lenya. His favorite niece just applied for an exit Visa, trying to get out through a small slit in the Soviet border. Her mother Lisa died recently, and Zoya had only Maya to think about.

She already applied to OVIR, the Government Investigating Agency on migration.

Victoria looked at her boys and shook her head. She would need her parents' permission to leave. "Dad would never let me go." She took a deep breath, "And he certainly would never let Dima go!"

She had had this conversation with her Dad many times. The worst was she did not have to convince him; he agreed. He knew there was no future for her and her kids in Soviet Russia, however, he would never tear his family apart. He had two daughters, and he could not choose the one to be with. "It is a long process, Zoya," offered Victoria. "You do not have to tell him now. Wait until you would get permission, if, of course, you would get the permission at all. And what would you do about Misha?"

Zoya was dating Misha for a while now. He recently separated from his wife. He planned to obtain a divorce, but like everything else, it was complicated.

"Misha had applied as well; his wife gave him permission already, and we plan to leave together. Maya is in a high school, and we hope to leave next spring, so she will not miss a school year".

"I am going to talk to Dad again tomorrow," Victoria said resolutely, "and to check with Felix if he got an invitation 'to reunite with relatives in Israel'. We are waiting for this letter for a few months now."

Zoya and Maya planned to go to Los Angeles where Zoya had an aunt who emigrated years ago. Victoria did not remember aunt Ana, but she remembered a well-known family story about how aunt Ana came to Victoria's Babushka to introduce her fiancé.

Babushka served a tea with her famous strudel and kept her poker face. When guests were about to leave, Ana had lost her patience and whispered, "Auntie Asya, what do you think?"

"He is a nice boy, Ana, but he is "bez shvantz".

Embarrassed Asya mixed Russian "bez," that meant "without," with Yiddish word for man's private parts. She paused and then added, as if Ana would not understand, "There would be no children, Ana."

For years, Lenya teased his Mom and wanted to know how did she make this diagnosis? How did she recognize young man's endowment or an absence of it? "Did you perform a doctor's exam Mom?"

Babushka just blushed silently.

Close relatives had whispered the story for years, praising Asya's insightfulness and wisdom as Ana's happy marriage remained childless. Now, from Los Angeles, she was ready to help her niece and her grandniece.

Victoria was right, it was a long process, and eventually, Lenya gave up. The line in OVIR, the Government Investigating Agency on migration, was months long. It was good that both, Felix and Victoria, were fired from their jobs at the first mention of emigration; they had to check in line to OVIR, like in every Russian state-induced line, every day. On a coveted day before Christmas, when they could finally bring the documents, Victoria had double pneumonia and a high fever. They had everything: the invitation from Israel from the people they never knew and forms from every school they ever attended, works they ever worked and addresses they ever lived, not counting Victoria dad's permission for her to leave the country and the mile-long questionnaire. They managed to apply; the last family to apply before OVIR closed for lunch and had never re-opened until the next year when there would be the new, much harsher rules.

They got the permission to leave the country a few days before Zoya's departure. It was May with new green leaves, aroma of lilies-of-the-valley, Victoria's birthday and a promise of incredible adventure.

"Zoya, would you please take a few my things with you in your luggage?" Victoria wanted to take some family heirlooms, her wedding presents, crystal and silver, however, official norms for taking anything out of Russia were extremely strict, and she expected customs to be especially vigilant considering how prosperous her Dad was now. She was sure "KGB (and the Customs) knew everything!" They packed her things in Zoya's small luggage and said goodbyes "till America."

Zoya and Maya left early that spring.

Lenya was desperate; he wanted to leave, but Ella could not. She was married and her husband Alex had a high government clearance; he would never be able to leave Russia.

Lenya would not abandon his younger daughter but, just in case, on his sleepless nights, he still fought all these questions; what to do with all the money, condominium, car, garage, plays on the stages, books? Everything that he worked so hard for all his life!

"You go, Victoria" he succumbed finally. "You settle and take the doctor's exam; you would work and build your new life. And then, you will bring us, the whole family to America."

They made plans; they figured it all out, the kids, the money, the dreams. The dreams, which had never come true.

EMIGRATION, EUROPE, THE 1970S

The fear and the rush of emigration ate into their daily existence.

First, it was a beautifully strange Vienna where every night Victoria planned how she would describe it to her Dad. She laid on the cot under the first-floor window and listened to the passersby, their German conversations, German laughs and German whispers, and she was ready to run; run from this horrible language and this awful city.

She took a deep breath and listened to the quiet, sweet breath of her children, the slight creak of the cot under turning Felix and unfamiliar breath of Pavel in the opposite corner of the room. She knew she had to take care of her family and she wanted to tell her Dad about the grand time kids had in the Prater. She would describe Vienna with its stately architecture and tell her "Papa" how they were all looking forward to getting to America.

In Italy, they were busy selling, moving to the seashore and worrying. They waited for the warrant, traveled and pondered their future. The sharp knife of emigration severed all their ties with the past.

Their existence was like an oil painting by the old master under the rain. It was lonely without roofs or walls, exposed to the elements; running paint dissolved by the reality. After a while, it could be a great abstract.

Victoria did not ask about Zoya. There was nobody to ask anyway. The night before they got their visas for the United States, she was surprised when an old acquaintance from Kiev told her that Zoya and Maya left for America only a week ago. "They left almost three months ahead of me, and they had a warrant to go to Los Angeles!

There is no way the HIAS would hold them here for so long!" She was sure the man was mistaken.

ZOYA
CALIFORNIA, USA, THE 1980s

Five years after Victoria and her family settled on the East Coast, she and Felix went to San Diego for vacation.

Victoria and Zoya did not see each other for all these years; however, they talked on the phone and even exchanged the occasional letters. Zoya sent a package with some of Victoria's things, and at first, Victoria wondered what happened with the rest, but time passed, and it was not important anymore.

"Can you believe we are almost five years in America?" she asked Felix. They stood on the beach and Victoria dipped her hand in the water shimmering in the sun slowly rising behind her back. They landed in California last night, and she was still on the Atlantic Time. She always thought it would be cool to name time zones after oceans, and today for the first time, she saw and dipped her hand into The Pacific.

Sleepy Felix started to head back to the hotel. "When do you want to leave?" He knew Victoria could not wait to see Zoya.

They drove out after breakfast, the roaring Pacific on the left, the warm sun on their right shoulders, a long way from the wintery East Coast, an eternity from Kiev.

"America is a God-blessed country," thought Victoria when Zoya and Maya greeted them happily at the door. Their three-bedroom tastefully decorated apartment was flooded with the sun; Zoya and Maya were putting the last touches on the beautiful table full of grand Russian, Jewish and American offerings. Misha smiled at the head of the table.

"Maybe she finally got a good day in her life," Victoria was happy for Zoya. Lunch slowly became a dinner; they had much to say, many people to remember, many stories to share. New bottles were opened, new dishes were served, and they were still talking. They forgot about the late hour and that Victoria and Felix still had to drive back to their hotel in San Diego.

Nobody noticed, but with every shot of vodka, Misha grew more and more angry and rowdy. He tried to tell dirty jokes not bothering with his language, and when Zoya wanted to stop him, he hit her in the face. What followed was outright awful, Felix tried to restrain Misha and hit him; Maya called the police and Victoria were heartbroken to learn that this was not happening for the first time.

Felix and Victoria were still in San Diego when Zoya obtained a restraining order; they were not officially married, and it turned out that his wife intended to join him in America.

"My God," thought Victoria, "This woman never had a good day in her life!" Zoya seemed to be a living antithesis to Victoria Dad's saying that life is like zebra, black, white and everything in between. Zoya's life was always black.

Nevertheless, there were white and sunny days, of course. Zoya was all smiles and happiness when a few years later Victoria and Ella came to Maya's wedding.

By then, Zoya married Jack. He was a retired widower with a big family, children, and grandchildren, which he adored. Zoya was an excellent homemaker, excellent cook, and a perfect step-grandmother, just like her Babushka. Everybody was getting along and happy.

Lake Tahoe sparkled on the background like a huge silver screen when a tall and handsome American promised Maya "to love and to cherish." The bride was gorgeous, the wedding beautiful and everybody drank to a long and happy life together.

ZOYA
CALIFORNIA, USA, THE 1990S

"Mom, you are coming with me," Maya was beaming telling her Mom about NASA award for achievement in developing space exploration; she was an accomplished aeronautical engineer.

"I would love to share my award with you, Mom; you are coming with me to Florida to get it. There is nobody in the world that deserves this more than you do."

There were happy tears in Zoya's eyes. Maya, her pride, and joy, Maya who spent years in the cast back in Kiev, Maya that she reared and brought up, now was helping America to explore the space. It was a dream that came true; it was the happiest day in her life. They were so excited about the ceremony in Florida. They both had a grand time planning the trip and buying outfits for the occasion.

The drinks were served on the terrace of a beautiful hotel in Florida where Maya treated her Mom to a penthouse suite. Their new dresses were perfect for a light breeze and a black tie reception later that night.

The late sun was still warm, and Maya was happy in her strapless dress, but Zoya wrapped a scarf around her long-sleeved jacket.

Suddenly she did not feel well; she was shivering. Maya noticed that her Mom became pale and came to her side right before Zoya got sick and fainted. Somebody called an ambulance and Zoya was taken to a local hospital. She spent there three days with Maya never leaving her side. They flew back to California on the private jet arranged by Maya; Zoya went from the plane directly to operating room. Maya took care of the things. She prominently displayed her NASA award above her Mom's hospital bed.

"Unfortunately, there was no any shade of gray in Zoya's zebra-like life" explained Victoria to Felix. "The white lines were very narrow, so Zoya hit another black line just about that time."

Maya's tall and handsome husband was so busy buying new homes and expensive cars he had no time to work, however, Maya would not notice. She spent her time between her work and her Mom. They divorced a few years later.

*****

A winding road lined with palm trees brought us to a whitewashed hotel with a red tiled roof. The grounds were like a lush exotic botanical garden. Our suite had a hot tub adorned with Mexican tiles, large bed with wrought iron headboard and a small balcony overlooking the pool.

The fragrant night fell silently on California. We soaked in the hot tub, rested and went to a restaurant for dinner. We settled by the fireplace at the table with an ocean view. Our waiter brought a warm woolen shawl for me, and I relaxed in a cozy chair. All day I was thinking of my cousin Zoya, her daughter, our lives and our plan to see them in California.

They visited us for my birthday and Ella daughter's wedding a few years ago. Zoya was battling breast cancer. She was still in the treatment but seemed to be doing well; she was a real fighter. She fought hard when cancer had spread to her brain. We knew that she was getting chemotherapy monthly and would have to do this for the rest of her life, but she did everything she had to without doubt or trepidation. Felix and

I had always admired how brave and confident she was. Still, I kept one of Zoya's secret for a long time, and it was a perfect time for the story.

ZOYA
LADISPOLI, ITALY, THE 1970S

It was hot late spring in Italy. "Not a good time to go through 'the change,'" thought sweaty Zoya. However, with her luck what else could she expect?

They left Kiev together with Maya and Misha, and he was nothing but trouble. Never mind, they had to visit HIAS thousand times to add him to her "warrant" for Los Angeles; he was useless when it came to selling something or finding an apartment. Besides, 'the change' really got her; she did not feel well, she was short of breath, and her skirt was too small for her.

Maya insisted on going to a doctor.

"We do not speak Italian," cried Zoya "How would the doctor understand me? And it will cost money," she added panicky and dizzy. Frightened Maya ran to a telephone booth and called for an ambulance.

They both were in a state of shock when smiling translator explained that Zoya is fine.

"No, not menopause, you are pregnant! Congratulations! And the baby will be Italian!" She was thrilled to deliver such great news.

They were not allowed to leave Italy and Misha was mad with both of them; with Zoya for "luring" him with her "warrant" for Los Angeles and with Maya for clinging to her devastated mother.

They sold everything they possibly could, and saved every lira, but a few weeks later Zoya went to the Hospital for the poor and without the language or anesthesia in the room with a few much younger women, delivered a perfectly healthy beautiful boy.

Every day Maya took a train to bring her poor mother milk and fruits and to look at her new brother. She could not believe it, but she loved him already.

"Now what?" cried Zoya looking at her new son. "How am I to find a job in America? And who is going to take us with the baby?" She had no answers; at least she knew they were going to her aunt and she hoped that the old woman would love the boy.

ZOYA
CALIFORNIA, USA, THE 1970S

California was not much better to Zoya than Italy. There was no love lost between Misha and Aunt Ana, and there was no love lost between Misha and his new son. Misha was most upset that Zoya could not work. However, the straw that broke the camel's back was not Misha but Aunt Ana: "You cannot live here! I am old, and the baby keeps me awake! It is too many of you, I had planned for two people, and now it is four, and a baby to top it all! Get out!"

Poor Zoya saw only one solution.

The room was small and brightly lighted with fluorescent tubes; there were no windows and not a sound came from the locked door. Zoya had never before was inside the bank, and the room frightened her. She was staring at the long gray box, but she did not see it through her streaming down tears.

Beside the safe deposit box, was a piece of paper; through her tears, it looked like a sail in a fog. A sail on the boat to the future. She stopped writing and looked at the documents in the box.

What should she write to her son? Would he open this box with her picture and her heartbroken explanation when he will be eighteen? Would he understand and forgive? Would his new Mom tell him about this box? What would be his new name?

She knew everything about the family when she signed the adoption papers yesterday, they seemed like nice people, but eighteen years is a very long time, and she wondered if she ever would see her son again. She wanted to kill herself, she did not want to live through today, she could not imagine trusting her baby to other people, but Maya still needed her, and thought about her daughter dried her tears. She would do what she had to do. She thought about her life, and she knew this was the worst day of all, by far.

*****

I looked at Felix. The flame from the fireplace reflected in his eyes, dinner was finished a long time ago and a waiter came around with a dessert cart.

"We should order dessert," I was smiling. "There is a reason I told you about Zoya; she had asked me to prepare you."

"Prepare for what?" Felix sounded skeptical. "What is going on Victoria?"

"Well, Zoya called me last night."

Felix's right brow went up as a big question mark, but he remained silent.

Maya was still divorced. Zoya's husband Jack died a few years ago, leaving everything to his children and grandchildren. He loved his family so much that unbeknown to Zoya he got reversed mortgage on his house and Zoya had to vacate the house after his death. After more than fifteen years of a happy marriage, he did not leave even one cent to Zoya in his well-prepared will.

I was just about to start with "Remember? Zoya had never had a good day in her life", but Felix's eyebrow was still up; he knew that with my two single cousins the possibilities were endless.

"He found her!" I could not hold off anymore. "Carl, her son, he found her and Maya! He is an adult now, of course, and he loves them!" The lights were dimmed, and the flames in the fireplace danced as in a fairy tale. The lullabying sound of the sea accompanied the fire.

"He was looking for his biological mother for years even though he had a wonderful large family right there in LA. Somehow, he found out about the safe deposit box, and the rest is history. Zoya and Maya are ecstatic, and I am as well. He is my cousin after all!"

Smiling from the ear-to-ear, Felix ordered dessert and champagne and made a toast.

I was expecting something about a new addition to the family and Felix came through, of course. "I'd like to drink to Zoya who finally got a happy day in her life and to my wife who is so good at keeping her family secrets."

We slept in that morning.

DAY 26, SEPTEMBER 22
SANTA MONICA, CA
CASA DEL MAR

Behind a thick fog, I could hardly make out the ship far at sea. "Flying Dutchman" I smiled to Felix.

"You might say it now, but never when we are on a cruise ship," Felix was busy feeding a small legion of robins around our table on the veranda. "She only shows up in the terrible weather, and it is not a welcome sign to see her at the open sea."

"So, how come in all our more than forty cruises had we never saw her?" I teased Felix. "Remember, those horrible storms in the Tasman Sea and the Bay of Biscay? And a hurricane force wind around Cape Horn, when our ship was literary lying on her side all night. That was pretty scary, and we were all ears when at dawn, the Captain on the bridge, still in his pajama, tried to calm down frightened passengers!"

Our breakfasts arrived on the beautiful plates, and we began to eat.

"Well, as you know, I had never got scared or seasick on any cruise," Felix had to prove that he was an experienced sea wolf and, of course, he had the last word. "See? Fog is going down, and this ship is not a "Flying Dutchman."

"OK, you are right," I agreed. "Fog or no fog, let us have a great sailing … on the highway to Santa Monica!"

I could not wait to see my "baby" Dave and our

grandchildren. Dave was way over forty, but for me the number meant nothing; I remembered the day and the minute when I saw him for the first time and loved him more than anything or anybody in the world; except for Dima, of course.

KIDS
KIEV, UKRAINE, THE 1960S

Victoria sat in the kitchen with a large mug of tea in her hands. The late fall was cold, wet and windy but Victoria's flannel long-sleeved nightgown was warm and cozy. It looked like a sail full of wind billowing around her very pregnant abdomen. In their bedroom next to the kitchen, tired Felix had gone to bed earlier. She was surprised when the coo-coo clock on the wall chimed midnight.

"Nothing helps!" Victoria was upset; she was a week past her due date. This afternoon, Felix following the advice of his "know-it-all" aunt, took her in the taxi up and down the cobblestone-covered boulevard, twice. However, it did not work.

"Maybe I should try to read my fortune in tea leaves?" thought Victoria looking into her tea.

She was desperate; this baby did not want to face the world. She finished her tea and got up ready to join Felix in their bed, which was now too small for the three of them. Suddenly she felt something warm and wet running down her legs; she was surprised that she did not notice spilling her tea, but then realized that her water broke.

Five minutes to eight on Tuesday morning, she delivered a healthy boy. He was big, quiet and adorable. And most important, he had a father!

Felix's Mom Olga passed away a year ago, soon after their wedding and now Felix had his own room. It was not the best way to get the room. He grew up in this one room with his Mom and grandfather. They shared the kitchen and bathroom with the elderly widow who had lost her husband to the war. She still was there when Felix moved his young family to his "apartment".

They had a problem, however; there was no way to fit a baby crib, Dima's bed and their sofa bed in this one room furnished already with a dinner table and a breakfront.

They tried to get rid of the table but they needed it for the baby bath at night, and they still needed to eat somewhere. They decided that for now, Dave would have to slip in his baby carriage but yet there was no place for Dima's bed. And they still needed to hire a nanny for Dave, if Victoria planned to return to her work and finish her post-doctorate thesis on the genetics of heart diseases.

Her parents loved and supported her, but she could not bring her family of four to live in her parents' place.

"Dima lived here all his life, and he has his bedroom," said her Dad. "It is not realistic for all of you and the baby to live in one small room."

"How are you going to take care of two small children, Victoria?" seconded her Mom. "Are you not going to return to work?" She retired recently and had all the time for little Dima while Aunty Rose still took care of the household.

"After you would move out, Dima would have his room back to himself. And where would be he sleeping in your one for all room?"

They were all right, of course, but Victoria could not imagine how she could live without Dima; she could already feel an emptiness creeping in her chest.

"Do you want to kill your father, Victoria?" Sarra raised her voice bringing the last argument. "He got a son that he never had. You know he would not survive to lose Dima, again!"

"What about me?" Victoria wanted to scream. "How would I survive to lose Dima? I am his mother, and I would never leave him!"

She did not realize she was screaming, crying, and yelling at her parents, but she knew, they were right. There was just not enough space for four of them in Felix's one room.

Felix was an eager Dad. He felt guilty and sorry to leave Dima with Victoria's parents; however, there was nothing he could do, and it was better for Dima this way.

Felix was the head of the household. He was ready to do anything for his beautiful smiling son who slept through the night. The nightly bath was a ritual on the dining table. There was no place in the communal kitchen or the bathroom for the baby's bath and every evening after the dinner, Felix cleaned the dining room table, boiled water in the large pot on the stove in the kitchen and carried it to their room to pour into the baby's small bathtub. He then would bring some cold water to mix in.

Dave was a few weeks old when on the trip from the kitchen with a pot of hot water Felix spilled a few drops on his foot. As he cried out, more hot water spilled until he dropped the whole pan on his both feet. He fell to the floor and crying took off his socks together with the blistered skin from his feet.

The ambulance doctor did not know whom to attend first: the moaning Felix on the floor, Victoria crying in horror or the screaming naked baby on the bed ready for his bath.

Felix spent next two months home singing lullabies to his son; his both feet bandaged like Egyptian mummies. He had all the time in the world; he would give his life for his son, never mind the skin from his feet.

After two months, Victoria had to return to work, and they were lucky to find a nanny for Dave. Maria, a tall, large woman, lived in a village and all her life worked at the collective farm. She had big hands that used to dig potatoes and a low, commanding voice.

Her girlfriend worked in the city as a nanny. "You gotta be crazy to work in "kolkhoz" now," she wrote to Maria.

She visited Maria a few times and bragged about her life in the city showing off clothes from the woman she was working for. "I do not have to work in the cold fields in the fall, no freezing out-house in the winter; they have hot water and a shower. They love my cooking, and I do not get up at night to the baby; Mom does. I told them right away I would not work at night. I take the baby to the park in a fancy carriage, and the pay is so much better."

Maria liked what she heard; it was stupid to dig potatoes in the collective farm, and one late fall day, she became a nanny.

A friend of a friend recommended her to Victoria, and that was enough. The room could hardly accommodate three of them, and now they had a nanny. Felix moved a breakfront to divide the room; their sofa bed and Dave's new crib went behind it, and every night, he pushed a dining table to the wall so that Maria could squeeze her folding bed between the table and the breakfront.

The trouble started in about a month when Felix found a few empty bottles of wine under a pillow in Dave's crib.

"I just found those" swore Maria. "I wanted to bring them to store to get the deposit back and to make some money. You did not pay me enough!" She was a tall woman with beady eyes and kerchief on her limp, thin hair; she did not apologize or explain; she was accusing and yelling.

"She has to go," whispered Felix in Victoria's ear at night.

"We cannot," begged Victoria. They both had to leave for work in the morning, and they did not have an alternative.

"Let us try for another week," Felix finally agreed." We will see what would happen."

"Dave is doing so well, he gained weight, and looks healthy," Victoria was always concerned about Dave. She was frightened when five-day-old Dave had his first asthma attack, and she felt guilty leaving him and going back to work. She was happy he had a nanny who cared for him while she was working.

203

He was a beautiful happy baby, sleeping through the night. Nevertheless, Felix was frantic, "She would have to go if she drinks; we cannot leave Dave with her. One more week, Victoria, I would give her one more week". They were afraid that Maria could hear Felix's tragic whisper behind the breakfront. He kissed Victoria's teared up face; they hugged and fell asleep.

Felix looked dark and upset when Victoria finally arrived home after work. She had a bad day, one of her patients was not doing well, and on the way home, she had to stand over an hour in the overcrowded bus. She just wanted to sit down and hold Dave and forget about everything, but Felix pulled her out of the apartment on the stairs. "They were not home when I returned, so I went to look for them. You know this seedy bar around the corner. I saw her through the window at the bar. She held Dave with one hand and drank straight from the bottle with other. They came home about half an hour ago, but I did not say anything. Guess, what she is doing now?"

Through the open door, Victoria saw Maria in the kitchen talking to Dave as she rocked his carriage and fried something on the stove.

"I had left breast milk for Dave," Victoria said defensively. She felt like a failure; she missed Dima terribly, seeing him mostly on weekends, and now she had a problem with Maria. What was she going to do? How was she supposed to work with the baby at home?

"She gave him your milk all right, but then she fried dark bread in the pork lard and gave it to Dave to suck on, instead of a pacifier!"

Felix was proud of his insight. "No wonder he gained so much weight! I cannot believe everybody thought it was cute that the baby's cheeks were laying on his shoulders!"

They had to move back in with her parents so that Victoria could go back to work; it was important for Victoria and her father. Lenya was proud of Ella who just started medical school and of Victoria working on her Ph.D. In his mind, essential things had to be done, children or no children.

Their little family was continually moving to Felix's apartment with a new nanny and back in with grandparents when the nanny would drink or steal, or not show up at all. Victoria loved her parents' roomy apartment, but mostly she loved Dima being right there when she was back from work.

He always waited for her in the hallway and tried to open the door for her. "Mama! There was an earthquake in Nicaragua," he could not wait to share the daily news with his Mom.

The family dinners on the weekends, which Felix called "grand rounds" because usually he was the only one not a doctor at the table, were anchoring a big household. Still, young grandparents loved to entertain, and most of the time there were friends at the weekend table: Cecily, their former schoolmates, and Babich; Ella would bring her fiancé Alex, Dima and Dave would be on their best behavior and Mom with the help of her girls and Aunt Rose would serve a fantastic meal. The people around the table were exciting and fun, and the conversations and poetry were abounded. It was the family at its best.

Victoria finally moved out when her father bought a new two-room condominium for her family. Now they had a room for the boys.

"You do not want to kill your father!" Sarra's old argument did not work this time, and Victoria started to pack Dima's things.

"For Dima's sake, Victoria," begged Lenya. He felt that he already lost one son; the one who looked like him, the one he chose and approved of, the one that he lost after only four short months of his daughter's marriage. He knew that he would not survive another loss. Victoria would; she already found another husband for herself, but he, he lost the son and now Victoria was trying to take Dima, his only reason for living, and he fought with renewed strength.

"Don't you understand that Dima is much happier here? The boy used to live here, and it would be easier for you too, now, that you are working on your dissertation." Lenya was relentless.

"I want to stay here!" cried Dima. He was an incredibly gifted red-haired boy looking just like his Mom. He was reading at two and a half, he knew the capitals and flags of every country in the world, and he could comment on his grandfather's new play with an understanding and an adult vocabulary. And he was very spoiled.

"I live here. I am not moving!" Dima had his own opinion; he did not need to repeat what his grandparents taught him to say. "Mom lives here too," he was too young to understand the complicated family's dynamics.

They were all right and eventually tired Victoria gave up. She had her hands full with frequently sick Dave, constantly changing nannies, work, and dissertation.

And then, there was Felix.

Things were not perfect with Felix. Life was chaos and cacophony of horrible reality when every mundane thing became a tragedy. Dave is sick; he needs to go back to grandparents; washer got broke, where to do laundry; the store did not have milk today; nanny is drunk … What a life!

Dave was her friend, her smiley confidant, and joy. He went to school when he was five-years-old, and on the first day, he made a marriage proposal to a blonde classmate who shared the desk with him. Dave sang and played the piano; he knew how to say a toast at the holiday table and how to go to buy milk in the morning. He was sweet and mature beyond his age.

"It is not happening," Victoria's neighbor Inessa was upset sitting at the table in Victoria's kitchen. "These tickets were impossible to get and they cost a fortune." They were finishing a long dinner, telling the stories of their lives, while Victoria was trying to decide what to do with Dave.

"Let's finish a tea and see if Dave would be asleep," they had tickets for the American movie, but the nanny did not show up for two days.

When Victoria returned home from the movie, the lights were on everywhere. Two hours earlier, she left Dave sleeping soundly in his bed and now she was shocked to see him in the kitchen hard at work washing the floor. Four small stools were upside down on the kitchen table, and a wet rag was tightly wrapped around floor brush.

"Dave, why are you not sleeping?" Victoria was shocked. "Why are you washing the kitchen floor?"

"I heard you were telling Inessa that you wanted a girl, not me," he almost cried, "I wanted to be a girl! And the girls wash floors!" He was a considerate man already. Both of them were sobbing, hugging, and laughing.

*****

I drove leisurely through Santa Barbara admiring elegant buildings, green streets and a picture-perfect waterfront. We had less than a hundred miles to make to Santa Monica, and I had time to take any detour I wanted. The fog, like a delicate lace curtain over the sea, was slowly dissipating. The highway was a typical Californian highway with always hurrying drivers and limited scenery. I was so far back to Dave's childhood that I took a wrong exit.

America has never failed to amaze me. It was a stylish suburb with spectacular homes and wide streets, and we sailed slowly in our big car through the other people's lives.

"Remember how we lived when Dave was a baby?" I asked Felix. "What a horrible, difficult time we had; the kindergarten where kids were always sick, lines in a milk store, supermarket and movies; angry people in the overcrowded buses, empty stores and "deficits." Were we crazy to think that we were well off or was it just in comparison to the others?"

The Los Angeles suburb was not exactly the place to get off the car and to kiss the ground for life in America, but I was close. Back there in my past life, I had to leave my baby with my parents because we did not have a space for his bed in our one room. I had to drag sick Dave on early winter mornings to my parents because I had to go to work. I had never had lunch at a restaurant with my girlfriend before we came to the United States. We had never had a family dinner out with the kids, except when on vacations!

I thought Felix was a mind reader when he turned to me, "Look at this house with curved front Victoria; it reminded me of our vacation in Yalta!"

KIDS
YALTA, CRIMEA, UKRAINE, THE 1970S

T he stately building with gently curved front was a famous Crimean Hotel and Restaurant "Oreanda." Victoria and Felix were spending summer vacation with their six and three-years-old kids on a seashore in Crimea. They rented a small room with two beds, one for parents and one for kids, with a small bathroom and no kitchen. Felix had to leave for the beach around five in the morning to secure two lounges near water and to wait for Victoria to join him when kids would wake up. They usually stayed until afternoon and went for an early dinner to "Oreanda," across the street from the beach.

People from every corner of the Soviet Union descended on Crimea in the summer, to fight for the lounge on the jam-packed beach, to swim in polluted waters of the Black Sea, to sleep in the crowded rented rooms and to stay in endless lines everywhere: restaurants, diners, and rare cafes. It called the summer vacation.

Victoria had never recuperated after Dmitry's death, and the beach was not her favorite place. However, after long dreary winter, kids would benefit from the sun and fresh air. She watched Felix playing with the kids in the water.

It was time to go for dinner, and Victoria waved Felix to get kids out of the water.

Dima came first, and she helped him with his shoes and then looked for Dave to change his shorts. However, Dave was not there.

She looked at Felix, still in his wet trunks, and took Dima's hand. She called Dave; first softly, trying not disturb nearby beachgoers and then loudly on the top of her lungs. They were standing on the crowded Black Sea beach looking with sheer horror for their beautiful three-year-old son. Every Dave on the beach came running as they called his name and screamed at each other frightened and devastated.

Suddenly, there was a commotion on the crosswalk leading to the restaurant. A tall man came out with a little boy, and as he started to cross the street toward the beach, they recognized Dave. Terrified and completely drained Victoria had to sit down on the sand.

"Is this one yours?" smiled the man. "He was in "Oreanda" standing in the line for dinner, but I thought he was too young to dine alone!"

"I had already changed my shorts and went to get us a place in the line," explained Dave, trying to free his arm from the stranger. He crossed a busy boardwalk from the beach to the hotel alone before, and he did not need a stranger to bring him back!

****

We checked in the hotel in Santa Monica, and I could not wait to see the family. Dave came with his kids, the boy and the girl, beautiful all American teenagers and we all had dinner. There was no waiting line at the restaurant.

We have lived in this country for so many years, but nothing can extinguish my memories of the past, the comparisons I made at every step. We got used to beautiful things, polite and friendly people, all the conveniences and services this incredible country had to offer, but still, at every turn, I remember and compare, and feel sorry about the years we had spent in the Soviet Union.

I am sorry for my parents who missed so many facets of the life. I am sorry for generations and generations of my family, my friends, my people who happened to be born and to live in a horrible place, in terrible times, whose lives were voided of joy and pleasure. They were lucky they did not know better, but every time I see something beautiful, taste something delicious, exercise my rights and my freedom, I share it with all these long gone beloved family and friends.

Felix slept quietly in our comfortable four-poster bed, the ocean shimmered gently under the light touch of the moon, and I felt so alone with my memories of the old times. Would my boys remember their old family and old homes? Would my grandchildren ever understand our lives, and who we were? Would they appreciate our decisions and everything we had to do to build a new life in America?

DAY 27, SEPT 23
SANTA MONICA, CA
CASA DEL MAR

It was our turning point. We drove forty-seven-hundred-and-eighty-five miles to get here and we were looking forward to the road back. We were not dead tired yet, although Felix said "close." The plan was to stay here for a few days, rest, enjoy the kids and start to drive back slowly.

I was retired now for almost three months, and I was thrilled that I did not have to go back to work and had all the time in the world to do what I want. I certainly did not want to get up at five thirty every morning to see patients in the hospital or to answer the phone on my nights on call.

"Felix! If we drive back slowly, do you think we would get back home before the first snow?"

However, Felix did not appreciate the joke; he just wanted to bask in the generous Californian sunshine and to breathe fresh Californian air.

On these fabulous first days of fall, when temperatures soared above eighty degrees, there were almost no sunbathers on Santa Monica's vast golden beach. Californians, spoiled by perpetual nirvana, did not care for the beach. We were left alone to soak up all this sunshine, to enjoy Turquoise Ocean and a perfect day. We hoped to save our admiration for the beautiful state of California and tan until home when New England weather and foliage would promptly pale both.

We went to the beach with the kids, and on the way back, I stepped on the decorative tile embedded in the stone walk, the dark red applique of animals' shadows. We all stood above it and our shadows mixed with those on the tiles like a double exposure. Here was Felix's head and there was the fox with a stolen fowl, there a mouse and a jumping frog and here were two small shadows of the kids; look, there it was, the elegant stork and threatening bear and here we were all together today.

KIDS
HAVERHILL, MA, THE 1980S

Victoria was excited and proud of herself. Today, she finally got the courage to "talk the talk," and nothing could stop her now, neither Felix with his open mouth, shocked by what she had just said, nor her surprised, but smiling boys exchanging conspirators' looks.

Her girlfriend Lana at the Kaplan's Center in Boston, where Victoria studied for her professional exam, told her about "sex education" in American schools, "all the horror of it."

"It was a special class at my ten-year-old daughter's school and a teacher brought anatomical charts and explained to kids everything about sex," she said to Victoria.

Victoria was surprised, "Nothing about bees and birds?"

Her friend looked at her with astonishment. "This is a Boston school, Victoria. Maybe in the suburbs, they talk about bees and birds, but here … you should hear my daughter; she knows more about sex than I do!"

There was no way Victoria would expose her boys to such "an education." She was fuming all forty miles back home. She passed the yarmulkes out as soon as they sit down around the kitchen table for a Shabbat dinner. She felt that these little cups made everything a bit cleaner and spiritual and today she needed help. She was lucky it was Friday, and the boys were going to Sunday school, so to wear the yarmulkes for a Shabbat dinner was a reasonable thing to do. She would explain about love and reproduction with dignity and decency, not with the anatomical charts.

"What the occasion Vika?" Felix was surprised.

Victoria took off her apron and looked at her boys, "I would like to explain to you how Mom and Dad made you," she started nervously.

"Daddy got a small seed, and he put it inside of the Mom's …" suddenly she was alarmed by Felix's reddened face; he was choking, and she could not figure out if he were laughing or dying.

Both boys were under the table, laughing hysterically. They were holding their mouths shut with their hands, so there was no sound coming from under the tablecloth.

Nevertheless, Victoria was determined to continue, "So the seed started to grow …"

"Are you insane?" finally managed Felix. "Dima is almost thirteen; what do you think?" His beautiful deep voice was booming, and kids finally emerged from under the table. Yarmulkes were not a big help and not the answer to sex education.

*****

Usually, I am a good sleeper. Some nights though, I wake up and with my eyes still closed, I see different icons opened and closed in my mind, and I explore them and then close and move on to the next ones. Those are the places and the times where my stories live. I see them in color or black and white with every detail clear and familiar. They are not dreams; I hear Felix softly breathe next to me or I feel just the first soft light of the morning on my face. Afraid to interrupt the story I want to keep, I cover my eyes with my hand or, if I am not interested, I open my eyes with the hope that my memory would not bother me anymore and my internal computer would go back to sleep.

We had a beautiful day with the family, the beach time and the dinner together. My grandchildren were eager listeners, and I managed to tell a few stories. Dave always appreciates my stories; I think he has a name for every one of them.

My favorite story was about my photographic memory and reading somebody else's textbooks in the bathroom. Suddenly my grandson said. "Ba," (that is what they all call me. When they were babies, "Babushka" with the accent on the first syllable was too complicated, so they shortened it to a simple Ba.)

"Ba, your memory is not as good as it used to be; it is the third time you are telling us the same story!"

DAY 28, SEPTEMBER 24
SANTA MONICA, CA
CASA DEL MAR

W e had dreamed about this trip for many years. Initially, when we were much younger, it was just the envy. "Wow!" we thought, "What an exciting idea; we just need the time." Then, when our "babies," one after another drove cross-country, we were ready to compete, "If the kids could do it so do we. All we need is time!"

We both worked, and for this trip, we, indeed, needed a time although, we had never expected to wait until we were over seventy. We had never expected to drive for fifty days, and we had never expected to take the trip we are taking. We folded in some important milestones: retirement, family wedding, and our fiftieth wedding anniversary. Every day is like a famous Faberge Egg. It is exciting and beautiful outside with sunshine and mountains, fields and ocean, great parks and incredible scenery but inside, there is a secret hidden, the old story of my life, my family, friends, places and times, thoughts and memories, love and pain.

This morning, I woke up with the early ray of sun feeling lucky in the plush bed in our fantastic hotel room in the glorious state of California.

In Russia, we called it "meschanstvo." It was a derogatory name for "petty bourgeois." Those who cared more for which plushy hotel they stayed in, rather than for what they saw on the way. Under the Soviets, people deprived of every simple necessity were brainwashed that only "cultural things" had any value.

It was honorable to stay for hours in line for the new book, or theater tickets, or in the line to a museum. Not always so, Felix's Mom read a secretly borrowed copy of "Doctor Zhivago" under her bed, afraid that somebody would see the forbidden book and would report her.

My Dad, who could afford to buy anything, never gave our Mom jewelry.

"What do you need them for?" he would ask. "It is such meschanstvo!" It was outright shameful to wish for furniture or clothes or, god forbid, jewelry.

By the mentality of our old country, it did not matter what hotel, motel or boardinghouse you stayed, a bed was a bed. For the same reason, bars were not a popular place in the country of alcoholics; why to pay fifteen dollars for a drink, when you can have the whole bottle for ten.

We became real Americans when I decided that on vacations we should reward ourselves, enjoy and live better, than at home. On this trip, we stayed at the fabulous properties that have much to offer to their guests: locations or architecture, historical rooms or incredible services, elegant restaurants or just the right pillow. I am sure, some of my friends would call it meschanstvo, but I love good hotels that feel like home. I love being American and enjoying the fruits of our labors.

Felix was still sleeping as I quietly admired our beautiful four-poster bed. I thought about the people who carved it lovingly, about people who came to this country, built it and called it Motherland, people just like us.

KIDS
HAVERHILL, MA, THE 1980S

Her boys were so different and yet they were the same, smart and talented, kind and very stubborn. "A half of their genes are mine," smiled Victoria. "Not bad!" Both, Dima and Dave always were "know it all" kids, and with a new country and a new language, they knew more than their parents did.

Victoria was ironing the boys' shirts when the mailman delivered an envelope with Dima's PSAT results. She was surprised that he delivered the envelope personally, not just dropped it in the mailbox, as usual. Victoria had no idea what it was and turned the envelope this way and that way trying to see why it was so important. That is how Tara found her when she walked in the door to check on Victoria.

"Of course he delivered it personally; every mom in town is waiting for the results," Tara tried to explain. She opened the envelope and exclaiming, "O my God, look at these!" showed it to Victoria. The piece of paper with some graphs and bold letters meant absolutely nothing to Victoria who was more concerned not to burn Dima's holiday shirt.

This evening, Tara and Molly came for a serious conversation. "Dima has to go to a private school," they declared. "He did incredibly well on his PSAT after only a few weeks at the new school."

"He did in English and Math better than ninety-nine percent of American kids," Molly tried to explain.

"He is a special boy. Are not you here because you wanted a better life for your kids?" seconded Tara.

"What do you mean 'private school'?" Victoria was frantic. "My medical license is not valid, and Felix just studies English!"

She did not understand, "Where would we get money?" She was getting upset. Both, Tara and Molly were talking together and repeating the same word, that neither Victoria nor Felix understood.

"Scholarship!" Tara tried to explain. "The money for school!" Molly seconded to no avail. Finally, Victoria got her English-Russian dictionary and looked it up. She still could not understand how "student's stipend" would help them to pay for school.

Education in the Soviet Union was free. Most of the students were even paid a small monthly allowance, just enough not to sleep under the bridge and not to die from starvation. All her student's years, her parents supported her, but for one semester, she managed to get a stipend. It was based not on academic achievement but her parents' salaries.

So the concept of scholarship or in translation "stipend" was foreign to her and only after spending weeks filling the forms for financial aid did she finally believed that there was hope for her boy.

They chose and applied to the six best private high schools in New England, filled all the forms and went for the interviews.

Of course, Dima knew better, when he was about to wear torn jeans and an old sweater for an interview at the Phillips Academy.

It was a warm day, and Molly was waiting in her new shiny car. She saw them and smiled coming out of the car. However, her smile evaporated when she saw Dima, "You cannot go for an interview dressed like that!" she was shocked.

She thought only for a second, "I still have Dan's bar mitzvahs suit," Victoria heard. "Wait here; I will bring clothes."

In a few minutes, she was back with her son's best and only three-piece suit. Dan was two years older than Dima, and the suit was too big. Victoria shortened the pants with her handy bobby pins, sleeves got new "inside-out" cuffs, and they all hoped that nobody would notice or scrutinize Dima's attire.

The interview lasted for a very long time, and Molly was just about to go to check with a secretary when suddenly the door opened.

"Do you know what your son is reading?" the woman who conducted the interview came straight to Victoria.

With a long wait and worries about Dima, Victoria could not understand a word the woman was saying. She felt so stupid; she was almost crying. It took Molly to explain to the woman that Victoria never knew what Dima was reading, only that she saw they were very thick books.

"I had never met a twelve- year- old boy choosing Sir Winston Churchill's seven- hundred- page biography as a fun reading!"

This year, their first year in America, Dima was accepted to five private schools, and four of them offered him a full scholarship.

*****

At dinner, I kept with the stories about Dima and Dave's childhood. Our teenage grandchildren were especially happy to hear about their Dad and uncle's misbehaving and mistakes. Apparently, those stories rang many bells.

"Well, these happened almost forty years ago," I was looking for an excuse.

"We had very little money when your uncle Dima was in the boarding school. He was home on vacation, playing with neighbors' boys and reading and I was surprised when he asked me for a new shirt. Dima was never one for the clothes, and I had to pinch myself and to ask him if he was my son, not some imposter.

'I had never asked you for anything," said Dima; but the boys at the school all wear this 'polo shirt.' I need only one, but it has to be the 'polo.'"

I had never heard about "polo" before this conversation, but the next morning, Dima and I went to a mall. He found the shirt immediately. It was powder blue with short sleeves and a tall skinny equestrian on the left chest. Everything was fine until I saw the price.

"Forty dollars?" I almost fainted. "I just bought a beautiful knit holiday dress for myself for nineteen! And it had the long sleeves!"

However, Dima was adamant; that was the only shirt he needed and, of course, I bought the shirt. I was very proud to be a good mother.

In a few days, when I packed Dima's suitcase to go back to school, I saw this shirt again. The equestrian on the left side was gone; a large hole took his place!

Dima was uncompromising; nothing made him feel guilty, neither my tears nor Felix's angry tirade.

"You do not understand, I needed this shirt, but I did not want the logo! I knew you would never understand!"

Dave was laughing, "Mom, why were you surprised? It is typical Dima. I remember when Dima was in high school we were in Florida in some museum. After leaving the museum, we were looking for our rented car in the parking lot. Dima pointed at the red Jaguar and said 'That is the car I would drive when I graduate from college.' I thought my older brother was a cool guy, but you were so surprised, you were speechless. I was in awe, 'Wow that is a great car!' Then Dima continued as an afterthought, 'I would remove the jaguar from the hood and repaint it gray.' Then we both understood; that was Dima. He would love to have the best, but he would never show off."

"All right, Dave," I started to plot my revenge for Dima. "Tomorrow would be your turn!"

After dinner, we said good-byes and watched Dave drive off with his kids.

"I cannot wait to see what story about Dave you saved for tomorrow," laughed Felix. "With Dave's history, I believe you have a great selection."

I tried to add some mystery to my smile, "I am sure we both are thrilled that Dave is not a teenager anymore."

DAY 29, SEPTEMBER 25
SANTA MONICA, CA
CASA DEL MAR

For the last four days, I watch pelicans' parade, row after row all day long. They were probably soldiers in some Pelican State. There is never one bird unless it is a seagull or a crow. Pelicans march or rather fly in lines, each squadron about fifteen birds, sometimes two lines flying side by side in opposite directions.

Who is in command? Who had trained them? At what military academy? Which one is a general or a sergeant who gives the orders? Who does not allow these magnificent birds to break the line seduced by fish or a wave and swerve away? It is hypnotizing to watch the ominous shadows their huge wings and long beaks cast on the sand.

These last lazy days in California, we melted under the sun, dissolved in the turquoise pool and indulged in ice cream until we shivered from inside.

I looked at the pool. The setting sun painted elongated shadows on the tiled floor. The lounges were lined up in perfect order, and the three men on them looked like clones, their color, the shapes, their position, their DNA, identical. Dave just like Felix, and his son, just like Dave. They had the same features and the same moves, the apple from the apple tree.

KIDS
KIEV, UKRAINE, THE 1970S

D ave was always a cute, easy baby. He had soft curly hair and a smiley disposition. Dave slept through the night; that is when he was not sick. He had his first asthma attack when he was a five-day-old and a long chain of pneumonia and ear infections as soon as he hit kindergarten.

He was a great companion and a caring child. He was also the only one who had the patience to wait for Victoria at the hat store, which she could never leave before trying on every hat and gathering every compliment. She was "a hat lady."

He got along with everyone, his constantly drunk nannies, his piano teacher and with retired Boris Babich who volunteered to help Victoria when Dave went to school.

Usually, Boris picked up Dave after school. They were a funny couple. Older, but still dashing Boris with his crew cut and ever-present tie and five-year-old Dave in his school uniform that was too big for him.

He was the youngest kid in the class. Kids started schools at seven, but Victoria felt Dave was brilliant and mature. He was way ahead of his age, and she pressed all the right buttons with the people she knew at the School Department. As with Dima three years earlier, she managed to get Dave at a prestigious English Language School.

Her baby's soft curls were gone, as demanded by the school's rules, and with his short cut hair, he looked a little like his tall escort. They walked hand in hand, although Boris had to bend down to reach for Dave's outstretched hand and thus, slightly bent and limping on his prosthesis, he walked his little friend home. They cooked their lunch together, ate in the kitchen, worked on Dave's homework and waited for Victoria.

KIDS
MASSACHUSETTS, USA, THE 1980S

Y ears later, in America, when Dima had left for boarding school, Dave became the backbone of the family; he cooked, thanks to Boris's lessons, did the laundry, cleaned the house and still managed to do a paper route. He was a sweet, mature beyond his age, reliable and caring boy.

The family's life in the new country fell in some cacophonic rhythm. A new language, kids, driving, sick and dying Lenya who was thousands of miles away, new friends, unknown foods, work, new music on the radio, exams.

Victoria passed her professional exam and was a first-year intern in the hospital in Boston. Felix worked many overtimes trying to get them on their feet. They usually woke Dave up for school and left the house by six in the morning for their forty miles drive to Boston in two separate cars. They had very different schedules with Victoria's night on call and Felix's overtimes. They did not understand the weather or traffic reports; there was only music on their cars' radios.

It was not easy to be just an intern after working for years at the tertiary care hospital with the M.D. Ph.D. to her name. However, Victoria wanted to become an American trained doctor, and nothing was too much to endure for that. She was embarrassed when during early morning rounds, a hospital operator beeped her for an outside call while the young resident grilled her on a "fever work up."

"This operator is paging me every morning the whole week, even though, I had asked her hundred times not to interrupt me with the outside calls," Victoria apologized to the resident.

"It is probably a pharmaceutical sales rep, and I have no time to speak to any of them." She felt like a little girl who did not do anything but still was in the wrong.

Half an hour later, she was paged again and this time on the overhead page. When she finally answered the phone, she heard an unfamiliar stern voice. "Good Morning, Doctor, this is the principal of your son's school." The voice was so out of place, out of what she was doing now, that she did not understand, what son the man was referring to.

"We are concerned what is wrong with Dave; it is the eighth day that he is out of school." Victoria lost her breath and her voice.

Suddenly, the gravity of the world settled on her shoulders, and she had to lean on the wall to keep standing. She called home, but there was no answer. For his parents, Dave was at school. She recalled that this morning, getting ready for school he was perfectly fine. He even brushed his teeth before Victoria left for work! She tried to call Felix, but he could not leave work early. It would have to wait until they get home in the evening.

They were lucky he just played hooky.

"What kind of a mother am I?" Victoria blamed herself. She did not have a choice, back in Kiev she had to work. Everybody worked; her Mom, her sister, her friends. No family could survive on one income. Only later in their lives, her parents could afford for her Mom to stay home, but by then, she retired.

The majority of her new girlfriends here, in the United States, were staying home, taking care of their families and children. They drove the kids for sports practices, arranged their sleepover nights and took them for a pizza with friends.

"Why my life is not like that?" Victoria wondered.

Her exams, her work, her years of residency always came first. She loved her children, she would give her life for them without any hesitation, but she had to do what she had to do and for that, nothing else was important.

Felix worked and they could get by but even a thought about life without medicine made her feel terribly empty. Obviously, she was not the right material.

Dave was grounded for two weeks.

Victoria's path to American medicine became the family Ariadne's thread; two years later, they moved from their "American crib," a small gracious town with a generous community, to a suburb with a large hospital and excellent academic program. Victoria survived her internship and got a position as a resident.

This fall they lived in the residents' housing across the street from the hospital. A cozy street was lined with the old trees, shielding their old, stately colonial from the hospital traffic. No more long drives into the city, no more room in the nursing dormitory where she stayed when she was an intern. She thought about this room at the old dormitory with sheer horror; state stamped linens, bed bugs and the victorious mouse on the table looking for morsels of food in a floodlight from the street lamp.

Now she was a resident, but the title did not improve her schedule. She worked thirty hours straight in the Cardiac Unit and then had twenty hours off. It was a grueling schedule with every other night on call, but she did not complain. She just did what she had to do.

It was a hot July day before the start of the teaching year, Victoria's first day as a resident, and they took a group photo in front of the hospital. They were young, and everyone wore a short white jacket.

In her late thirties, Victoria was, by far, the oldest resident; but she felt and looked like she belonged with all these young American doctors. She was proud, and she sent the photo to her Mom as proof that now she was a full-fledged doctor in America.

The letters were coming faster now, "Maybe the Russians do not read all of them," thought Victoria. Mom did not have even to go to the main Post Office in Kiev to make a telephone call; she could call from the apartment.

Victoria was sure her Mom would be proud of her achievements, and indeed, she was. Sarra was thrilled her daughter was a doctor; however, she was most concerned about Victoria showing up at work without stockings.

"How little they understood there, back home, what it took to pass the exams, to get the residency and to survive," fumed Victoria "and the only thing she noticed were stockings, or rather the absence of them!"

"Your Mom never took the garbage out without putting lipstick on," Felix tried to console her. He wished his only problem would be his wife's stockings. He still worked overtime, took care of the house, cooked and cleaned, with Dave's help, of course.

On a sunny afternoon late fall, as Victoria started her night on call in the Intensive Care Unit, Dave paged her. He came back from the school with a fever and a sore throat.

"Please, Dave, drink fluids and gargle your throat. Dad will be home soon, and I will see you tomorrow." He was almost fourteen then and could take care of himself.

Dave was slightly better by the next day, and Victoria, after a short sleep at home, asked him again to rest, drink fluids and with a kiss, she went back to work.

She was on call every other night. Felix took care of Dave in the evening, but he too rushed out of the house to work early in the morning.

The next three days, as his parents came and went, Dave spent alone laying on the sofa in the living room. He ran a high fever, his head hurt, and he did not want to watch TV; he was weak, and he slept most of the time.

When Victoria returned home in the evening, Dave still had a very high fever, and he did not look good. With sudden fear, Victoria realized that she could not "doctor" Dave anymore. They tried to bring him to the hospital across the street by car, but he lost consciousness every time Felix and Victoria tried to set him up. They, finally, had to call an ambulance for this short ride.

That night they almost lost him; his white blood count was critically low, and the Emergency Room doctor called for an attending- on- call. It took a few hours for the attending doctor and a called- in- consultant to make a diagnosis.

"Is he going to die?" Felix's voice was a hardly- laudable whisper.

"No!" wanted to scream Victoria, but she only shook her head. She felt like she was under water, she was drowning while she tried to swim up. "No!" She tried to whisper this time, but she had no voice. She could not lose Dave; she would rather die right here, right now. She leaned on Felix and sobbed.

Dave spent five days in Intensive Care with measles. Back in Russia, he was never immunized, they did not have hypoallergenic vaccines there, and his asthma was a significant contraindication for immunization.

He managed to start a small epidemic in his school where some kids were also not vaccinated because of their parents' ignorance and unfounded prejudice.

*****

I looked at Dave. He was in the pool with the kids, looking handsome and healthy. Nevertheless, I still felt guilty.

Years ago, we went to the Canary Islands to celebrate Dima's thirtieth birthday. It was a big undertaking, with Dima working as an Editor-in-Chief of an American newspaper in Kiev, Dave living in California and Felix and I flying in from Boston. At the birthday dinner, I made a toast to my sons. I was very nervous when I told them that I gathered the whole family for this exotic celebration because I felt guilty for taking time from my children for my own life and my work. I told them, I felt guilty because I did not remember if and how many children's books I had read to them at night, that I had never had time to take them for a sport practice, that I knew very few of their friends, and that often I had no time to cook dinner.

They looked astonished and speechless but only for a moment, "Mom, are you kidding?" Both of them were talking at the same time.

"You were the best Mom of all! You were always there for us!"

"You did everything you had to do for us!"

Then, finally, Dima came up with, "You even tried to teach me to sing!"

That evening was my triumph and prize; not only Dima turned thirty, but apparently, neither he nor Dave suffered any ill effects of a hard-working mother.

And yes, I did teach Dima to sing. Dave was just born, Dima was three years old, and I spent endless hours washing and ironing Dave's cloth diapers. "They have to be ironed on both sides," that was the doctor in me. "Now would be a great time to spend with Dima," intervened my "motherly side."

Dima could read by then, he had a beautiful, occasionally, very loud voice but he could not sing. His late father was a musical prodigy; he played a violin, and he could sing the whole Tchaikovsky's concert by heart.

I always sang and thought that if I were growing up somewhere else, not in the Soviet Union, I would be an opera diva. My dad was a great singer with a low, velvety baritone.

For months, ironing diapers, I tried to teach Dima to sing. I was sure it would be an easy and pleasant task. Unfortunately, Dima did not inherit any musical genes from his parents; life is very unfair!

DAY 30, SEPTEMBER 26
SANTA MONICA, CA
CASA DEL MAR

I woke up with a smile.

"What?" Felix demanded. His cheek was pressing on his left eye and kept it closed although, the right eye was looking at me with unmistakable suspicion.

"What? " He repeated with a doubt reflected in his voice. He was all ready for whatever my smile meant. "Let me guess; you do not want to leave?"

I laughed, "What the matter? Did you have a bad dream? Of course, we will leave tomorrow; we got a package from Caroline yesterday with the rest of our trip all booked".

For the last month, we followed Caroline, our travel planner's instructions to the point and so far, all her suggestions were sound.

I turned to Felix; he was awake now and both his eyes were open, however, he still was suspicious about of my smile.

"I thought about our kids. Sometimes I can remember their every step, from the first word to the marriage. I remember everything about them; how they looked, dressed and what songs they sang; what they ate and who they dated; and in every vignette of their lives Dima is always stubborn, and Dave is always sick. I am, probably, an awful mother."

Our last day was a regular Californian day, where one does not need to look at the window to know the weather; clear skies with a picture perfect lonely cloud, gentle sun, and beautiful people; how can anybody complain?

I looked at the two young people and a middle-aged man at our brunch table; I could not believe they were my baby Dave's children and our grandchildren. I did not have answers to such mundane questions, as "How did it all happen? How did we get so old so quickly?" and "When did the time go"?

It was "the anniversary" day; the day we had arrived in the United States almost forty years ago. We had left a terrible country to bring our children to the best one, we worked and traveled, we lived eventful, interesting and exciting lives, we kept family and friends, we built the house, and we planted the tree. Not a bad score for about four decades. Tomorrow we will start to drive back home.

KIDS
KIEV, UKRAINE, THE 1970S

The hot summer day in Kiev was gorgeous, although Victoria did not have time to notice. For the first time, they were leaving for vacation, the typical family with Mom, Dad and two little boys. Victoria was surprised that everything was ready; all morning she packed Dima's small bed and a chair, Dave's crib, Dima's clothes and Dave's diapers. She got hers and Felix's belongings and food; they had to bring everything for the kids and themselves.

It looked like they were leaving forever, although they would be only forty minutes away by the local train at the "dacha" as Russians lovingly called summer houses in the suburbs.

They were all tired and needed a break from the close living at her parents' apartment. Her Dad rented this small house for Victoria and her family, and her Mom got a big van to move them. As usual, her parents came through.

"They wanted to get rid of us," Victoria smiled. "They even did not mind Dima leaving with us."

It was dark by the time they settled. The house was in the woods about a mile from the railroad station. It was an incredibly small house, a far cry from a real "dacha";

just one big room with a double bed and a large table, tiny kitchen with gas stove, sink and a small refrigerator. A dilapidated wooden shack at the end of the yard served as an outhouse. There was no phone or television. The adults were busy trying to settle: they were exhausted by the time kids fell asleep in their beds.

Victoria woke up at two in the morning. It was utterly dark, and this darkness was broken by the horribly familiar sound. She recognized it immediately; on her first night on-call, she had lost a patient, a young woman who died of a severe asthma attack.

Dave did not cry, he was nine-month-old, and when she picked him up from the crib in dim light of one bulb, he was blue.

It took her only one minute to decide what to do. She gave Dave the asthma pill; she warmed the water on the stove and made him a drink. She was carrying him upright wrapped in the blanket as she tried to calm him down. She did all this while Felix ran the run of his life to the only pay phone in the village at the railroad station. He ran on the unknown road without lights praying that he would find this phone before it would be too late. He called the ambulance and Victoria's father and ran back home.

They pressed a warm cloth to Dave's chest, and they tried to calm down Dima, who woke up in the middle of the night in unfamiliar place upset to see his Mom crying.

Victoria was scared out of her mind. Felix held kids while she ran through the moonless night to the outhouse at the end of the yard. They were waiting for somebody to come and to take them away from this horrible spruce and pine forest that Dave turned out to be so allergic to.

Lenya stormed in before the arrival of a local ambulance. He drove forty miles from Kiev at night; the last ten miles on an unpaved road. It seems her dad was always there when Vika needed him. He was her protective wall to lean on, to hide behind and to reach for all she wanted to reach. He was her father.

*****

It was our last evening with the family, and after the dinner, we all went to Santa Monica Yacht Harbor. A beautiful moon hung over the ocean, and the Pier was bursting with fun and people, open souvenirs stores, restaurants, and attractions. We could see tall Dave and the kids ahead; the two of us looked short compared to them. Everybody in my family was tall; my parents, Mom's sister and brother, even Ella, my baby sister, was always taller than I was.

"Poor girl," joked my parents' friends, "They did not water you enough when you were young." Or maybe it was the war.

We stood at the pole that marked the end of historic Route 66 and took the pictures on the pier with a giant Ferris wheel behind us making its slow rounds. The kids wanted to ride, and we said our goodbyes and walked back to our hotel. We took a few steps down to leave the pier, and suddenly the sounds and the lights disappeared. It was dark and quiet, and it was just the two of us. We could hear the ocean. It was exactly a month since we left home and we both felt it was time to go back to another shore, to another ocean. We went to the beach and touched the water. It was our goodbye to the Pacific, to California, to Dave. He was no longer "the baby." Felix's hand was on my shoulder; we kissed in the middle of the boardwalk and walked faster. We were going home.

DAY 31, SEPTEMBER 27
LAS VEGAS, NV
HOTEL VDARA

We settled in the car and already pulled out when I noticed that my car keys, stored by hotel parking attendants for the last few days, were missing a keychain, a sentimental present from Felix. He did not mind at all, but I was fuming all the way through Los Angeles. I called the hotel but got no answer or an explanation.

I drove through "Jesus is the way" signs, barren hills and strip malls. Why was I so attached even to smallest things? Where was the way of Jesus?

Nevada reminded us of the South African bush, the same long empty fields, and cacti although, the colorful, neat houses behind the wire fences were all American. We even saw the sign for Zzyzx Road and tried to figure out what language the inhabitants spoke? There were more sands, pitiful shrubs, military antennas and even dark low mountains on the way.

Only when Felix took the driver's seat did I realized that all morning there was no sun on my left shoulder. For weeks going west, I got used to a leading light of the morning sun on my left side; it was my constant companion and a warm friend, but now, we were driving east and the sun all but abandoned our car and us.

TALES FROM MOSCOW
MOSCOW, RUSSIA, THE 1950S

Victoria loved Moscow. In her childhood memories, Moscow was a small village she visited with her Babushka. She vaguely remembered a little train and a big old wooden house. It was late fall, red and yellow leaves covered a vast lawn and the street behind the tall fence was empty.

For Victoria, this sprawling house outside of the city was Moscow. She remembered her Babushka's sister and brothers and their children, fun and loud people. Over the years, she visited many times, with her Dad, alone and later with Dima before their wedding, but the best, she loved visiting with her Babushka.

The Moscow part of the family treated her Babushka like the Queen. The long table was covered with a white lace tablecloth; silverware shimmered under the soft yellowish light from a single electric bulb hanging from the low ceiling. The cord and the bulb were hidden inside the large silk lampshade called "abajour". Beautifully decorated with lace and fringe, it was casting strange moving shadows on the pristine tablecloth. Old crystal was ringing with every toast as the "Muscovites," Babushka's younger sister Fanny and her two brothers Yasha and Abram with their families sat around the table. It was a large clan with children and young grandchildren, with the stories of love and death and life in Moscow.

Fanny was a pleasantly plump beautiful woman with a regal head; she wore her hair piled up in an elaborate updo and held her head high. Her husband Markus was tall and big with an impressive large beard. He was a former "kulak," and his front yard was not so pristine in the nineteen thirties when KGB came to look for hidden gold and dig out the whole yard. They did not find anything; nevertheless, he was arrested. After his surprising return after only a few months, Marcus had one explanation; he survived because he did everything in the name of Lenin and he demonstrated how he did it, showing a Soviet hundred rubles note with Lenin's portrait. He favored young Vika and always had some candies for her in his pocket.

Fanny's two children, Jenny and Lenya did not look anything like their mom. Jenny was short, very nearsighted with thick glasses sitting comfortably on her round cheeks. There was something wrong with this branch of the family because Lenya, or Lusik, as everybody called him, was also extremely nearsighted. Victoria did not know for sure, but she recalled the whispers that Marcus was a cousin of her Babushka and therefore his wife's.

Babushka's two younger brothers, Yasha and Abram, settled in Moscow long before the war. Always smiling, good-natured younger brother Yasha got to medical school and became a gynecologist. There were no doctors in the family and Yasha was always eager to tell why he decided to be the one.

"Well, I have to tell you," he always started with a kind smile, which wrinkled his round face. "I was not a good boy. We were working on the machine when I heard a scream in the house. Asya was my favorite sister, and I thought I recognized her voice. I ran into the house and heard some voices, but the door to the bedroom was locked. Something was not right there, behind that door. I was a short boy, and the keyhole was right in front of me. That is how my father caught me, watching through the keyhole the birth of my nephew Lenya. I told him right away I will be a doctor, but that did not prevent me from the punishment". At this point, he laughed and his face gathered in myriads of wrinkles like an accordion.

The older brother Abram studied to be a teacher.

At the students' party, they met two beautiful sisters, and within a month, right before graduation, both of them got married. Romantic Abram and his new wife went to teach kids in Siberia, while fun-loving Yasha with his wife stayed in Moscow, close to his sister and the family.

The life after the war was not easy; the cities were in ruins, the families destroyed, the orphanages overcrowded with homeless kids. Yasha, who delivered thousands of newborns, and his wife, a teacher who adored children, did not have their own and by the end of the war, they adopted a baby girl.

Little blond Tanya was lucky to get out of the orphanage, to have food and loving parents, beautiful dresses and a big family. Yasha was a famous doctor with significant practice; even Kremlin Clinic frequently summoned him for an emergency consultation on the Party leaders' wives.

The war had never reached Siberia where Abram became a school principal. His wife passed away from cancer, and he lived alone with their young daughter Inna. He had never remarried, devoting all his time to Inna's education.

Now, his seventeen years old daughter was his crown achievement. Not only she was all "A"s student, she also held the first place in the whole country's Scientific Olympics in Mathematics, Physics, and Chemistry; she was a beautiful girl with dark curly hair that she braided in a long braid and huge eyes the color of the spring "forget me not" flowers.

After graduation, Inna and her father left their home and school in Siberia, the place they had lived all their lives, and settled in one spare room at Aunty Fanny's big wooden house outside Moscow.

A little Victoria was in awe when she saw Inna for the first time. Not only was the girl beautiful but she also wanted to get to Moscow University! It sounded like a dream to little Victoria although, Inna's hope for the best University in the country was utterly crazy. There was no way a Jew would get in, no matter how talented she was.

When seventeen-year-old Inna met her family for the first time, Aunty Fanny could not hide her admiration; she whirled her niece in the welcome waltz right there in the hallway before Inna put her suitcase down.

The whole family reunited for a welcome dinner at the big table with the best of Fanny's cooking. However, Inna was not there; she went to apply to University before they unpacked their luggage; she was excited and sure, she would get in. She would stop at nothing.

The brutally hot Moscow summer spewed chewed green leaves, crumpled grass, and melted asphalt. The heat was hanging in the air like an old gauze curtain, suffocating brave souls venturing outside. Stonewalls of the university were hot as a Russian stove, but the halls were crowded with fresh graduates dreaming to get in. The university was their ticket to a better future.

The high school graduates could apply only to one school a year and had to take the exams to get in. If anyone failed, she or he could apply again to the same or to a different school next year, but this meant losing a year and the older boys at nineteen would face a mandatory draft to the army. The colleges, or "institutions" in Russia, were highly differentiated; each one prepared for a specific profession only: the engineers, the teachers, the doctors, the lawyers, the actors, the journalists, the diplomats.

At seventeen, the high school graduates had to choose their professions and their future. They had to make up their minds and make their choices. Inna, for one, had no problem; she knew exactly what she wanted to do. She would be the teacher, like her parents.

In the summer heat wave, life was not easy in Moscow. Downtown, or at the center, as Russian called it, the yard-keepers in the long white aprons were watering melting asphalt all day long and even outside of the city, it was hot.

The other kind of heat and melting was happening at the "dacha", right under the noses of Fanny and Abram.

Fanny's son Lenya had a nickname Lusik. He returned home after a business trip, and when he stepped out of the second-floor bathroom with the wet towel still around his hips, he almost ran into a girl he had never seen before. She was just about to open the door he was trying to close behind him.

"Sorry," she whispered hurriedly and disappeared, but he managed to notice the thick braid and eyes the color of the spring "forget me not" flowers.

They were introduced at the dinner, and it was amazing to see how alike they were, both tall and dark. Only Lusik hid a shy smile under his large glasses when Inna had an open and determined smile on her beautiful face. They were first cousins, and they fell in love at first sight.

Inna graduated from a high school with the highest honor, the gold medal and she was exempt from the exams to the University; she just had to have an interview.

To everybody's incredible surprise, in spite of the "fifth line" in her passport, Inna was accepted to Moscow University.

"The fifth line" or "the fifth paragraph" in the Soviet passport was detrimental if you were a Jew. Every passport issued in the Soviet Union had the fifth line with the nationality of the owner. Granted, it was after the last name, the first and father's name, date of birth and place of birth. Nevertheless, there it was.

Being Jewish in the Soviet Union did not mean faith, but nationality and Jews had to list "Jewish" on the fifth line.

Every little clerk, every small party chief, every yard-keeper knew who you were. The government jobs, titles, admissions to universities and foreign travel were off-limits to you, because on the fifth line in your passport in blue ink was clearly written "Jewish".

This summer Inna beat the curse of the fifth line and got to the best school in the country. She also got the best-looking boyfriend in Moscow, the first in her life.

The whole family was in an uproar. His Mom and her Dad stood the united front against their children. Victoria's Babushka was summoned from Kiev to help in the fight and to try to talk the common sense to "the kids."

"You are first cousins!" screamed sisters in unison, "you live in the same house for this very reason! You are already a family, and you love each other as a family!"

"Jewish law allows it," fended "the kids." Lusik smiled and shrugged his broad shoulders, but Inna, in the heat of her first love, did not know any limits. She was a winner, the University student, and she was not about to lose this battle.

By the new academic year, Abram stayed alone in the guest room, and across the hall, Lusik's room was missing the owner. "The kids" married the same fall.

*****

I looked at Vegas from the twenty-seventh floor of my next century's room and remembered Las Vegas of 1980th when we saw this town for the first time. Then, it did not look as elegant and impressive. We saw casino for the first time in our lives, and we ate at the "all you can eat" buffets for less than three dollars. So yes, we were more than impressed.

I guess we had changed as well. I looked around the room, which had every possible gadget. Behind the window, fountains of Bellagio danced higher than the Old Faithful in Yellowstone, Eiffel's Tower was lighted up better than in Paris, and Rio sparkled brighter than real Rio de Janeiro. We drove three hundred miles from Santa Monica and arrived into the future, which was amazing. Our hotel Vdara, an incredibly modern and elegant hotel of the next century, left us speechless.

We settled in the very futuristic bed, and I kissed Felix good night with a fifty-year-old kiss. Some things never change.

DAY 32, SEPTEMBER 28
LAS VEGAS, NV
HOTEL VDARA

Far below our window, Las Vegas looked fresh and clean in the morning. The pools at Bellagio were still uninhabited. The hottest and the driest place in the USA seemed deceivingly fresh and inviting. No wonder, when the Spanish scout Rafael Rivera came to a grassy green valley that became Las Vegas, he named the place "the meadows" in Spanish. He was lucky that the nomadic native tribe, which lived here for thousands of years before, did not care to name this hot and dry place.

We planned the whole day of exploration, eating and gambling and took a side exit to the beautiful Bellagio. Did I mention the nomadic tribes? The contemporary ones called tourists were all here, under spectacular ceilings, among exotic trees and dancing fountains.

We took a cover at the small table of the cozy café, enjoyably empty between breakfast and lunch.

"It feels like a date" smiled Felix. "Lucky me; at our age, dates are hard to come by."

"Too bad there was only one cafe in Kiev when we were young."

"Yes, I remember, the Czechs had a Pavilion at the Exhibition Hall, and after they were done, they built a small glass-walled café on Khreshchatyk. The place had the best coffee in town!"

I closed my eyes and saw two young women seated at the table in this café many years ago. I was wearing a long gray suede coat and high black boots; all from my recent trip to Poland, an outfit to see and to be seen in. It was my girlfriend Ellen's birthday, and we waited in line for over an hour to get the seats for a cup of coffee. Through the floor to ceiling glass, we saw the street, window-shopping people, quiet trolleys and a woman selling late fall flowers. A small car stopped right in front of the café. A dashing, tall man in a three-piece suit and a stylish fedora went straight for the woman with flowers and bought a small bunch. It took me a few moments to realize that was my Dad.

"I saw two beautiful women sitting at the window and could not drive any further!" He smiled mischievously.

"Dad! Have a cup of coffee with us. It is Ellen's birthday."

"So sorry, I have a patient to attend; these flowers would be for Ellen then," he sat on the edge of the stool and wrote a few lines on Ellen's paper napkin. He kissed her hand and my cheek, and rushed out. His car pulled out shortly. There was a short poem for Ellen scribbled on her napkin.

"The flowers and the poem!" Ellen was pleased and surprised. "Your Dad can make any woman happy, even now!" I opened my eyes.

"Are you Ok?" asked Felix. "Where is my date? You seem far away Vika."

"I just had a date with my Dad, and as you know, he is still above the competition."

TALES FROM MOSCOW
MOSCOW, RUSSIA, THE 1960S

"Your Dad was here!" whispered Jenny's son Ilusha and pulled Victoria out of the room. He looked like a big conspirator, "Listen, Victoria, I overheard what he told my Mom about you."

Jenny with her husband Michael and son Ilusha lived now in the very heart of Moscow, in the old building on the elegant street across from Conservatory. It was just a few short blocks from the Red Square. Beautiful old buildings that housed many famous musicians and writers lined the street, so there was always a chance to bump into a celebrity.

Jenny's family moved to this one room in a-three-room-apartment from her parents' large house outside of Moscow.

Jenny was much younger than her cousins, closer to Victoria's age and when Victoria started to travel to Moscow alone, she loved to stay with Jenny. They were friends, and they could talk and share family secrets for hours. This summer's visit was a gift from Lenya to his daughter for her first year in medical school.

The long hallway of Jenny's apartment was damp and deserted. A lonely sunray danced in the tall window at the end of the hallway, lighting up a large kitchen. An old woman was standing next to it, at the door to the small room. She wore an ancient robe, and her hair had not seen a comb lately. Victoria had seen this typical communal hallway and the woman many times before.

"What did you hear about me?" asked Victoria suspiciously. Although she could not wait to hear what Ilusha had to say, she did not like the old woman in the hallway listening to their conversation.

"Do not pay any attention," reassured Ilusha. "She is always like that. She lost all her family in the war, and she lives alone. She wears nothing but the old robe and does not talk. Mom brings her groceries since we moved here."

"Hey, guys, come back, dinner is ready," Jenny called from the room. "Later," whispered Ilusha. "I am hungry."

The table sparkled with Fanny's crystal and silverware.

"Remember the old house?" asked Jenny. "These were Mom's wedding presents. She cannot move anymore, her back is terrible, and doctors do not pay any attention if you are over sixty- year- old."

"I know, I just worked a month at the hospital," said Victoria. "It is awful; one nurse and one nurse's aide for the whole floor of sixty patients, ten people in the room, no linens or clean pajamas. The patients were all very sick; I felt terrible for them."

"What did you do there?" asked Ilusha.

Victoria took a deep breath. "You know, this was my first year in medical school. I wanted to be an actress and my last two years in the high school Dad and I had argued nonstop. First, he did not want me to go to Theatrical School at all. He took me to all premiers of his plays, to show how poor and hungry the real actors were, not the famous ones. Then, he was afraid I would not get into any school and would have to lose a year, so we made a deal. He would let me try for an 'art' exam in Theatrical School a year earlier. The one that you have to sing, dance, and recite poetry, to show that you have a talent. If I would pass, then the next year I could apply to Theatrical Institute, but if I failed, I would have to apply to Medical School, because my grades were excellent."

"Well, it was a complete disaster," continued Victoria. " I recited the famous fable, and I thought that I did well; I played piano and sang this latest hit 'Moscow Windows,' and it was good too; but at the end, the Chairman of the panel told me that I have no talent; 'none whatsoever,' he said. I ran away in tears and hid at our friends' house for three days. I thought I would never survive such humiliation. I did not want to hear what my Dad would say. So the next year I did not argue with him. I got to medical school, and after this first year, we have a month of 'practice' working as nurses' aides."

Victoria did not enjoy telling this story, although the people around the table were her family, she felt like a loser, in spite of finishing the first challenging year of medical school and loving it.

They started to clean the table carrying dirty plates through the long hallway all the way to the kitchen. The strange woman in the old robe was still there.

"I loved what I did last month," Victoria said with the pride in her voice. In all her eighteen years of life, she had never made up her bed at home and Aunt Rose nicknamed her "the princess to be served", but the last month she did not mind changing patients' beds, helping them to walk and serving their meals. She loved to help and to take care of the patients; she felt happy when she could help and the patients appreciated her work.

"Before I left for Moscow, I wrote a letter to my Dad, thanking him for recognizing my real calling in life and guiding me to it, for helping me to fulfill my real dream," she was not a little girl anymore, she knew what she wanted to do.

After the dinner, Ilusha did the dishes in the kitchen and Victoria helped him dry the china.

"I can't believe you are such a fool!" Ilusha was almost screaming. "We love having you here, and happy your Dad let you come to Moscow. He was here last week, and he told Mom how he had arranged for you to fail on that exam to the theatre institute, so you would have to go to medical school! He knew the head of the panel and asked him to fail you. How could you be such an idiot? You have talent, Victoria! What are you going to do with it now? Do you want to keep changing sheets in the hospital? You have to quit the school and go back to the theater!"

She was shaken; she always believed she had the talent. Even in the "Youth Theater" at the Pioneers' Palace, she always had the leading roles.

She was humiliated at the exam, but now, she was indeed vindicated. She loved this last month working in the hospital; she was sure she made the right decision. She was happy. She only wanted to know how her father could foresee all this.

She laughed and left Ilusha to do the dishes.

"It would be good for him," she thought, "not to listen to adults' conversations."

She remembered the story Jenny told her when Ilusha was just a child. "We were going to Moscow from the dacha. Ilusha was a beautiful little boy, spoiled and bored he was not behaving while we were waiting for the train. I tried to bribe him and promised to buy him a train. At this moment, the real train arrived, and my little boy became hysterical, 'I want this train, the real one!' He screamed at the top of his lungs. We could not quiet him down all the way home!"

"He did not change much," thought Victoria.

*****

"I do not like boats," I informed Felix as we looked at the strange abstract pile-up of colorful small canoes in front of the hotel. "I like trains."

We headed back to our room after quick dinner and an even shorter visit to the casino.

I have a theory that some people always win and some always lose. Unfortunately, we belong to a second category. Felix even rubbed the shiny belly of Buddha in the posh lobby of Aria Hotel, but all in vain. I would love to know what makes the same people win again and again. If it were not the skills or a character, then I would have to become religious and believe in God.

The night air was warm like a scarf on my shoulders, but we had to go back to our room to pack. We walked the shiny floors, looked at the lighted ceilings, rode futuristic elevators and said goodbye to Las Vegas.

I was still multitasking, applying cream to my face, writing my nightly email about our day and sneaking a look at the never sleeping still sparkling with lights Vegas.

Sleeping Felix suddenly sat up and looked at me, disoriented. "What time is it? Should I get up?"

"It's only midnight, Felix, go back to sleep. We are off to Mount Zion tomorrow."

DAY 33, SEPTEMBER 29
SPRINGDALE, UT
ZION NATIONAL PARK
HAMPTON INN & SUITES

W e left urbane Las Vegas, skyscrapers, straight streets, fountains and manicured lawns and drove about hundred and fifty miles through sands, cacti, and occasional palms to The Oasis. It was not the oasis in the desert, just the resort.

The transformation was incredible; the hills grew up to become mountains and green colors slowly turn to pink.

I was surprised when we hit a corner of Arizona; somehow, I expected Utah to the east of Nevada. I saw a sign "Entering Arizona" and a lonely police car on the divider. I slowed down for Felix to take a picture of the state sign and proceeded to drive seventy five-mile-an-hour.

The white highway patrol car followed and flashed his lights. A very young and friendly police officer stopped me for going too slow! That was a first for me. He was apparently bored and wanted to know everything about us. How did we get our car with Massachusetts license plates to Arizona? When did we retire and what were we doing before? How did we survive for fifty years but most importantly, how did we survive driving in the car together for over a month? At least, he did not ask Felix for the proof of citizenship.

"I was very tempted to tell him, that my handsome, but

very Spanish looking husband retired from the field work," I teased Felix. "Then, I decided that I was not tired of you yet. At least, you let me drive."

I was delighted to get a warning for driving slow! I planned to frame it and hang it on the garage wall. I wanted it to go permanently on my driving record right next to my old ticket for driving at the ridiculous speed of one hundred and two miles an hour on Mass Pike that almost cost me my new American medical license!

A friend of ours was singing at Carnegie Hall, and we got a personal invitation from the Governor of New York Mario Cuomo to the concert followed by a VIP dinner. It was a black-tie affair, and during my lunch hour, I could not suppress an urge to check out Bloomingdales. I was driving a very new electric- blue- two-door Volvo that in my opinion looked and handled like a Lamborghini, so ten- mile- drive to the store was just a stroll. I took Mass Pike and in a few minutes noticed an unmarked police car behind me. I changed to the right lane, but it was too late; he flashed the lights and pulled me over.

"Nice car," he sounded friendly so far. "License and registration, please."

I was just about to tell him that I am going to a nearby hospital to visit a very sick patient when his face went red. "Your license has expired!"

"I am very sorry; I was not notified," I almost whispered as my prospect of getting to the store started to evaporate.

"Miss, your license expired over six months ago! Get out of the car; it will be towed now!"

"Officer, please, what am I going to do in the middle of Mass Pike? I am a doctor! I have a heavy doctor's bag, and I am wearing high heels; can I please drive next mile to the Rest Stop to get to a public phone at least?" Right there, my trip to Bloomingdales expired along with my license!

Where did his initial friendliness go? He was towering

behind my window obstructing the sun. "Leave the car right now, I had already called the tow service," he was not kidding.

A sign for the Rest Stop was calling ahead, but I would never make it there in my heels. I was frantic, and suddenly I thought of the solution to the problem, "Felix!" The man was my eternal savior, the stick to lean on. "I have to call Felix; maybe he is home for lunch!"

There was no time for deliberation, slowly I got back in my car and turned it on. As in slow motion, I pressed the gas pedal and flew to the rest stop. In my side window, I could see the stunned face of the officer. I drove straight to the phone booth. My hands shook as I dialed my home number, "Felix, please, save me!" My voice trembled more than my hands. "Please, come pick my car, my driver license has expired!" I was lucky he liked my homemade lunch and was home.

I put the receiver down and opened the door of the soundproof telephone booth.

Police sirens and flashing lights deafened and blinded me. Three police cars surrounded the booth and my car. There was a police officer aiming a gun at me behind each open door of every police car. Dumbfounded, I raised my hands, and they rushed to surround me. I did not care; I was even not afraid of aiming at me guns! "Felix, please, Felix," I begged soundlessly. "Please, come to save me!"

The tow truck arrived first. It looked like a hearse for my car. Stunned, I quietly got into my car. I was about to close the door when the officer put his gun through the window. He was livid, "Get out of this car immediately!" What did he want from me? I had to pull up my opened window!

"I just wanted to take my things," I offered meekly looking into aimed at me a gun barrel and carefully getting out of the car. The tow truck started to lift my car.

Felix's car flew into the Rest Stop. The brakes were still screeching when Felix got out and went straight to the officer.

"Put this car down now!" His low voice was quite commanding in spite of the situation.

"She does not have a license to drive, and we will tow the car," the officer was seriously pissed off now.

"This is my car, and I have a license," Felix designed the Patriots missiles, and he was afraid of nobody. "Put this car down immediately; I am going to drive it out of here." Obviously, he was well trained by his past encounters with KGB.

"You cannot drive two cars," almost yelled officer somewhat losing control. "And she does not have a license!" He was furious, now with both of us; he was not used to losing his battles with the motorists. Not with the Russians, anyway.

"It is a Rest Stop, officer; just so you would know," Felix said victoriously. "I am going to drive my wife in my car to the registry, renew her license and come back to pick up my car here. Is it OK with you, officer?"

It took the officer a long time to write up my tickets, all seven of them. There was a ticket for operating in danger, a ticket for operating without a license, a ticket for not obeying a police officer and a ticket for leaving a place of incident and more of the same. The CEO of the hospital was shocked when I reported what happened. Nevertheless, he helped me to find the right attorney and to settle the case out of court. An attorney and a court fine cost a lot of money, much more than the best designer's black tie outfit.

We entered Utah without a police escort. The roofs looked like the beach umbrellas hidden behind cacti and green shrubs; occasional cypresses graced the road. The sky color of forget-me-not spring flowers hung over the signs for Buffalo Trails Trading Company where Indian pottery and turquoise jewelry mirrored the deep blue sky. Shy, maiden-like river, appropriately named Virgin, ran quietly along the roadside, embellished by greenery sparkling on the sun.

We anchored at the gate of Zion Canyon in magnificent Springdale, Utah, population five hundred and twenty-nine.

If you ever saw a view, which caused your heart to jump, your chest to squeeze and your soul to soar, then you will know how I felt in Springdale. The unique beauty of the mountains, canyons, and valleys was overwhelming.

However, man cannot live on view alone. At the restaurant across the street, we ate simple and delicious dinner in silence. One would not be laughing in front of the Mona Lisa or Pieta, the same held true for this view. There should be a vaccine to help us to deal with incredible beauty, to prevent us from being awestruck by it, on the other hand, maybe not.

The spell was finally broken in the room when Felix watched the news, and I tried to tell him the family stories. There was nothing joyful in the family tales about the life in the Soviet Union; it was a hard and frightening life of gloomy existence. There were love and family, and friends, and art, of course, but every crumb of happiness was poisoned and destroyed by the lies and corruption.

MOSCOW, RUSSIA, THE 1970S

The secret was out.

"She was always very secretive," Jenny was crying, angry with Inna, her cousin slash sister-in-law.

It felt good to confide in the visiting Victoria who was family and a friend yet she lived in Kiev, very far from the Moscow clan.

"You would not believe it, Victoria. He is a big shot in the Party, and he is married. Inna turned out to be so sneaky; they carried out this affair for years, right under the nose of his wife. And Lusik did not suspect anything either." Jenny took off her glasses and delicately wiped her nearsighted eyes with a lacy white handkerchief.

She was right; Victoria did not want to believe. "I remember how much they were in love; they fought with everybody to be together! Even my Babushka had to come to talk to them. Maybe it is just a rumor, Jenny."

Victoria was a grown-up woman with two children and the problems of her own.

At least, her marriage to Felix failed not because of the affair. Although, now she was not sure.

KIEV, UKRAINE, THE 1970S

Two new nine-story- high buildings in the center of Kiev faced each other. Large balconies called loggias added a lot of glass and some style to the boring architecture. The condominium was commissioned by Ukrainian Television and designed by Dmitry's uncle. Victoria's Dad bought the sixth-floor- apartment for Victoria.

Writers, composers, and actors working for the TV studio occupied most of the units. Felix was away on a business trip when the apartment was finally ready, and Victoria led by her lack of patience decided to move in. Her Mom got her a small truck and a driver who promised to help. Victoria packed their belongings, the driver loaded the car, and Victoria with Dave on her hands moved to a new chapter in her life.

The elevator was not working, the telephone was not connected, but Victoria was thrilled to have two rooms, a balcony, kitchen and bathroom, water and electricity all to her own family. "Dima, Dimochka would be living with me now," she almost sang inspecting her small heaven.

She was dragging a heavy box to the sixth floor when a tall, handsome stranger offered to help.

"We are neighbors, I presume." He was freshly shaven with a faint smell of colon. His hand, with long fingers, was cold when he shook Victoria's sweaty palm. He picked up the box and carried it without any effort to the sixth floor.

"I look like hell," thought Victoria. "Why is he so nice?"

The man put the box down and inspected her sparsely decorated two-room-apartment. He noticed Felix's boxer gloves prominently displayed on the wall above a sleeping sofa in the living room, "So you are married, pretty girl," he acknowledged with a sigh. "Then why are you and not him moving the things in?"

Victoria laughed, "He is waiting for everything to be done, including a rug on the floor."

"My name is Phillip, by the way, and I live on the second floor. I am divorced and available just in case this husband of yours does not show up, and you decide to hide those threatening gloves." He took off his hat and bowed slightly.

"What a gentleman," smiled Victoria running downstairs to pick up her next box.

Her husband finally showed up and was pleasantly surprised with their new apartment. He loved the already connected phone, quiet elevator and rug on the floor.

They became fast friends with Phillip who was a well-known jazz composer and pianist. He entertained in his cozy studio lavishly and had many exciting and famous friends. Phil, as they called him, was frequently on the tour accompanying and playing with different bands. He usually left his plants and a cat in Victoria's care.

The day, when yet another of Dave's nannies left, was a disastrous day. Never mind the nanny was always drunk and lazy and went to bed before Victoria would finish cleaning up after dinner. At least, she would help Victoria with Dave's bath.

This fateful evening, when the nanny was gone, Dave was sick, and Victoria had an important meeting at work the next morning. There was no way she would drag sick Dave to her parents tomorrow. She could hear a small washer humming happily in the kitchen.

"I have to ask Felix; maybe he could stay with Dave tomorrow," she plotted; however Felix could not.

"I have a job too, you know."

Victoria was beside herself, and Felix got very angry. "It is always about you, and your work and your dissertation, and your parents, Victoria. It does not matter that your child is sick, it does not matter that I work too; everything is always about you and you alone!"

It was unfair; she yelled, cried, and yelled again. Dave woke up, he still had a fever, and he cried; the washer in the kitchen was not humming but screeching, and she could not stand Felix who was watching TV in the middle of all this mayhem.

"Get out, I can manage alone without a useless husband," roared Victoria and went to check on Dave. She heard the door slam. No TV was on in the living room.

Sick Dave was very hot, and Victoria rubbed him with a cool cloth. Suddenly she noticed the silence in the kitchen. "The laundry is probably ready," thought Victoria. "I'd better hang it on the balcony to dry overnight".

The washer was full of soapy water with wet laundry; a small puddle started to form on the floor. Victoria tried to restart the old washer, but it did not cooperate.

"Felix," thought Victoria. "Where did he go when I need him?" She sat next to the dripping washer and cried.

"What did I expect from him anyway? He would rather spend time with Phillip downstairs than at home with Dave and me!"

Then she remembered, Phillip was on tour and left his keys with them. She went to look for the keys, but they were not on their usual place on the hallway mirror.

"Maybe I was too unfair to Felix," she felt sorry and thought about apologizing. They were stressed with Dave sickness, the nanny leaving without notice and their daily arguments and problems.

"He brought me flowers this morning," she looked at the pretty bouquet in the crystal vase. She felt guilty for yelling at Felix but most of all, she was sorry for herself.

"At least now the nanny is gone, and there would be no one sleeping on the cot next to our bed tonight" strategized Victoria. "Maybe I would be able to make it up to Felix."

She checked on Dave who finally fell asleep, touched his forehead and realized that his temperature broke. He was breathing quietly and seemed comfortable. She returned to the kitchen, but she could not bear a thought of dealing with unwashed laundry and growing puddle.

She smeared on lipstick and went to Phillip's apartment to apologize and to bring Felix back. She took an elevator down and looked into the eyehole on the door. She could see the light inside; of course, Felix was there. She pressed the bell. Fast shadows moved in the apartment, but nobody answered the door. She was ringing and ringing the bell to no avail.

She felt the anger as a fire raging in her chest. "Dave is sick; I am desperate with the child and the laundry, and he is free in Phillip's studio! He is a terrible father and even worse husband. Why he is not opening the door?"

Suddenly she knew. "O, my god, he is not alone!"

She pushed the door with her hands, she jerked the door handle, and she pushed and pushed the door with her shoulder. She was enraged and furious, but somewhere inside her, ice calm slowly raised to her head. She knew exactly what she was doing.

After two locks gave up, the door finally opened. Victoria calmly moved Felix out of her way and went to search the apartment.

"There is nobody here, Vika," Felix trailed behind her.

"If you were alone, you would open this door a long time before I broke these locks."

She was almost smiling when she found the acquaintance, the woman from the next building, hiding on the balcony. Galya was a short, plain- looking single mom. Victoria knew her only because her daughter often played with Dave outside in the sandbox. She had a job at a TV studio, and Victoria saw her once at a party at this very same apartment.

Victoria looked at the scared woman and sneered; this cliché was so beneath her. She left and took an elevator to the sixth floor.

Dave was still sleeping as she loaded Felix's clothes into a suitcase.

When the doorbell rang, she picked up the heavy crystal vase with flowers that Felix brought this morning. She opened the door and tossed the vase with water and flowers straight into upset Felix. The vase shattered with a loud pop splashing them both with water. Victoria picked up a suitcase and wanted to send it right after the vase, but Felix stopped her and came in.

"Victoria, you are completely nuts; nothing happened. The only mistake I made was not to open the door right away. She came to see Phil, and we were just talking where you showed up. I knew you were crazy but why to break the door, and for what reason exactly?" He was almost crying.

Still seething Victoria took her wedding band off her finger. She went to the balcony and threw it into a wild shrubbery below. "I do not want to see you ever again. Leave now!"

*****

I looked at Felix comfortably sleeping on the bed. My heart was beating fast and loud, and at this minute, I was as young and furious as over forty years ago. Felix had always denied that anything happened in Phil's studio apartment that night. It did not make any difference after all.

Youth does not believe in experience, does not think that things will change with the time. The decades passed since this memorable evening. We were lucky to save our marriage, to renew our union, and find our almost lost love.

I looked at my husband who every day tells me how much he loves me, who brings me flowers every week and writes love poems for me in three languages and my heart slowed down and filled with tenderness and love.

I quietly got to the bed beside him. We had an early start tomorrow.

DAY 34, SEPT 30
SPRINGDALE, UT
ZION NATIONAL PARK
HAMPTON INN & SUITES

I always knew that we were the travelers. Not like everyday tourists who flocked to Rome and Paris, London and Bangkok, Sydney and Buenos Aires. Everybody knew and visited these cities, had a map or souvenir to prove it and recited fluently places and attractions.

True travelers admired incredibly beautiful Brisbane, stately Santiago, enchanted Kyoto, and full of life and history Manaus. They crawled the dunes in Namibia, visited villages on the stilts in Ghana, sailed through Marlborough and Milford Sounds in New Zealand, played with lemurs in Madagascar, rode camels in Petra and took underwater photos in Tahiti.

There are legends and tales of Yosemite, and crowds in Yellowstone, but until the itinerary from our travel agent, we did not know anything about Zion National Park.

We were almost an hour early for the date with our guide and much too early for the touristy crowds because we did not realize how close we were to the simple gate of stone boulders with the iron plaque "Zion National Park," chained to the wooden crossbar.

Dark and mysterious mountains surrounded us. The late September morning was cold and invigorating as the first rays of sun lighted up the cliffs. The sun was getting higher, but we were still shivering in awesome solitude. A majestic light show was playing out in a deep canyon that pioneers called "color country." Pink and white interlocked with deep wine, embellished by dark green at the bottom, when immense mountain slowly gave up its deep crevices and threatening heights to bright light and sunshine. There were no more secrets or mysteries.

TALES FROM MOSCOW
MOSCOW, RUSSIA, THE 1970S

Victoria still did not know where it was going. They were separated but still married; they loved and took care of the kids together, they were friends with their own lives and their significant others.

She did not want to judge her Moscow cousins. Inna and Lusik were married and had two girls. Heredity was not very kind to them, the older girl Alla was born with Down Syndrome and was very nearsighted. The younger girl Bunny was an angel; blond with beautiful blue eyes she was a darling of the family, but she too was legally blind. The family was heartbroken, and everybody burned to say, "We told you so," but had a heart, and a pity, and watched in silence. The girls were the fruits of two incestuous marriages between cousins in two consecutive generations. Were Jewish laws so smart to allow it?

Inna, the principal of one of the best Moscow schools, and her retired Dad spent all their time and efforts to give the girls a normal life. There were no schools for special needs children in the Soviet capital.

Life was not easy for Inna when at the Party meeting she met a distinguished, handsome CEO and fell in love all over again. They were smart, and they managed to keep the affair secret for years, but now, when it was discovered, he was threatened with expulsion from the Party, loss of his career, livelihood, and family.

Inna took the girls and moved out of her home. The parents, cousins, aunts and uncles, mothers and fathers-in-law, the whole Gordian's knot of the Moscow clan was devastated.

A visiting Victoria was leaving Moscow with a heavy heart. She had no solution to the failed marriages, upset and confused kids, passions of new romance and suicidal affairs.

The Moscow family's demise cascaded over the years.

In spite of Inna's hopes, the handsome communist choose his Party membership card and publicly denounced their love.

Lusik had a fatal heart attack a year after the divorce; he was in his forties.

After Lusik's death, Inna had parted with the family. She lived alone for the rest of her life; her father helped with the girls. As principal of the prestigious Moscow school, Inna devoted all her time to work. She died at 85 in her school office.

Babushka's beautiful sister Fanny, who suffered undiagnosed and untreated back pain for years, did not want to outlive her son. She was not able to stand; she hanged herself sitting next to the radiator.

Her husband Marcus remarried a young woman. A few years later, after his death, the big family house on the quiet street outside of Moscow with all its content went to his new wife and her sons. Jenny was tied up in the endless and hopeless litigation for years.

Two brothers Yasha and Abram lived to old age. Abram buried his two granddaughters; Alla died at age eighteen of leukemia, blind Bunny was killed by a drunk driver who tried to park on the Moscow sidewalk.

Good-natured, always smiling Yasha continued to work until his late seventies; his patients adored him. He lived alone after his adopted daughter Tanya threw him out of his apartment. She beat him up, threw anti-Semitic swears, and accused him of wanting to make her "a dirty Jew."

Jenny's son Ilusha got married young and named his son Lenya. The name still held its appeal for the family. A few years later, after a fight with a militiaman, Ilusha ended up in prison for years. It was incredibly sad to see what happened; a solid branch of the old tree suddenly dried out and was ready to fall.

Before Victoria left the country, she brought her sons to see Moscow and the family. They stayed with Jenny and her husband, the lone survivors of the love tsunami.

They toured the Moscow's all the prerequisite tourist attractions; Victoria telling them that this was their last chance to see Moscow. As they walked the beautiful old street, Victoria pushed the front door of the nearby building. The boys followed her inside. It was a stately building with a wide marble staircase.

"Your grandfather Lenya had many friends in Moscow. One of them, Peter Markowitz was a famous music critic, and he lived in this building. Many famous musicians, composers and the members of the Union of Soviet composers lived here."

"I don't remember how old I was, probably five or six years old, the most," however she could see Peter in a fur-lined coat and a bright bow tie, her young Dad in wide-brimmed hat sailing above his tall figure and her red winter coat and terribly cold hands. "After Dad and I visited with Peter, we were coming downstairs, when a tall old man walked in from the street. I was little, so everybody was tall and old. The man wore a winter coat, black fur pie-hat, and the gloves. Peter, who was seeing us out, introduced Dad and me to the man, who took off his gloves, bent over to me and shook my cold hand. He asked me something, I do not remember what, and smiled. He left, and we went to the street.

"Victoria, never wash your hand again," said my Dad seriously. "Serge Prokofiev just shook your hand!"

*****

We met our guide and started with a spectacular morning shuttle ride through the Zion Park. We did not know where to turn first. The names of the majestic mountains were equally sacred: the Three Patriarchs; the Court, Angel's Landing, The Throne; all of them awoke religious awe.

Led by our intrepid eighty-four-year-old guide, we took a Virgin Riverwalk to The Narrow. Even the capital N in the "Narrows" cannot describe the immenseness of the six thousand feet tall mountains with only twenty feet of sparkling clear cold Virgin River between the cliffs. The river did not have banks, only the walls of the canyon as if nature knew that less is more.

The eighty- four- year- old docent, who supposed to sit in his office, was not pleased with our lame and watchful attitude. He was way ahead of us; he wanted to hike, to climb and to conquer. We were too slow for him, and we did not want to waddle in the cold knee-high water with stones- lined- bottom.

For being lazy tourists who would not hike, our guide awarded us with a scenic car ride to the top in his twenty-year- old Honda.

We went on roads that I do not want to remember, through yet another "narrow," the one-way tunnel with a cutout window into the other side of the canyon, which was only an arm-length away. We emerged on the other side of the claustrophobic tunnel to abundant sunshine and summer temperature. We were on the top of the mountain, literary the arm-length close to every stone, every wrinkle, and every splash of the color on the cliffs around us. It was remarkable beauty, majesty, and elegance, a fascinating cancan of lights and shadows.

We were not out of danger though in that old Honda, driven by the old man, on the high canyon road with a deep ravine on one side and oncoming cars on the other. I tried to keep my eyes closed but noticed Felix's surprised face.

"You never sleep in the car, Victoria, what's the matter?" He turned back from the front passenger's seat.

"I closed my eyes in the utter horror and fear to end at the bottom of the canyon! I do not know who is older, our driver or his car!" Thank god for my Russian, docent could not understand me. "Please, give me my phone, Felix. I want to have it on me, just in case we end up on the bottom of the canyon; not that it is going to help us anyway."

We were safely back to the gate, as our guide was laying out the program for the afternoon: another walk, another drive, and maybe a hike to the sunset. The old man still wanted us to explore, and he looked at poor me with pity and contempt. However, I had had enough; I did not want to see another mountain as long as I live. My all senses were flooded, all circuit breakers were shortened, and my back was not happy with all that walking.

"What is the best way to Lake Powell, Arizona? We are driving there tomorrow," I asked innocently, planning our escape.

"O, just under hundred miles. Take the road through the same tunnel on the mountain, and you will be there at no time," he was smiling.

We went to a local supermarket and bought a bottle of Scotch, cold cuts and cheese.

For the rest of the day, we drank and mapped our alternative, about two hundred miles longer route out of Springdale with no mountains roads. We were visually and physically overwhelmed, almost crushed, by the beauty and majesty of Zion Canyon, however, by the end, we became the Zionists, of course.

DAY 35, OCTOBER 1
BIG WATER, UT
LAKE POWELL
HOTEL AMANGIRI

W e drove the extra miles through pretty countryside with Indian reservations and row after row of cute low mountains looking like pink pressure cookers with covers. All to find the hotel without an address and a sign; the address in our GPS was in a different state altogether. We had to call for directions three times while driving in the circles within two miles of the hotel. Finally, the friendly concierge informed us, "If you are in Arizona, you are too far. Please, turn around and after a road marker "two miles" take an unmarked mountain road on the left."

The unpaved road curled around stone formations in every shade of red, white and yellow only to end up in front of the closed gate with yet another endless stony road behind it. By some miracle, the gate slowly opened and after a few minutes, we arrived at a small landing in front of the wide granite staircase. There was no hotel or even a sign in site. As we were contemplating where we should go to look for the hotel now, the car doors opened and two young men greeted us, "Welcome to Amangiri!" They were holding silver trays with champagne flutes. "Please, feel free to browse or to visit with our concierge while we unload your luggage to your room."

The view from the floor to ceiling windows did not need

any enhancement by champagne. Large pool with floating lounges hugged a huge monolith beautifully painted by the best impressionist, Nature itself. The guests who, unlike us, did not have a problem locating the hotel, lunched at the tables around the pool. "Sir, your wine just arrived on a private plane from Germany," we overheard a waiter informing a patron.

We took a tour of the property where every structure was built of the local stone incorporating the slope of the mountain. Nothing here looked man-made. Large candles in glass cases lit the pass.

Our room was no less impressive. Small pool with goldfish and an apple tree full of delicious apple were in the entryway. Massive walls, all granite, supported a high ceiling. We admired an enormous bathroom and an outside deck with built- in lounges around a fireplace/ grill. A bowl of fruits on the table and refrigerator with all kinds of snacks made us feel welcome. It was expensive but well deserved after years of honest and hard work. On a shelf was an artfully framed large black and white landscape. On the background, like a double exposure, I saw another life, another place, another time.

CAMARADERIE
KIEV, UKRAINE, THE 1940S

f the "blue blood" were a contagious disease, then Monya had it. There were no "blue blood" Jews in Ukraine, and although Monya's father Abram Solomonovich Levin came from a very well to do family and studied at the prestigious Heidelberg University in Germany, he was not "blue blood." Abram Levin was a tall, wide-shouldered man with straight straw-blond hair and intense blue eyes on a broad rectangular face with a strong chin. Little Victoria had to tilt her head back all the way to talk to Monya's father as if looking at the sky.

The story, which made Abram Levin's blood blue, was that while at the Heidelberg University, handsome Abram met and became a good friend with another student from Russia, the Great Duke Constantin. The two spent much time together and helped each other with their studies. The expatriate Duke, who was a part of the Tsar's family, got as a graduation present from the Tsar a tour around the world on the Royal Yacht.

The University, well known for its liberalism, taught its students well and the Duke invited his Jewish friend Abram Levin to sail with him. However, the good ideas of a liberal education were short-lived in the Tsar's family, and an invitation was standing only under the condition that Abram would convert and become a Christian.

After the Christening, newly minted Alexander, aka Abram, traveled the world in a glorious company of "blue blood"; however, The First World War and Revolution brought him back home where he promptly converted back to Abram and married a wealthy Jewish girl, Sofia.

Sofia's father owned sugar plants. Beautiful Sofia, with her dark eyes, updo hair and waspy waist, was used to the finer things in life. Handsome well-educated Abram was her true love along with the gifted Tsar's fine china, crystal, and silver he brought home from his trip.

Their only son Solomon was an exact copy of his father. His parents adored him, but there was no Heidelberg University or Grand Duke in his future; considering his birthplace, he was lucky to be accepted to Kiev Medical School.

The new Medical School students, Lenya, Jack, Misha and Solomon (shortened to simple Monya) met on their first day, on their first lecture on human anatomy and became friends. This friendship guided their future and lighted up their lives until the very end.

They looked funny walking in the middle of the street, their hands on each other shoulders. Crispy new doctors' diplomas filled them with pride and hope. Three tall and one short Jewish boys, they were the doctors now. The late June night was warm; they had just danced the night away at their graduation, and the world was full of joy and promise.

They had no idea what had happened when the first German bombs fell on the streets of Kiev. In no time, the graduation's class was loaded into two tracks at the railroad station.

"Don't you understand?" pleaded Lenya at the local military office. "We are the doctors and would be much more useful on the battlefield as doctors rather than soldiers." When he returned to the station, the bomb had hit one of the tracks with less than a half of his classmates surviving the carnage.

Monya was running. He wished he would be thin, short, and easy to hide. He tried to find and join the Red Army by heading to the West, but the Germans were everywhere, and he had lost all hopes. After months of hiding during the day, he walked into a small village at night and knocked on the first door.

In the morning, he erased "n' in his last name. Now his Diploma said S.A. Levi; his straight yellow- blonde hair and blue eyes helped his transformation to doctor Savely Alexandrovich Levi.

The German army rolled on to the East and North in its victorious "blitzkrieg" and on its way had left a loyal Czech battalion in a village near the Ukrainian town Kirovograd. Germans were everywhere, and there was nowhere to go.

"It is better to lay low here, where it seems like the world's end," decided Monya. He found an abandoned hut and wrote "Dr. Levi" on the door.

The priest, one of the first patients of the young doctor, was impressed. Not only was the man a good doctor, but a good company as well. On long winter nights, they played cards with Czech officers. The players usually gathered in the church and between rounds, they listen to Monya's stories about Christianity, holidays and the Great Duke, a friend of his father, Alexander. Time stalled in the godforsaken Ukrainian village behind the front lines.

After a fiasco in Stalingrad, retreating Germans were angry and brutal. They checked and rechecked, and hunted Jews and communists, partisans and sympathizers and Dr. Levi was ordered to come to Kirovograd "to chat." Monya considered running, but he knew he would not get far in the dead of winter. He was also worried what would happen to Ana, his blond fifteen-year-old assistant, the daughter of the neighbor whose door he knocked on over two years ago; he was secretly in love with her and would not leave her alone. He went to Kirovograd.

The winter wind was merciless, and dark sky promised more snow. Monya stood on "the Platz" in front of Commendatory and could not take another step.

"I will never see the light of the day again!" the thought was beating in his mind like a frightened bird in the cage. It endlessly repeated an ugly tune of a German song his German card partner Otto played in the church last night. "They will kill me! They will kill me", he almost whistled to the tune. He looked around at the dreadful gray town, gathered all his will, straightened his tall figure and entered the building.

The Gestapo officer sat behind the imposing desk of his predecessor, the previous owner of the room, the District Secretary of the Communist Party.

"Doctor Levi, welcome; I have heard a lot about you."

Monya felt terribly alone at this large scarcely decorated room with a gloomy winter day behind high, floor to ceiling, windows.

"Please, take a seat; I have a few questions," said the Officer, "about your family." He almost whispered, and Monya was ready to repeat all the "blue blood" stories he ever knew, when suddenly the officer yelled, "Jude! Dirty Jew! Communist!"

Monya jumped out of his seat. He was ready to get his hands on this bastard, but aiming straight at him gun barrel stopped him.

He backed up to his chair and said quietly," You have the wrong man, officer. Please, check my documents. I am doctor Savely Alexandrovich Levi."

He noticed a small side door opened and his last night's card partner Otto entered the room. Monya's heart sank; now he was against two Germans and had no chance.

"Documents?" Gestapo officer smiled sarcastically. "Documents? Take off your pants, Doctor!"

The circumcised man was a sure Jew! No one else was circumcised in the country of socialists and atheists.

Monya slowly rose from his chair, "Pants? You want me to take off my pants?"

With the last words, he tore off the buttons on his fly and dropped his pants, exposing warm blue long johns.

"Go on, doctor!" ordered the officer, his gun on the desk in front of him.

"I would never be able to reach for this gun with my pants down," Monya contemplated bitterly.

His cheeks flushed, his voice boomed when with "Here are my pants for you!" he tore his long underpants only to expose yet another layer of boxer shorts. He was swearing loudly, fumbling with his clothes, when Otto whispered to the officer, "It is enough; could not you see he is a real 'muzhik' (a Russian peasant)?"

Shaken and exhausted but alive Monya returned to the village. The cold winter sun was sparkling on the fresh snow, and Ana, beautiful Ana, was pacing nervously in front of his office.

She was tall and shy, a daughter of a local fisherman. A long blond braid crowned her fresh face. She was smart and kind, and she volunteered to help the doctor in the office. She was fifteen and in love.

There was no time for romance, but they were young and tomorrow was dark, gloomy, and not predictable. Monya was busy with sick and wounded, and Ana stayed in the office after a long day. It was too dangerous to walk anytime, but especially, at night.

Otto knocked at the door before sunrise. "Doctor, for your ears only! We will take all the able female workers to Germany tomorrow. Freight cars are already at the station. Please, send Ana home to pick up her things."

They did not have a plan, so they just hugged and cried. Finally, Ana got up; she had to say goodbye to her parents. She knew what to expect; her girlfriend served as a sex-slave at the brothel in Germany. She wrote two letters to Ana, warning her to avoid German roundups; however, the last message was over a year ago, and then Ana hoped that the war would be over soon.

Surgery was not Monya's favorite subject, and he tried to avoid operating room when he was in the medical school. He was not a star student, and he did not plan to be a surgeon. Nevertheless, just like when he stood on the Platz before Commendatory, Monya stood in his hut now in front of an improvised operating table. His hands were shaking, the emptiness in his chest made him lightheaded, and he was whiter than pale but determined Ana on the table.

She was not afraid. "Monya, please, cut me where my appendix supposed to be! I will be fine, I am strong and healthy, and I will not go to Germany!"

When soldiers came for Ana next morning, she could not move after emergency surgery to remove her inflamed appendix. She was pale from losing too much blood and had a huge fresh incision with amateurish sutures on her right lower abdomen.

Two springs later, at the end of the war and as soon as Monya's parents returned to Kiev, Monya brought home his young pregnant wife.

She loved her new parents, Kiev, his Jewish friends and Royal China. However, for the rest of her long life, most of all, she loved her Monichka, Doctor Solomon Abramovich Levin.

*****

"You are all set," concierge informed us. "I was able to secure a tour on the Lake Powell for you in the morning." The sun was ready to retire in the crib of pink mountains, and strange music on the large deck accompanied its descent. Was it music at all?

KIEV, UKRAINE, THE 1950S

By the time Victoria was five, "the gang" of her Dad's medical school classmates had over ten years of friendship under their belts, so Victoria had recognized them as a family and called them the uncles. Later, as the young and handsome doctors got married, there were aunts as well, but they were not as important or as much fun.

Lenya and his friends usually gathered in his one-room apartment, sat in a tight circle around a small table, drank and talked. Victoria grew up with them and their stories. Her Dad had a student photo of four of them, and Victoria remembered them just as they were in that old picture, young with smiley faces and curly, far from gray, hair.

They all went to medical school together, survived the war, and were jobless and poor in a Kiev destroyed by the war.

They defended their country and did not have time to complain or to blame; they rolled up their sleeves and went to work. They worked as handymen or roofers, moonlighted in Emergency Rooms, taught at colleges, treated patients and built their lives. At night, they told jokes and sang old Russian romances.

Comaradery

Handsome Misha Bonferman was a kind and quiet man who usually did not say much. He was the youngest in the family of four brothers, their mother's pride, the only doctor in the working class family. He was the only one of four brothers who returned from the war.

He was the first to find a job, making home visits. He married his blond high school sweetheart, and they settled in his mother's apartment. They had two children, a daughter, and a son, a young happy family. He gave his heartbroken mom grandchildren to help her back to life; however, life was not kind to him. Misha had a fatal heart attack at work when he was not yet forty-five. His mother survived all four of her sons and lived a long life. Ten years later, she danced at her granddaughter's wedding. Victoria and her Mom were there. It was the fateful night when Victoria met Felix.

Jack came from an old Kiev family. He was tall and handsome. His blond hair was straight and fell on a high forehead, shading his beautiful blue eyes. He was the only one who paid attention to his clothes, and he always looked elegant and dashing. His mother Maria brought up her two boys alone; she was one of the best beauticians in the city. When they returned to Kiev after the war, her younger son, Igor, was still in Music School. Jack, the doctor, was looking for work. He was lucky; he was single and still lived with his Mom. In the hungry years after the war, every week he faithfully delivered a present from his Mother: a half a cup of semolina for Victoria's breakfast. Apparently, women in Kiev still valued a good facial.

Jack's younger brother became a famous Ukrainian composer, but in this far-away 1948, he was playing accordion at the wedding of Lenya's sister Mila.

Jack was the dream of every woman and the life of every party. He got married and divorced and enjoyed his single life. As soon as Lenya got a position at the Dnieper River Steamship Line's clinic, he helped Jack who was a Urologist to get a job there too. They were real friends.

The usual evening party in Lenya's room was in full swing. They did not need a reason for the party; friendship was enough. Everybody was eager to eat and to talk, to discuss literature and politics. The literary crowd mixed with doctors, beginners with celebrities; they were young and poor, no one was rich then.

The famous conductor of the Kiev Symphony Orchestra Nathan Rachlin usually stayed after visiting Lenya as a doctor. He was Lenya's private patient getting his course of intravenous injection of glucose and vitamins, and he loved to chat with Lenya and his friends.

There were Anatoly Polyakov, the famous movie director from Kiev Movie Studio, promising young poet gorgeous redhead Arnold, Diodor Bobir, well-known translator of Ukrainian Poetry with his wife Masha who translated French Poetry to Russian and who always brought her tall black poodle Mishka waiting for scraps of food. Boris Babich felt very much at home next to Felly May, the prominent journalist earlier imprisoned for cosmopolitism. An always-hungry writer Serge Shwarzoid was there as was Victor Nekrasov who just published his new book "In the trenches of Stalingrad." They drank shots of pure alcohol and smoked papiroses (a cigarette with a mouthpiece) called Belomorcanal.

"You have to meet this woman, Jack," Lenya was having a very private conversation with Jack at the crowded table. "She is lovely," he persisted. "Her mom was our professor at the medical school, you should remember her!" Jack did not remember and was not about to give up his newly founded freedom after divorce. He already had his mom on his case trying to marry him off again.

"Lena was married and had a son. Her husband had died suddenly at the dinner table; he was only twenty-seven then, and it was a real tragedy. Lena is brilliant, and she teaches at medical school too. Can we, please, go for dinner somewhere on a double date; I cannot invite her to this apartment." Lenya loved being married; he did not understand "What is your problem, Jack?"

The evening of the date was cold with a steady rain, not like the late April rain was supposed to be. Lenya and Sarra, Jack and Lena were drenched and squeezed in at their corner table at the noisy restaurant. Lenya bravely tried to entertain his friends, neither of whom wanted to be there. To add to the damage, Jack stabbed his Chicken Kiev way too hard and, in revenge, it sprayed everybody at the table with hot oil. The famous dish hopelessly ruined their dressy outfits. Guilty Jack saw Lena home, and to Lenya's surprise, the next day he was raving about the great time they had. The rest was history. They loved each other for the next fifteen years.

Jack remained handsome and fun; he was Victoria's best friend.

"What was this new dance you were dancing, Victoria?" he asked at the party for Lenya's birthday.

"It is a new dance, Uncle Jack, called rock-n-roll. You have to step like that". Teenage Victoria was eager to teach Uncle Jack the latest craze.

Three hours later, she was awakened in the middle of the night by her Dad. "Victoria, get up!" Her Dad was bewildered and angry. "There is Jack on the phone for you, and he does not want to explain to me why he is calling you at two in the morning!"

"Victoria, darling, thank you for teaching me that dance," excited Jack almost screamed in the phone. "There was no taxi and Aunt Lena, and I rock- n- rolled all the way to our home. Took us over two hours, sorry for the late call."

*****

Felix showed me a small flyer announcing a presentation by Navajo Indians, and we rushed outside on the patio.

The older man, Brown Horse, had a red bandanna and massive turquoise and silver bracelet on his left wrist. He presented his young niece and nephew dressed in beautiful, colorful costumes. She played the drum, and the boy showed us the ritual dances. In one of them, he personified various images of birds and animals by artfully arranging numerous plastic hoops, while he was dancing to the drum roll. It was fascinating. Then, Brown Horse explained how we could reach happiness, joy, and peace.

When Brown Horse insisted that one could reach perfect equilibrium and tranquility by conquering one's fears, I was immediately sorry that I did not drive the treacherous route nine west from Springdale, Utah.

He almost convinced us to convert to their beautiful and straightforward religion with its beauty, its healing miracles, and its taboos. Unfortunately, he also told us that The Divine Being extended its advantages and restrictions only to the Navajos. They were sure they were "the chosen." It is always helpful to listen to the other side.

We walked back to our room on the pass lit up by the candles. The shadows of the past danced on the beautiful falling- asleep- mountains; colorful people of Brown Horse and black and white shadows of my memory creating a fantastic double exposure. I could see them clearly in the darkness; they all stayed alive as long as we remembered them.

DAY 36, OCTOBER 2
BIG WATER, UT
LAKE POWELL
HOTEL AMANGIRI

"We will be at the Grand Canyon tomorrow!" I could not hold my excitement.

"Good Morning would be nice," said Felix still half-asleep.

"Come on, Felix, get up! Today we have a boat ride on the lake right after breakfast, but a grand day would be tomorrow, at The Grand Canyon.

The view from our room was majestic. The sun, like Felix, was not quite up yet. It was still hiding behind pink mountains; however, the first rays managed to escape and to add a pale blush to the rare high clouds. The tall dry grass rustled in the mild wind. It was all peace and quiet in the Land of Navajos.

The concierge promised to drive us to the boat. From a distance, a small bright patch of the blue and turquoise lake among the rocks did not impress us. We were too busy admiring blankets and lunch "to go" provided by the hotel.

The concierge deposited us with all the stuff safely on the boat. He introduced us to our Captain Bryan and off we went. Nobody warned us what we were up to, so we settled to see the Lake Powell and the Glen Canyon Dam, second in height only to Hoover.

The day was sunny, with some autumn breeze and our boat

was fast. The lake looked like a great river with dendrites of the canyons. We took turn after turn on the elegant Antelope Canyon where the Lake looked like an Enchanted River in ancient Egypt. The water was emerald green and reflected tall cliffs of every possible shade of pink, brown, yellow and black silently towering above us. We were alone on a small, now slowly moving boat and we whispered in complete awe. We admired beautiful marines and envied the owners of elaborate houseboats. We sailed through the Navajo Canyon flooded by the Lake, hypnotized by majesty and beauty of the woman's face painted on the cliff by Nature. Was it a portrait of the Navajo Goddess, the Queen of this matriarchate society? Neither our Captain nor we had the answer. In spite of the warm sun and all the jackets and blankets, courtesy of the hotel, we were cold to the bones, sailing through the wind combing clear and cold waters of the magical lake.

We were smitten and speechless, overwhelmed and dazed by all the beauty and splendor. Maybe we did need a vaccine against beauty that makes us cry.

Back at our patio at the Hotel, we warmed up and had our lunch by the outside fireplace. We soaked in the hot tub and went for a late dinner. It was just another day on the road.

THE CAMARADERIE
KIEV, UKRAINE, THE 1960S

"No! No! No!" Lenya's cry woke up Victoria and Felix at five in the morning. They did not hear the phone ring, but they found Lenya standing in his striped pajamas in the middle of the long hallway with the telephone receiver in his hand. He was sobbing. He tried to cover his face quivering in the unimaginable pain, with his other hand. Jack died in his sleep at age forty-eight. Lena went on to become a professor, well known in the medical world academician, and the director of Victoria's Ph.D. thesis on the genetics of heart disease.

A few years after Jack's death, she remarried a world checker champion, Iser Kuperman. She remained very close friends with Lenya until his death.

Monya died at the bus stop while waiting for the bus; he was not sixty yet. Until the end, Ana was dreaming of leaving Russia but, without Monya, she had no chance. Their daughter and granddaughter are still living in Kiev. Misha Bonferman's family moved to America. The fateful marriage that got together Victoria and Felix did not last.

*****

In the cozy dining room of the restaurant, the fireplace was roaring with playful flames. "Do you think our parents ever saw the working fireplace?" I asked Felix.

"Of course, they did." Felix thought for a second. "Well, maybe, not."

"I am sure they had read about fireplaces and perhaps saw them in the museums." I was bewildered now. "Such a small thing. They were robbed of everything, even the simplest pleasures".

In the dancing light of the fireplace, I could see them clearly.

Our small dining room that converted to my and Ella's bedroom at night. My Dad is presiding at the head of the table with a bottle of vodka and small glasses next to the plates with potato salad and herring. My parents' friends are all there, telling jokes and laughing loudly.

"Victoria, a tea kettle is boiling in the kitchen," Dad is trying to be diplomatic getting me out of the room. "Can you, please, go and shut it off?" Apparently, the anecdote is not suitable for my fifteen-year-old ears.

They would fit right here, next to this fireplace at the large table in the room with pink Arizona mountains behind the window.

All my life I had envied my parents. I desperately wanted to learn how they got all these incredible friends and how they managed to keep them for the rest of their lives. I was afraid I would never have friends like their classmates from medical school, loyal friends, and wonderful doctors with stellar careers in a country difficult to survive in. They all had died before their time. They survived the war, Soviet reality, Stalin and antisemitism; but in their forties, fifties, and sixties they were dying of broken hearts, fear, horrible diets, and hopeless life.

People find their friends when they are young, at schools and colleges; they share their plans and dreams and accept each other, as they are, simple and single.

It is hard and almost impossible to build a real friendship later in life. Especially, when you change your country and the language. We were fortunate.

Not only we met new real friends at the new land, but we also kept them and our old friends from Russia, for the last forty years. We love them, trust them, and think of them as our family. We keep them just as my parents did, for life. We are so lucky to live in the country that we love and respect, the country that took us in and became our true motherland, treated us fairly and gave us every opportunity to succeed.

DAY 37, OCTOBER 3
GRAND CANYON NATIONAL PARK, AZ
HOTEL EL TOVAR

I t was a small river with a big name, Colorado River. We stopped to admire the smooth walls of Powell Dam and took in the last glimpse of the incredible lake Powell with a sad parting sigh. I drove on the winding roads south through blooming yellow desert and vast Indian lands with trading posts selling colorful jewelry and beautiful crafts. A trivial sign "Grand Canyon" at the T-intersection was not grand at all and displayed arrows in the opposite directions, "South Rim" and "North Rim".

If the Earth was flat, somebody could post a sign "End of the Earth" and people would just stop casually and turn in the needed direction. We turned south.

A light wind was nothing to us, but after million- years of tedious work on the stone, it created amazing monsters and sphinxes all along the road. We drove a time machine through centuries and millennials to the core of the country.

DAD
GORBASHOVKA, UKRAINE, THE 1930S

Revolution and Civil war destroyed and changed everything, but did not scare Asya who kept her family in the relatively quiet harbor of a Ukrainian village. Her children were outstanding students, and Asya decided that now, when her younger brother Yasha became a doctor, her son would be a doctor too, just like his uncle.

However, Lenya, the tall and handsome teenager, had in mind quite a different road; he was sure his destination was the theater.

Victoria could never understand what genetic confuse happened with her father. How and where did he inherit his dreams and talents? From whom and on what Olympus did he acquire them?

Ambitions, strong will, and spectacular memory came, without question, from his mother, but his booming singing voice and perfect pitch, a talent for poetry and storytelling combined with intelligence, eloquence and great looks were gifts from the gods. These were generous gifts for a seventeen-year-old boy from a god-forsaken village.

The new Soviet order was simple; there was no place in any school for the son of an artist and a homemaker. The only thing that mattered was provenance; the schools were for the children of working class; excellent school records and talent meant nothing. To get an education, Asya's boy had to have "proletarian roots," and his mother would stop at nothing.

"Volf, pack your brushes," she said on the warm June night. They were just finishing their supper of boiled potatoes and salad of cut tomatoes and onions. The room became still, and a light cotton curtain that separated the parents' bedroom from the dining room did not move.

"We are moving to Kiev."

Volf's near-sighted eyes followed his wife, who was cleaning the table. Even at night, her arms were flying, and she was still full of plans and energy.

"Eleazar has to go to school," Asya was not pleading, she merely told her family what to do. She always used their Yiddish names when she was excited or angry.

"To medical school," she added not looking at her older son, who was scribbling a few rhymed lines on a piece of paper. His sister Mila started her school homework on the cleaned dinner table.

Asya looked at her family; she did not want to move to an unknown big city, but her boy, her love, and pride, the best student at his school, had to get an education. She was sure Lenya had to go to medical school, and for that, he needed a proletarian family.

Next morning Volf quit his job at the fine china factory, Asya packed boxes and tied bundles, and the family boarded a train to Kiev.

To secure the needed "proletarian origin" for his son, Volf found a job as a metalworker at the big plant. He was the same slim, shy and quiet man he was about twenty years ago when they got married. He wore the same black suit and the same cap, hiding his thick glasses. He did not like a tram that brought him to the plant; it was too noisy and shaky.

He knew he was lucky to get this new job; "For Lenichka," he smiled at his wife. However, he had no idea how to operate this frightening machinery; it was worse than a tram.

He missed his quiet place by the window and his fine brushes made of the best sable fur; he missed dusty Gorbashovka and green grass in his yard. He lasted all of two days; on the third day, he almost died a victim of a horrible industrial accident. He came back from the hospital without his right arm. He will never paint beautiful flowers again.

After the accident, with his father being a real proletarian now, Lenya was accepted to both Medical and Theatrical schools. He loved theater, but his father's arm was a too steep price for the theater school. With his mother's approval and his father's kind smile, he became a doctor. For his parents, no cost was too high for their son's doctor diploma.

*****

I took off my sunglasses to read the sign "The first view of the Grand Canyon," it was silly and exciting at the same time. After Yellowstone, Yosemite, Lake Powell, and Zion we did not need a warning.

The view stunned and numbed us. It made us mute. It felt sacrilegious to open the camera, to smile or to talk. We witnessed Mother Earth's divine show played for the billions of years.

The late sunset painted the last shadows in the canyon, and we retreated to the splendid Al Tovar Hotel and its impressive restaurant. We were beaten and subdued by the grandiosity and proximity of the canyon.

Only once, in my life had I experienced something remotely similar. We were on vacation in Hawaii on Kauai Island. Somebody suggested to us to go to the best beach on the far end of the island, beyond the military base. We decided it would be a fantastic day trip and we drove to the end of the highway armed with a map and a bottle of water. Felix got a bit nervous when we hit a dirt road running among fields of tall sugar cane.

"On the map, this road looks only a few miles long," I informed him cheerfully.

The time was before cell phones and GPS. The last civilized life we saw before leaving the highway was the military base. Tall cliffs bordered the sugar cane fields on the right, and as soon as we were on the narrow dirt road, nothing but the sugarcanes were all around the car.

Felix drove slowly, and we did not see another car for about seven miles when suddenly the sugarcanes parted.

An incredibly wide beautiful sandy beach was in front of us. It ended up on the right with the cliff going right into the ocean and on the left with no end to sand and waves. Turquoise waters crowned with foamy white crests were rising and falling in huge waves licking spectacular beach. There was nobody on it; we were completely alone, small and defenseless against all that powerful, majestic nature. I felt like a Lilliputian in a country of Gullivers, overwhelmed, threatened and scared, small and miserable compared to Nature.

It was unbearable to be alone against all these elements, and we left. We surrendered; we were no match to the cliffs and ocean, to the sun and wind and even to the endless swatch of the warm white sand. We deserted and drove back seven miles of the dirt road ashamed by our capitulation and in awe of the majestic Nature that had beaten us so easily without any fight.

I turned off the light and looked out. The Grand Canyon laid quietly under the window.

DAD
KIEV, UKRAINE, THE 1940S

I t was a great mystery that even Lenya himself could not explain. He could hypnotize. With his velvety low baritone and piercing brown eyes, he could make anybody fall asleep and to do extraordinary things on his command.

It all started as a joke on his sleepless nights on- call when the nurses noticed that the young doctor could make patients so comfortable they would fell asleep. He was as surprised himself as the rest of the staff when the patient in deep sleep could hear him and follow his orders. First, he tried to explain it by being a great actor. "Maybe with my great performance I could put the public in a trance," he joked with his friends. However, they were doctors, and they needed a better explanation.

The lecture hall in the medical school was jam-packed with the faculty and students. Everybody wanted to see the show of hypnosis. Sarra stood at the very top of the Auditorium. She even brought Victoria who knew this place very well; every holiday she participated in the concert, reciting from the stage her father's poems.

Now, it was Lenya's turn. He brought on stage a pretty young woman and introduced her to the audience.

"This is my patient Mrs. B. When I first met her, she was in her first trimester of pregnancy and had a severe case of morning sickness that we treated successfully with hypnosis. She kindly agreed to help me today to demonstrate the power of hypnosis."

He helped the very pregnant woman to the comfortable armchair and invited volunteers to observe. The Chief of the Department, Professor Ivanov sat at the long table. Three other medical doctors joined him on the stage. Lenya talked to his patient in his soft voice, and within a few minutes, the woman seemed to be in a deep sleep. Lenya asked the jury for a coin. Doctors were surprised, thinking that he needed a special one, but, finally, Professor Ivanov fished a few kopecks out of his pocket.

Lenya placed the coin on patient's forearm telling her that it was a hot iron. Within seconds, the arm under the coin became red, and a small blister started to form, but the patient did not wake up. The audience held its collective breath.

Next, Lenya asked the patient to raise her leg. He told her that leg is very strong and she cannot put it down. He invited three students from the audience to push the leg down. However, a thin pregnant woman held her leg up as if it was made of steel. When Lenya woke her up, she did not remember anything and was surprised to see a small burn on her forearm. The old Medical School Auditorium could not recall such thunderous applause.

My parents. The war is over

Professor Ivanov was the first to congratulate Lenya; he could use this magic for the benefits of his patients.

*****

"You know, Felix, he was the doctor by God." I had no idea if Felix was sleeping or not.

"He always looked distinguished, but when he hypnotized, he was magnificent. I remember he had a headband, just like Ear, Nose and Throat doctor use. Instead of a mirror, his band projected different colors with small rotating color bulbs; like a Christmas tree. He treated many patients with hypnosis, morning sickness, and different phobias. He even treated my girlfriend Tala when she was afraid of exams, and I was allowed to sit in the room the whole time!" In the dark, I could see the twinkling lights on my Dad's forehead.

DAY 38, OCTOBER 4
GRAND CANYON NATIONAL PARK, AZ
HOTEL EL TOVAR

The long day started with a tour of the Grand Canyon in the morning. We met our guide from the Field Institute in the Lobby; she was a tall, very thin, grim woman by the name Slight. We felt like school kids going on vacations, anticipating the sweet taste of making fun of the teacher. Holding close distance behind the guide, I even whispered to Felix "We are lucky to have a guide with a crazy name Slight."

The early sun was still low, and canyon kept all the deep secret shades of yesterday's sunset. It looked like an inverted hologram of an unearthly colossal mountain that fell down, top first. It looked like so many different things to so many different people who photographed, painted, wrote and sang about it.

After the tour, we settled our over seventy-year-old bodies on a wrought iron bench above the canyon and inhaled in unison. No matter what time of the day, sun or no sun, it was incredibly beautiful and intimidating in its majesty place. The river looked like a shimmering snake, the mountains looked like castles, ships, and temples; and even the bird high above us was huge and slow, a regal eagle. Soft, strange music played in "The Hopi House," and nostalgic smoke of barbeque seeped through the kitchen window of El Tovar. I thought about Indian wigwams with the blazing fires on the cover of my favorite childhood book.

DAD
KIEV, UKRAINE, THE 1940S

What makes the man a womanizer? His childhood adoration for his mother? The obsession with the art and the beauty; or lust and low morals? Whatever the cause, Lenya could not help but love women.

"Ninochka," as everybody called Doctor Nina Alferova, moonlighted in the same Emergency Room as Lenya.

It was a summertime in Kiev; the streets were clean after a warm fresh downpour. St. Andrew's Church floated above Andriyivskyy Descent, its turquoise and gold dome shaded an elegant old mansion across the street.

Lenya stopped in front of the stately staircase and checked his jacket. This morning, one of his patients gave him a small chocolate bar that was now in the jacket's front pocket. The thoughts were dizzying in his head as if on Marry-go-round. It took him three weeks to convince Ninochka to invite him to her home. Her husband perished in the war, and she had a little girl, the same age as Victoria. She lived in a grand house that did not need a memorial plaque.

Lenya was ready to kneel and to kiss the steps that were in front of him. His role model, the talented writer, Doctor Mikhail Bulgakov used to live in this house. The thought of walking into Bulgakov's house sent shivers along Lenya's spine, and this thought by itself was even more exciting than the evening with Ninochka.

He looked at St. Andrew's Cathedral hovering above him. He almost felt sorry he was Jewish. Would it not be nice to ask St. Andrew for forgiveness and to walk upstairs with clean conciseness? He tried to forget about Sarra who probably was still at the library and Vika planning her next mischief. He touched the pocket again and ran upstairs.

Ninochka was even prettier without her white coat. Her daughter Irina was a quiet girl with sad blue eyes that always followed her Mom. Ninochka served the tea in the old china cups, while Lenya tried to charm her with his war's stories. He waited for the right moment to give the coveted chocolate bar to Irina, but every time he reached for the pocket, he thought about Victoria. She would be thrilled with this small bar. He drank the tea, his hot palm padding the pocket with melting chocolate. Ninochka laughed and flirted awkwardly, but her blue eyes were just as sad as her daughter's.

He hurried home before Victoria's sleep time, half-melted chocolate in his hand. He hugged his daughter, looked into her delighted eyes, and felt forgiven for his little indiscretion.

*****

"Dad loved us, me and Ella, so much," I wrapped a scarf around my shoulders; it became chilly on the patio. We came back to our room and Felix settled with a drink and a book. The canyon behind our window drank night air and listened to the night voices.

DAD
KIEV, UKRAINE, THE 1950S

On a dark and rainy January day, Lenya came straight to the room without taking off his coat and hat in the hallway. He was wet and pale, a wet newspaper in his hand. The brim of his hat looked like a small lake, and the water was coming down in front of his face, but Lenya did not notice. Aunt Rose scurried around with the mop, but he did not see her. He quietly put newspaper on the table and almost whispered, "We all will die."

On the front page, Victoria could read in big black wet and running letters "Vicious Spies and Killers under the Mask of Academic Physicians."

Sarra came from the kitchen where she was cooking dinner. She looked at the newspaper, at her husband who got up and they locked in the mournful embrace. They both cried.

The rumors about Birobidzhan and arrests were crawling for months. Nobody knew anything; however, somebody told about new camps in Siberia for deported Jews, trains ready to transport thousands and lists of the apartments freed of their Jewish inhabitants. Nobody wanted to believe, but there it was in black and white in the Party newspaper called "Pravda," and it started with Jewish doctors!

They all came that evening, Lenya's loyal friends, classmates from the medical school, and colleagues from the clinic. They were terrified of the danger but even more of the necessity to write and sign the letters blaming other Jewish fellows- doctors.

Lenya could not understand; just recently, he wrote an ode for Stalin's birthday, and now the party arrested hundreds of Jewish doctors calling them terrorists, American spies, and the fifth column.

It was a miracle among the other impressive miracles by the Jewish God, along with the parted waters of the Red Sea and the lamps burning for eight days; Stalin died suddenly in March. The event did not extinguish an anti-Semitic epidemic; however, the morbid idea of resettling millions of Jews to Siberia was buried together with the dead dictator.

Two years later at the Party Congress, the trial was called fabrication.

The life was complicated under the socialism.

*****

I was still thinking how my Dad made it from the big dusty yard in Gorbashovka, where my grandmother cooked on a wood-burning stove, to professor at the medical school and successful playwright.

The childhood incident with the horse when he ended up sitting in the dust before the stable, surprised to be alive, left the scar; he loved horses but was always afraid of them. And that was exactly, how I felt about these beautiful animals.

"I rode the horse twice in my life," my voice was soft, but Felix heard it.

"Victoria, this is a very old joke," he was deep into his book and annoyed by the interruption.

Felix rode a camel a few times, in Morocco and in Jordan, and was not intimidated or afraid.

We were in Petra, Jordan, and in spite of the over hundred-degrees heat, we decided to walk. It was a slow winding road down to the famous Library.

As soon as we stepped on the pass, the world became real chaos. Fast two-seat carriages sped down on both sides of the road. Pompous tourists rode horses and camels; donkeys pulled small one-seater carts; and everybody passed us with yells, whistles, and laughter.

On the Plaza, Felix rode a camel, and I took pictures. We still needed to make it back, now uphill, still in the unthinkable heat. We proudly declined numerous offers of the rides; we were regulars in our gym, and we were in good shape.

The one and a half mile walk was draining. There were

still carriages and carts, donkeys and camels but we were preoccupied with our sour thoughts of how stupid and arrogant one could get. About half a mile before the gate, I set down on a bench.

"You can carry me from here, or you can bury me here," I informed Felix in a soft voice. "I cannot make another step."

It was close to the gate, and at this point, all the available Jordan's camels and donkeys were serving other exhausted tourists.

It was a miracle, but after about half an hour, Felix found two young Arabs with two horses. Their exorbitant price was still less than the cost of my burial in Petra. I hopped in the saddle right from the bench; however, my feet were about ten inches shorter than stirrups. I put my bag in front of me and hold to the saddle for my dear life.

"Vika, take a picture," yelled Felix who had mounted another horse. At this moment, our little company started to move, and my hands' knuckles gripping the saddle became the color of my white horse. The camera was in my bag, and there was no way I could ease my hold on the saddle. The horses were walking on the edge of the road; I looked down into the steep ravine on my right, "When did I have my last Tetanus shot?"

The thought was timely as suddenly I saw two- horse carriage aiming straight at me. By sheer miracle, the two-horse wagon passed us, and we continued our slow climb, interrupted only by the handler lightly slapping my horse Sarah and Sarah's following short-lived canters.

Eventually, I took a deep breath, fished my camera and took the photos. By the time we reached the gate, I was sweating much more than I would if I walked on my own two.

That was the story when I rode the white Arabian horse named Sarah twice, the first and the last time.

Grand Canyon, El Tovar, and Felix were deep in sleep when I turned off the light. However, the images of the day stayed with me. In my mind they shifted and mixed, my Dad rode the horse on the slopes of the canyon, and my grandmother's wood burning stove was in Petra; in the Library, little Lenya held a piece of lard in his outstretched hand while a huge eagle was circling over. I tried to shake the images off and get some sleep.

I was glad we would be leaving for Sedona tomorrow.

DAY 39, OCTOBER 5
SEDONA, AZ
ENCHANTMENT RESORT

I t was supposed to be a short and easy drive. A measly one hundred and twenty miles separated majestic Grand Canyon from the old Arizona town. We planned to arrive in Sedona before lunch and eagerly anticipated a leisure two-day stay.

The first hundred and fifty miles were a breeze with mountains hidden behind the spectacular greenery. It was all fine until we reached the Oak Creek Canyon. Suddenly our GPS screen started to look like Chinese Labyrinth, and our speed dropped to fifteen-mile an hour on this scenic but unnerving drive.

When we finally arrived in the town with an enchanting woman's name Sedona, to a place very appropriately called the Enchantment Resort, it was late for lunch and too early for dinner. Our large casita with two bedrooms, two bathrooms, and two patios was only an arm -length from pink mountain slope. We donned thick, luxurious robes and decided to rest.

We settled on our clay-walled patio with wicker chairs and wood floor. We were already drunk with clean, high-desert air. An alleged psychic energy of the pink mountains was upon us.

DAD
KIEV, UKRAINE, THE 1950S

Four apartment buildings formed a square with a large inner yard. Victoria was returning from school when she suddenly saw her father. He was running! Her tall, handsome and always self-confident father was running! He was crossing the central square of their apartment complex in broad steps; his face pale and distorted.

An early fall afternoon was sunny and quiet, and the sight of her running father with a huge dark shadow running behind him was shocking and frightening. Victoria saw that he was trying to catch up with a couple who, apparently, just left the doctor.

"Police!" was her first thought. Private practice was prohibited and severely punished by the Government. She knew her father could not refuse to see a patient. His private patients waited weeks and weeks to see him on weekends or before and after his work. She used to wake up in the morning to a steady whisper of full "waiting room" in their hallway. In the early morning along the narrow long "corridor," on the kitchen stools, sat three or four figures; they stared curiously at the ghost of a girl in the nightgown, the doctor's daughter, trying to sneak unnoticeably into the bathroom. Sarra opened and closed the door, made sure there was no police in sight and that neighbors would not notice the morning traffic.

The monthly salary of an average Russian doctor or engineer was around one hundred rubles a month, and a worker at the factory made even less. At five to twenty rubles for a visit, only the desperate could afford a private doctor. Everybody understood it and treated these dark figures on the kitchen stools with the utmost respect.

They were a strange couple, the people her father was after. A thin young woman with gray skin, pale lips and a frozen smile and a tall, distinguished older man dressed in an oversized coat. His hand was on the woman's shoulder. To protect? To worm her up? To hide?

Her father finally caught up with them, a tight pack of money in his outstretched hand. There was a tense, but a soft conversation with reserved gestures and the money traveled to a side pocket of the oversized coat.

It seemed that money made his coat heavier and even larger. The gray fabric almost swallowed the owner who grew older and shorter during the few sentences exchanged with her father.

Lenya walked back home with his head down, his eyes full of bitter tears.

The young woman was his patient with end-stage cancer. In the Russian tradition, the grave prognosis was mercifully hidden from the patient and Lenya discussed her fatal, untreatable disease privately with her husband. The man, a successful executive from a nearby town, knew about the diagnosis but still could not accept the verdict.

They had two small children and a dacha. She was an integral part of his life, career, and survival. He pleaded with the doctor to do everything possible to save her, but Lenya did not have any hope. Departing, they left an envelope with the doctor's honorarium. When Lenya saw five hundred rubles in the envelope, he started to run after them.

Victoria still remembered his pale, teared up face, "You cannot bribe death!"

*****

I saw so many patients who trusted him with their lives, who believed that he would help and save them. He was not just any employed by State physician. He was God's gift to hundreds and hundreds of hopelessly ill and forgotten patients who were frantically looking for a cure and salvation in the long lines of Soviet Clinics or on the empty shelves of State Pharmacies.

My father was the Doctor. The one who believed in looking, listening and smelling the patient, the one who worshiped his old stethoscope, made of sandal tree, the one who knew that patients should feel better even after just a conversation with a good doctor.

Was it my father's shadow behind him when he ran in the yard or was it death by herself who frequently runs alongside a physician? All my life I fought with her for my patients' lives. I won many times however I lost plenty.

My father's old stethoscope, which lived comfortably in his chest pocket for many years, has an honorable place on my desk. The wood is warm and smooth; it feels alive.

Our casita is quiet; a half-empty bottle of tequila is still on the kitchen table. It is our vacation after all, and we ordered our dinner in. My eyes are half-closed with overlapped double images of Oak Creek Canyon and patients waiting to see my

Dad, clay-walled Ukrainian huts, and small color lights of Dad's headband, huge dark shadow overtaking the pink mountains and my smiling grandchildren back in California. Time to go to bed.

DAY 40, OCTOBER 6
SEDONA, AZ
ENCHANTMENT RESORT

We were lucky it was not one of us; it was our car, which needed tender loving care. Suddenly, this morning, Felix realized that after a rigorous six-thousand- mile drive our car might need an oil change.

My poor, usually immaculate car was loaded like a camel in a desert. The fifty-day trip would do it to any vehicle; we needed it all, suitcases and bags, water, tonic and much higher spirits to accompany us on our long nights at the hotels, even the back pad that, thank God, we did not need. Our jackets for the cold mountains morning or an occasional pouring rain were littering the back seat. However, the most important were bags with all those cute toiletries that I collected from our every stay at every great hotel. I could almost taste the stories I would tell to my visiting grandchildren about our incredible cross-country drive while preparing a delicious Jacuzzi bubble bath for them.

Thinking of home, we planned to meet Caroline, our Travel Agent in Santa Fe. After that, and a three-day rest in Tennessee, according to her plans, we would start a real drive home, doing more miles and driving more hours every day. We should be safe back to Massachusetts (O, sweet home!) by October 16. While we were waiting for our car to be serviced, I was home already, back home in Kiev on Christmas.

DAD
KIEV, UKRAINE, THE 1970S

Christmas was one of the best days of the year, and not because of Jesus's birthday. Christmas had been "canceled" together with the Russian monarchy and the old calendar since nineteen-seventeen when religion was proclaimed "opium for the masses." The New Year was much more suitable for the communists. There were New Year trees and New Year vacations, Grandfather Frost and Snow Maiden and even an Old New Year, which everybody celebrated fourteen days after the real one.

Russia accepted the Victorian calendar three months after the Revolution, about four hundred years after Europe and in the process lost almost two weeks.

Nevertheless, Lenya's Birthday was on December 25, on Christmas day, and preparations started many days ahead.

The whole family was involved; Sarra called Zoya for any available delicacies and Lenya went to visit Monya's wife Ana, now Director of Personnel at the meat plant. Ana was always ready to help, and Lenya left the plant through the back door with all kinds of meats wrapped in newspaper; it slowly leaked some pink color through the fishnet bag.

Ella and Victoria, the press team, got a poster-size piece of thick paper and created a wall newspaper with photos, poems, and congratulations.

Mom

Dad

Smaller tables flanked the extended large dining room table, and long planks wrapped in blankets rested on the chairs on each side, creating more sitting spaces in between. Dressy tablecloths covered this L-shaped banquette construction.

Slightly aged Lenya and his elegant wife entertained frequently and lavishly. They had a special holiday dinnerware, crystal, and silverware. Not that it was available in the stores, but they knew right people in the right places who knew how to get "the deficit."

They both aged well; Lenya was still very handsome with a full head of beautiful wavy gray hair and large brown discerning eyes. Sarra stayed tall and attractive; she was a classy chic woman with impeccable taste.

"Aunt Rose and I will be responsible for the main course. I will make meat roast and potatoes, pate and tongue," Sarra planned.

"Ella, as usual, will be responsible for salads and desserts. If I can suggest, 'the old witch' salad made of marinated onions, cabbage with pomegranate seeds in sour cream and herring covered with cooked vegetables would be nice. Too bad, it is December, and we can only dream about spring vegetables to make any other salads. Also, Ellochka, (that was the diminutive for Ella), can you please think what to make for desserts? Victoria, you are going to lay the table. Nobody can make it as beautiful as you can. Please, play your magic; we have a big crowd tomorrow."

Sarra counted the guests, "The relatives, our local friends, guests from Moscow, Arbuzov and Zorin, and a lot of others. Please, girls, do your best," Sarra delegated the duties.

The evening was always a terrific fun celebration with toasts and jokes, stories and anecdotes, fancy imported cognacs and lousy Russian vodkas, plenty of simple and elaborate dishes. Glorious Sarra served, a consummate wife and hostess.

Lenya sat at the head of the table. A tall, beautiful New Year tree sparkled behind him with color lights. He was the best toastmaster both emotional and clever. After dinner, he sang old Russian romances and Yiddish songs in his low and sexy baritone. Everybody was in awe of Lenya's talents, and so many celebrities, famous and talented people around the table loved and admired him.

"He is the one and only!" whispered proud Victoria to Ella. They were leaning on the wall at the dining room; there was never enough space at the table, and they needed to help their Mom.

Victoria watched her father; she loved him so much. He was the best, and he was her Dad. How much lucky could one get?

She did not know then, that for the rest of her life she would be searching for the best, the man exactly like her father. She did not know then, that it would be an impossible task to find a giant of a man like that. She did not know then, how many mistakes she would make, how many impostors she would meet and how difficult it would be to find even small parts of him in other men.

She did not know then, what unimaginable grief would be to lose her father and that forty years later, she would still swallow tears thinking of him, missing and loving him.

He was not one to keep his secrets. As soon as Victoria was old enough to understand, he told her the story about Nina and chocolate so she would know how much he loved her. In his heart, he was an actor, and he made such a funny performance that even taken aback Sarra had laughed.

He loved women, regretted it, and asked his wife for forgiveness. She loved him wholeheartedly and selflessly, and she always forgave him when he needed absolution.

They were a beautiful, full of life couple. They cherished their family and friends. They went a long road from nothing to prosperity, from patriotism to complete devastation and disillusion with socialism and their Russian existence. They loved each other for forty years to the very end.

Sarra had never left Lenya's side when he was in Moscow hospital for the final leg of his life. He was only sixty-five. For weeks, she slept in a chair next to his bed, leaving only for a quick shower. She fed him and ate hospital food with him when he could eat; she did not eat when he could not. She washed him and shaved him, read to him when he wanted to listen and prayed with him.

Lenya believed that his love for his family would save him and Sarra trusted him; Lenya believed that his grandchildren would save him and they prayed to their grandchildren together. He dictated letters to Vika and the family, his last poems and his last thoughts. On his last day, he scribbled his last words to Victoria himself with his shaking hand, "Yours, until my last breath …"

*****

"To those who drink for the first time under this roof, to good health and many happy returns!" The glasses were not as fancy as my great-grandfather's ruby-red Passover glass made in Germany, but reciting his favorite toast, we clank them anyway.

Russians cannot drink without making a toast. Even if it is as simple as "to a good health" or "to you," there is always a toast, a wish, respect. My Dad borrowed and embellished his grandfather's favorite toast, which he invariably started with "At my Grandfather's table, the first toast was always raised to a guest who was visiting for the first time".

Dad would go on and on with all the good wishes to the guest, "let the drinks and food be plenty, let there be no ill effects from the drinking; to your good health and many happy returns." It was a great way to start a party, to make one's first visit enjoyable and to put the guest at ease.

I had borrowed the toast when I served the first drink to my first guest under my first roof.

A few days ago, in California, Dave had borrowed the toast as well. There was no red with gold ornaments great-grandfather's Passover glass that usually adorn our family table on Jewish Holidays, but Dave and his teenage son, the seventh generation of the family, toasted us in the best tradition of the family.

Now, sitting under the roof of our lovely casita in Sedona, we raised our glasses to our good health and many happy returns. I looked at the jewelry box sitting on the table between us. It was a present from Felix for our anniversary.

We debated the matter of a present for many miles over the last few days. Felix threatened to spend one dollar for each year of our marriage. I furiously disagreed, "Considering the hardship of marriage, your character, children and Grandchildren, I expect no less than ten dollars per every year of marriage!" We laughed and bargained and settled somewhere in between. Felix is a very generous man indeed.

In a jewelry box shone a bracelet made of one of the enchanting stones of Apache Indians, blue as the sky, turquoise. It was a perfect gift for a Golden Anniversary.

We all are happy now. Our car with changed oil. I am wearing a beautiful new bracelet, and both of us have the good fortune of family traditions and marriage still alive.

To Santa Fe tomorrow.

DAY 41, OCTOBER 7
SANTA FE, NM
THE INN OF THE FIVE GRACES

The road was long, all four hundred and twenty miles of it. We drove out of Sedona on the same labyrinth-like Oak Creek Canyon Scenic Road. I was driving leaving the scenery up to Felix; however, deep green canyon and high mountains draw little appreciation from him.

"We are driving for six weeks, Victoria," Felix tried to explain. "We saw every incredible canyon and every gorgeous mountain, and after six weeks my admiration is wearing off."

I did not answer; I was afraid to ask if he still admired me … after fifty years.

The landscape became more manageable as soon as we hit "Historic Route 66". We entered New Mexico, "the land of enchantment." There, we crossed yet another Continental Divide, but by then, I had lost the count how many times we did it already. We found route twenty-five north, and arrived at the hotel tired and confused by the winding narrow back streets of Santa Fe.

In the hotel, our "Magnolia" room was a burst of intense colors from Morocco, Spain, and Mexico with fiery reds, emerald greens, and midnight blues tiles, depicting peacocks and flowers, sun and full moon, parrots and fishes. Vivid purple and orange ornaments in the wild combinations of

Indian and Mexican crafts blinded us. No wonder Santa Fe's nickname is "The City Different."

Founded by the Spanish in 1610, Santa Fe is the oldest capital city in the United States. Between Indians and Spaniards, the town had changed allegiance a few times until after twenty-five years of being a Mexican territory, it became a capital of the forty-seventh State.

Desperate for some rest, I laid down on the inviting quilt covering our bed. The fabric was soft.

VICTORIA (CLOTHES)
KIEV, UKRAINE, THE 1940S

She did not care about clothes. Shorts suited her just fine except for the case with the stolen apples. However, this dress was as soft as a cloud. It was made from the white silk of a German parachute. Victoria had to wash her hands to touch it.

Her dad's patient, Tatyana, embroidered it with lovely blue forget-me-not flowers. Tatyana was young and very sick, and she told Victoria that the flowers on the dress were to remind Victoria of her.

Tatiana died a few months later. Every January 25, at The Saint Tatyana's Day by Russian Calendar, usually the coldest day of Russian winter, when sparkling white snow reminded Victoria her first white silk dress, she thought about Tatyana and the beautiful dress embroidered with lovely blue forget-me-not flowers.

VICTORIA (CLOTHES)
KIEV, UKRAINE, THE 1950S

Her first stockings were not hers. Victoria still felt the blood rushing to her face when she remembered "the stockings" fiasco.

In the eighth grade, she begged her Mom to wear Mom's new stylish skirt to school "only once, Mom, please!"

Sarra was thin and tall and Victoria short and plump, so the black and turquoise gingham skirt, with two rows of shiny large black buttons on the front, was inches below Victoria's knees. Nevertheless, the class dame sent her to the Principal's Office, where she was given a lecture on a proper school uniform and was told to "Come back with your parents."

Even her Babushka noticed that Victoria did not have much luck with clothes. She always confronted Sarra, "Victoria is a big girl now, and she should dress appropriately." Later at night, Babushka complained to Lenya, "Vika does not have a decent winter coat." It was obvious; she was counting on his support. She was right, and Lenya himself called his tailor Tovarisch Herman.

He even carried a large packet with his old winter coat. Victoria stumbled behind her parents. She did not want a new winter coat by Herman; he was a man's tailor! And she did not want Lenya's old black coat.

Tovarisch Herman, an old Jewish tailor, looked like University professor. He wore a three-piece-suit and round glasses, hiding his kind eyes that saw everything. When Sarra proposed to turn the coat inside out and adjust it to Victoria's size, he sat down. Everybody understood it was not a good sign.

"Doctor, you know, I respect you very much; you are a good client and even better doctor. This coat already turned inside out once, and the fabric has only two sides; moreover, this seal fur collar looks rather like a red fox. Now, I just got a new fabric, let me make a good suit for you."

They were ready to leave, when Babushka, the voice of reality, said, "It's already cold, and Victoria does not have a coat. Please, Tovarisch Herman."

Victoria wore this coat for the next few years.

She was already in medical school when her parents bought her a new fur coat. She was delighted to show the thing off at school when one of her friends greeted proud Victoria," Finally, you are dressed in your national costume, Victoria!"

Sarra had her own dressmaker, famous Clair, who was always a talk of the Kiev's fashionistas. Sarra with her beautiful tall and slim figure was Clair's favorite client. She copied for Sarra the latest fashions from the impossible to get "Moda" magazines. Victoria was in heaven, waiting for her Mom to try a new dress and looking at the beautiful magazines in Clair's large one room in the old multi-family apartment.

"I asked Clair to make your prom dress, Victoria," announced Sarra one May morning. "It will be our present for your graduation." It was beyond anything Victoria could dream of. It has just happened that last week, three boys asked her to be her prom date!

*****

We found a quaint French restaurant around the corner. The red wine flickered like an imprisoned flame in the large crystal glasses, and the bread was warm and crunchy.

"How did I get so lucky?" I felt content looking at Felix's face still handsome in the dim candlelight. I pulled a light shawl over my bare shoulders, air conditioners were not my best friends, and suddenly, I remembered another shawl and remarkable story of human kindness and generosity.

VICTORIA (CLOTHES)
KIEV, UKRAINE, THE 1960S

Victoria opened the door and let her Dad's patients in. The tall older man was quite handsome with gray temples and deeply settled blue eyes. Victoria could see that he had lost a lot of weight recently as his elegant jacket with a silk handkerchief was too big on him. His wife was a portly woman with freshly coiffed hair and a stylish outfit. A beautiful coral mohair shawl covered her shoulders protected her from the autumn draft.

Since Dima's death, she did not care about anything, especially, about clothes; she was widowed and pregnant, and she did not need and did not want anything. However, later this day at the dinner Victoria commented how warm and fluffy and how gorgeous this shawl was.

"She got it in "Berezka!" Her Dad, who had never care about anything material, who thought that clothes and jewelry were "meschanstvo," called his patient's wife to ask where she bought this shawl! He stepped over his own principles for her! Not that Victoria or even Lenya himself could go and buy the shawl in "Berezka," which was "the currency store."

Every corrupt socialistic or communistic country in the world, from China to Cuba, from the Soviet Union to Africa, had these stores, where the local money meant nothing. Only a selected few, like local Party leaders, foreigners or celebrities with legally earned and brought to the country foreign currencies could exchange it for so-called coupons. It was the Soviet version of the best American Department store with the Sears prices.

Lenya opened the door when the doorbell rang later at night. The wife of his patient was at the door. She held a packet in her hands; safely stored in the original plastic bag, was a coral mohair shawl.

"Doctor, this is for your daughter, please! I want her to wear it in good health."

She firmly rejected the offer of money and left. For years, wrapped in her favorite gorgeous light and fluffy warm mohair shawl, Victoria thought about this woman. Only women who grew up in the Soviet Union could understand and appreciate her sacrifice. The women gave as a present her pride and glory, the best shawl in town. At that moment, Victoria became a true fashionista.

*****

Our Magnolia room was mysterious and sexy; the scintillating tiles were sparkling under the warm moonlight.

"Why was I so infatuated with clothes? What did they give me in exchange for a ton of money?" I thought about my enormous closet; years ago, we rebuilt and expanded our house because I needed a much larger closet. We were still under construction when one of my partners, Peter, asked me to show him what we were doing with the house. We drove during our lunchtime, and I showed him the unfinished house, still without floors and windows.

"I loved what you are doing with the house," he said on the way back, "especially this two-bedroom guest suite next to the master bedroom."

I laughed, "This is not the guest suite, Peter. It is my new closet!"

I loved shopping for clothes. Maybe that was why I always remembered the book that I had read many years ago. The book was about a young woman who grew up in poverty and became a big star. It was "a nylon century," and she wanted to have everything. She acquired many needed and not so much needed things and eventually she ended up in her old dilapidated family home in the heart of the night. She got drunk there and was eaten by rats.

The writer Elsa Triolet, a Jewish woman, born in Moscow, lived in France and her novel made a big impression on me. She loved clothes and even when she could not afford to spend money, she always managed to buy the beautiful new things. Feeling guilty after buying something new, I often joked that rats would eat me too. Nevertheless, I survived my extravagant shopping sprees.

"What are you hiding in this closet, Victoria?" exclaimed my friend, a psychologist, after seeing my closets. "What childhood wounds, sins of your youth, losses, and lies are you nursing in your closet?" However, I saw only designers' labels.

The quilt on our bed was soft and inviting, and we were asleep before our heads hit the pillows.

DAY 42, OCTOBER 8
SANTA FE, NM
THE INN OF THE FIVE GRACES

Santa Fe was a beautifully flamboyant, livable and very expensive town. Dazzled, we walked sidewalks shaded by the trees and stopped at every colorful store minded by the locals, Indians, Mexicans, Turks, Afghans and everybody else. The shops' windows were bursting with turquoise, corals and silver jewelry, fabulous color glass and pottery. We sat on The Plaza, took an open tour bus, visited famous Canyon Road and had lunch under cover of the trellis in our own courtyard.

For the last thirty years, we traveled the world visiting more than a hundred countries. We planned the trips and decided when, where and how. About a year ago, when the idea of retirement settled in my mind, I decided it was the time for the coveted cross-country drive. With our golden anniversary approaching, we plotted our fifty- day drive, one day for every year of our marriage.

Felix and I unfolded a map of United States and got immediately lost where and how to go, where to stop, what to see, what's important and what's not, should we rent a car or just drive ours, should we have a reservation or stop on a whim? We had thousands of questions with no answers. I tried to ask friends, concierges, and agents with no luck.

"You will be able to plan it when you would get there," was the best anybody could do for us.

I am not a big fan of writing to magazines and asking for help. However, after a few months of futile attempts to plan our trip ahead of time, I looked in my favorite travel magazine and found a list of the best Travel Agents in the USA with specific areas of interest and expertise.

I chose five travel agents specializing in the National Parks because there was nobody on the list specializing in the whole country or cross- country trips. I was still working, so one Saturday I wrote the same letter to all five of them explaining that we are "two older people, both in our seventies," and we plan to drive across America for fifty days for our fiftieth wedding anniversary. I asked for the ideas, guidance, and suggestions.

The same evening, I got the first call back. Judging from the young woman's voice on the phone, she was professional and experienced; she was even excited for us.

"My name is Caroline. It is a challenge not only for you but for me as well, but I will plan your trip from A to Z and will take care of all your needs," she said.

I have to confess; I was taken aback when the next day she asked for my American Express card number including my secret code. I even called American Express and asked what my liability would be.

"If you provide the information voluntarily you are responsible for all the charges," the agent informed me sternly. Nevertheless, I did it anyway.

For the last six weeks, we lived by somebody else's schedule. Somebody else planned our trip, mapped our roads and made our reservations.

Caroline was everything I had heard in her voice during our first telephone conversation and more, much more. Two weeks before the departure, we got a packet with two books that outlined the two first long legs of our trip.

Each book had a few sections. The first section mapped our drive for each day, with suggestions such as which scenic drive to take and where to stop for incredible views, second, our reservations at the hotels, many in historically significant suites. Caroline reserved dinners, booked tours and lectures and provided advice for the day- drives and other entertainment. The third part was a narrative of the place, its history, importance, local attractions and whatever additional information would be helpful for the tourists like us.

As soon as we got our itinerary mapped, we spread the map again and traced our routes by days, by attractions, by stays in the hotels. While I searched with great enthusiasm when and where we would stay and what we were going to see, pragmatic Felix looked at the hotels' charges and sightseeing fees. His eyebrows almost met his hairline when he asked incredulously, "Did you tell her 'Money is not an object?'"

For the last six weeks, these books were our bible and endless source of information. I was waking up and going to bed with one, quoted it in my nightly blogs and envied myself on my luck to find such incredible guidance. I could recognize Caroline's voice on the phone, I had her cell number on my speed dial, and I loved her E-mails; she was always worrying if we had enough rest, did we like the tour, did we see everything she planned for us to see.

After working together on this trip for about six months, we became friends and later today, we were finally meeting Caroline in person. Our itinerary brought us to the town at the same time Caroline was there for a meeting. She made a reservation for dinner, and we could not wait.

VICTORIA
KIEV, UKRAINE, THE 1950S

Victoria was almost seventeen when she had her first date. She never wondered why she did not have a boyfriend until then; she had many friends, boys and girls alike, and she spent plenty of time with them but always along a lot of company. They usually hung around somebody's room when parents were away; sometimes they went to the movies. They all lived on the same streets, went to the same schools and knew each other since childhood. By the tenth grade, some of them almost dated, but that was rare, nearly a crime by the moral standards of the fifties. Hormones were not allowed to talk before graduation from high school.

Victoria loved her friends, especially her best girlfriend, shapely Dora, who just started to date a handsome, tall outsider Mark. Victor was the troublemaker and Yasha, tall and soft-spoken, was a talented self-taught illusionist.

Last year, after the government announced that graduates with two years of work experience would have preferential treatment at the college admissions, most of her friends transferred to the "evening schools" and looked for work. Fifteen- and sixteen –year- old kids from doctors' families went to work as nurses' aides on ambulances. That was the best their parents could do to give the kids a better chance for their future education.

"All the boys got crazy," whispered Dora sitting next to Victoria in the movie theater. The "Thunderbird" was their favorite movie theater, only a block from their home and they were about to see their favorite movie. It would be the eighth time they came to see "Some like it hot" or in Russian translation "Only girls play jazz," and they had been in the ticket line for three hours.

"They are all in love with this girl, Ellen. She works with them in the ambulances," whispered Dora.

Shy Yasha brought Ellen to their next gathering. She was a beautiful girl; her dark straight hair and long bangs swung around her face like a curtain framing almond-shaped gray eyes. She had a wasp waist supported by a wide red belt and a full skirt resting on a starched underskirt caressing her long legs. She was the dream of every boy who Victoria knew at the time, and there was no way for plump, naïve Victoria to compete with such ravishing beauty.

"Vika, do not pay any attention to Ellen!" Dora, as usual, tried to save the situation." Why do not we have a double date with you and Mark's friend Vlad?"

Dora could always get her friend out of misery and Victoria agreed instantly; she could not possibly hope for any date while gorgeous Ellen was in the picture.

Her hormones were still asleep but her curiosity was not, and she was sure one date would be enough, just to brag about dating a real man.

When after a few dates, tall and moderately handsome Vlad asked Victoria if he could be her date at the prom, she was grateful and flattered. She was the Komsomol Secretary in charge of the prom, and she sang at the concert; however, she still worried that her fabulous prom dress, made by famous Clair, would be supporting a ballroom wall if she did not have a prom date.

On Saturday, they all gathered at Victor 's to listen to new contraband- Elvis Presley's disk, which made its slow rounds on the brand-new tape-recorder, which belonged to Victor's older brother. Victor invited his school friend Ron who was a big fan of American music. They knew each other for a long time, but this was the first time Victor invited Ron to hang out with the gang.

The voice on the tape and the song hypnotized Victoria, especially the only English word she could recognize: "Love," repeated again and again.

In a small, poorly lit room, they danced all night swinging softly to the American tune. As the night grew older, the embraces became tighter, and some boys even managed to steal kisses from their favorite partners, but Ron was new, and he kept his distance, although he danced with Victoria all night.

A sweet perfume of chestnut blossoms followed Victoria on her way home. The aroma stuck inside her nose, scratched her throat and made her dizzy. Or was it Ron's look, when he asked her for her phone number. She tried to remember the song she loved so much, but instead, she remembered Ron's blue eyes and the only English word she recognized "Love, Love".

Ron called the next day; he met Victoria after school on Kiev's very own Red Square, under the street clock. Ron was holding an enormous bouquet of red tulips and lilacs.

"This is for your belated birthday, Victoria," Ron was smiling pressing flowers in her hands. "I have my sources, and I know it was last week. Unfortunately, I did not know you then."

Nobody ever gave her flowers before. Victoria felt her heart dropped; it was beating hard and fast somewhere in her feet glued to asphalt. It was pounding hard in her sweaty palms, and her chest, which was just about to explode. She took flowers with shaking hands, looked in Ron's blue eyes, admired for a second his sensual smiling lips and suddenly she heard her own hoarse voice, "Would you come with me to my prom?"

Ellen became a constant fixture at every party, every birthday, and every get-together of the gang. Behind her back, Yasha called her "my girlfriend," although, she made clear that she was not attached to anybody in the group. Poor Yasha bought a new shirt, learned new, more complicated tricks and signed up with the local concert organization. He was now "an artist," which was a great achievement compared to the rest of his friends who continued to clean patients' bedpans in the ambulances.

"Can you do me a favor, Victoria?" asked Yasha. They were sitting on the cement fountain brim in front of Victoria's building. The fountain had never worked, and Victoria sometimes imagined what would happen if it suddenly started to spout high beams of water.

Yasha was waiting for his Dad who had an appointment with Victoria's father for a private doctor's visit and Yasha decided it was a good time to make a deal with Victoria. She was responsible for the students' concert at the prom, and she worried about it all the time.

"I would be happy to help you, Vika. I am a professional artist now, you know." Yasha felt he needed to apologize for his blatant bragging. "Can you, please, talk to Ellen and tell her that you invited me to perform at your prom because I am so good?"

Victoria thought for a moment. "Of course, Yasha; you are, and everybody would love to have a magician at the concert. It would be so much fun; can I please, be your assistant?"

And that was how she ended up with three dates for her prom.

*****

We finally met Caroline, our Travel Agent, who turned out to be everything we had expected and more. She was very professional, well informed and friendly. Moreover, to our delight, she was a gorgeous outdoorsy blonde girl from Montana. She was fun; the dinner was a blast, and we had a great time.

To Oklahoma tomorrow.

DAY 43, OCTOBER 9
OKLAHOMA CITY, OK
HILTON SKIRVIN

There was absolutely nothing between New Mexico, Texas, and Oklahoma. Of course, there were vast swathes of the desert, some hills, occasional fields, but nothing memorable or impressive. Unless you call impressive the mile-long trains, the mile-wide irrigation machines and the red -roof slaughterhouses stretching for miles.

Felix comfortably reclined in his passenger seat with his eyes closed and I was bored.

"Hey, Casanova," I touched Felix, trying to interrupt his bliss. "You bragged so much how popular you were with the girls when you were young, where exactly did you do it?" I tried to find an explanation for my late start on the dating stage.

ROMANCE
KIEV, UKRAINE, THE 1950S

They all lived in one room with their parents; they could not go to the hotel or motel. There were women —on —duty who sat behind the desks on every floor, right on the stairway landing or in front of the elevator, if a hotel was lucky to have one. They were sitting there not to welcome or to help but for the sole purpose to check the guests' passports. Both guests had to have a stamp in the passports that they were married to each other; otherwise, the woman would call the police.

They could not make out in the movies or on the park benches; the self-appointed moral guards were everywhere. They did not have cars with comfortable back seats, there were no coffee shops or fast food places, and they were not allowed to the restaurants before age eighteen.

Felix's mom was a deputy director of a large radio plant and she, her father and Felix lived in one room in the two-room apartment.

It was the end of December and his grandfather Gedale, a short religious Jew, hiding his yarmulke under a cap, just brought from the market the whole sack of potatoes for the winter.

"Dad you should not do this, why didn't you ask Felix to help you?" Felix's Mom, Olga, was upset.

"He is busy in school, Olga; and now he is a boxman too," the Russian was the old Gedale's third language, after Yiddish and Hebrew.

"Felix, busy or nor, I would like you to come with Grandfather and me to celebrate New Year at Motik and Ida's place." Motik was Mom's brother, and he lived nearby with his wife Ida, who was a doctor.

Felix was glad to hear that his mom and grandfather would leave for the party; now he could make his own plans for New Year. "Sorry Mom, I did not know you and Zeide planned to go to Motik; I already promised Michael and Shved to celebrate with them."

He and his two closest school friends were inseparable, however now, the different plan ripened in Felix's mischievous mind. He recently met a group of friends with real girlfriends, the girls from a local club, and now he would have a room for the holiday all to himself. He could not possibly miss this opportunity.

The New Year party was in full swing, with plenty of vodka and the girls when about five in the morning Felix went to the bathroom separated from the bathtub by a thin plastic cloth. He heard a small noise behind the cloth, and he picked up a short broom to take care of a stray mouse.

He pulled the curtain. In the dim light of the pre-dawn New Year, Felix saw his mom and his grandfather sitting fully clothed in the bathtub.

The party at Motik was canceled earlier that day. His mom and zeide loved him so much they did not want to spoil his New Year plans.

*****

307

"You had your own room," Felix suddenly woke up. "It had a nice sofa-bed with a funny name." He straightened up in his seat, his eyes bright; a sly smile curved his lips. In my peripheral vision, I saw young Felix on the prowl when he was full of life and fun, gentle and mischievous, loving but always leaving. "Remember, we would stay in for days at the time, living on canned peas and champagne?"

"Sorry, the assortment was not a strong point at the grocery store around the corner."

We both laughed grateful for these days when we did not want to get out of my sofa bed and to part, even for food. I had an endless supply of canned peas, which I fried with a good chunk of butter on the skillet and Felix would run to the store; by afternoon in the liquor department, there was nothing but unsold champagne.

"You played guitar, and we sang 'Foggy morning,' the sad old romance by Turgenev." I tried to sing in spite of the cruel job that old age did on my vocal cords. "We loved old romances, Gypsy's and the students' songs, but this one was our favorite."

"When I was on business trips you sent me crazy telegrams with quotes from "The twelve chairs," which had always got me into trouble!" My husband was alive and animated; he sang a few notes and looked at me. I bet he saw me as I looked then.

We smiled at each other thinking about the last fifty years, the years we stood by each other caring, supporting and staying friends. We loved with passion and sometimes hated even more, we cheated, forgave and held onto each other like the alpinists on a cliff tied with the same rope. It was an amazing journey, and we were on a home run.

VICTORIA (ROMANCE)
KIEV, UKRAINE, THE 1960S

Victoria stood on the stage holding a large carafe. She plastered a fake smile on her face, but inside she swallowed her tears and screamed at the top of her lungs, "My dress! My beautiful moiré dress! It is ruined!" She was heartbroken, especially, because the beginning was so perfect.

Yasha did not expect all these troubles when he offered Victoria, the role of assistant. Victoria's friends applauded Yasha's every turn on the stage; however, he could not concentrate and had to improvise when a trick did not work out, as it should. Then, Victoria did not realize Yasha's double- wall pink jar was not what it seemed to be and, trying to convince the public that it was empty, Victoria spilled pink water all over her new pale blue prom dress.

She got off the stage, wet skirt clinging to her knees like a dead silverfish. Vlad tried to cover the ruined dress with his jacket; however, Ron had a better idea. He led Victoria up to the top floor.

The school was strangely quiet at night with only faint music floating from the ballroom. Her prom that started so gloriously with three dates ended up with a stage fiasco and a wet dress. They settled in the dark chemistry lab, and the wet dress dried up very quickly in the heat of the night and the first love.

This hot romantic summer, they spent together every day. Ron brought her flowers; Victoria wrote poetry, each poem a love letter to him.

When August exhaled crisp autumn breeze, Victoria left for a medical school three hours by train from Kiev. She cried all the way to her new home and her new life. She returned home for vacations and occasional holidays, but after a few months, her love poems found new heroes. In two years, by the time Victoria transferred to Kiev Medical School, they were just friends.

*****

The flat, quiet road was easy to navigate. Felix drove, and I relaxed in the passenger seat. We had our lunch at the roadside café, and two hundred miles to Oklahoma seemed easy.

The long winding roads of our lives were exciting and challenging, full of unexpected stops and dangerous curves. Since our first romantic summer, almost every birthday I got flowers from Ron. Our friendship lived through my and his marriages, emigration, children, and grandchildren; we danced at each other seventieth jubilee and on every holiday, my telephone rings and a familiar voice- now from New York- says, "Vika, your voice has not changed; you still sound eighteen."

I was born in the spring when nature is hearing the first rings of an alarm clock but does not want to get up yet. I was born in May when everything is young and fresh after a morning shower, alert and smiling, dressing in the best vibrant colors and ready for action.

In my age, I am still stupid enough to love my birthday. Why everybody remembers that day is beyond my comprehension, but the day usually starts at midnight the day before, because Felix and Ella are always the first. "It is already your birthday in Kuybyshev and even in Kiev," Ella would say. In the morning, I invariably would find lily-of-the-valley from Felix on my bedside table.

Sam usually called early; the last years he lived with his wife in Germany. When I was still in the medical school, he was a celebrity football player. He was gorgeous, with long dark eyelashes curling up above blue eyes and muscles in all the right places.

He was an excellent storyteller with a devoted audience of my mom and Ella. I believe that only his superb sense of humor helped him to survive when my father screamed "Nyet!" to Sam's proposal of marriage to me. He was the funniest guy, even after working in Chernobyl the first year after the disaster and getting sick. We were friends until his death last year.

The next call usually came from Israel, from Felix's best friend, Sasha. We had visited him and his wife there a few years ago. Last year after wishing me all the best, Sasha asked for Felix. "Wait a minute, please; he is taking large trash bins out of the garage."

"You are kidding," Sasha doubted. He knew my husband very well; they were best friends for many years.

"But of course, he does." I forgot how undomesticated Felix was years ago. "He is a happily married man, and he does a lot of things in the house."

"Victoria, we are all happily married men," smiled Sasha on the phone, "But if we would be smart then, all these years back, we all would marry you." I knew then that my best birthday compliment just arrived. Sasha passed away suddenly last year while fighting multiple myeloma.

Volodya would call mid-morning; Kansas City is an hour behind, "Did you think I could forget your birthday, Victoria?" Then would come a long tirade about a new car, new trip or plans for the next birthday; his was not far away from mine. He died planning his eighties jubilee.

Despite being three hours behind, Zoya called in the morning. It is hard for me to imagine my birthday without a call from her. She succumbed to metastatic cancer after a twenty-year-long fight.

Galya, Dora, and Ellen are all gone for a long time now.

"We are so lucky to celebrate every day, not just the birthdays," I thought.

Felix pushed the brakes, the car stopped in front of the hotel, and I was back to the present. We drove about five hundred and fifty miles that day, one of our longest drives so far, and settled in the old Skirvin Hotel downtown Oklahoma City.

Beautiful red lacquered grand piano graced the Red Piano bar. We ordered drinks and waited for the music to start.

After our long drive, we felt old and tired. Shiny red lacquer grand piano almost hypnotized me; I hoped it would save the night. But music did not come, and our drinks made us both grouchy. We took two different elevators upstairs but ended up in the same bed. Felix's familiar body was warm and comforting, enveloping me with his hand all in the right places. O, the bliss of the long marriage! Good night.

To Hot Springs, Arkansas tomorrow.

DAY 44, OCTOBER 10
HOT SPRINGS, ARKANSAS
EMBASSY SUITES HOTEL

"It is going to rain all three hundred miles to Little Rock," Felix predicted unhappily. He was a real believer in the forecasts by local TV stations. However, the sky did not cry over our departure as we took a leisurely road east back home.

We still had another week to travel, but compare to routes we had left behind, it seemed like a short and easy drive. Even our itinerary bible, the third and the last book by Caroline, was not very extensive or exciting, no fantastic State Parks or fabulous hotels. We just had to drive back home and not to kill ourselves from boredom in the process. All we needed were places to stop, to sleep, to eat, to rest, and at the end, to come home exhilarated and rejuvenated for the next fifty years.

I was driving through beautiful countryside, lakes and forests to Hot Springs, Arkansas. We drove over the railroad bridge; even trains here were shorter and more manageable, so to speak.

"What do you like about the trains?" Felix asked almost as an afterthought.

Why did I always like trains? "They have faces. They are different, memorable, and distinct. Planes are all the same; how many flights can you remember? Trains are our fellow travelers; they are part of the story. "

TRAINS
KIEV, UKRAINE, THE 1940

T he overcrowded train rolled through burnt fields and bombed villages. The war ended two years ago, but people still were trying to get back home. Soldiers were looking for their displaced families; civilians, back from the long journeys east, were trying to find their homes demolished by war; homeless "invalids of the war", amputees without legs, propelled through the carriages on small wooden platforms on wheels, asking for food or money. A small group of two families with young children was out of place in this human beehive, but they had a purpose and they were determined to make it.

There were no jobs available in Kiev for a Jewish doctor and Lenya became increasingly worried. He had a big family to support and a few lectures in Culinary School on proper food handling were not a big help.

Monya, his best friend since medical school, returned home with his new wife Anna, a sixteen- year- old gorgeous Ukrainian girl, and their newborn daughter. He survived German occupation in a small village, saved Anna from deportation to Germany and married her with her parents' blessing. He too could not find a job in the city.

The late spring was unusually hot and hinted at a gruesome summer. Even virgin white candles of Kiev's famous chestnut trees were yellowish and crimped. There was nothing to do after the end of the school year in the dusty suffocating city and Lenya and Monya decided it was a perfect time to improve medical services in the deep of Ukrainian vastness. They packed their wives and daughters and headed to Anna's parents, to the village thirty miles away from the closest railroad station. That is how Victoria remembered her first train.

The train carriage was packed to the brim with the people. There were three rows of wooden shelves; six in each open compartment and three perpendicular shelves along the hallway. Two top shelves were for laying only; they were too close to the ceiling for the person to sit. Nevertheless, people were sitting on every inch of every shelf, their dirty socks, boots and leftovers of shoes swinging in front of the faces of people on the lower shelves, pieces of rugged luggage in between.

For the first few hours, their small group had a "standing room only" space between the shelves; but mercy was upon them, and when somebody left on one of the stations, Sarra got a seat. Victoria, sitting in Mom's lap, remembered the whole mass of human bodies swinging to some exotic rhythm of the rolling train, remembered the nauseating smell of dirt and sweat, poverty and human tragedy, but most of all she remembered feeling incredibly hot.

Lenya got her just in time before she almost died of a heat stroke; using his gun, he cleared up the top shelf, as people fought for every inch of it. He got a cold-water bottle to cool Victoria and stood guard of his very hot daughter all night. Victoria still could feel the warm shiny wood of the shelf she laid on that night on her very first train.

Both doctors' families got off the train the next day and spent a bountiful summer in the serene village on the river between two mountains. The villagers were thrilled with the care provided by the young doctors "from the capital" and donated plenty of fish, eggs, chicken, milk and bread to their small community. Monya practiced Dermatology and Lenya treated everything else. Once he had to use a GI tube and that made him a doctor who treated "with snakes"; after this, his popularity and authority were unsurpassable.

Anna's mother had only one big pot on her old Russian stove. She cooked Ukrainian borsch in it all day and after they ate dinner, everybody washed their feet in the same pot at night. It was evident that Lenya did not give her any lectures on food handling. Victoria slept on the top of the warm stove; it was a magical place for a four-year-old with a vivid imagination.

After a few weeks, they returned home tanned like peasants, with sacks and baskets of food for the whole family.

TRAINS
KIEV, UKRAINE, THE 1950S

Suburban trains were the sign of summer. Sarra usually volunteered to work at the young pioneers' camp or at the children sanatorium, so she could keep her girls with her, away from the suffocating city. Victoria and Ella stayed there with their Mom for the whole month. On the weekends, Dad came to visit. The girls would meet him at the station when the train emptied its carriages in the morning and loaded people back for a trip to the city at night. Dad would bring a present from Babushka, the most delicious fresh strawberries layered with sugar, so they would survive for a few days on Victoria's bedside table. Sometime Mom needed to go back to work for a meeting on the weekday and they had the whole train car to themselves. Victoria would sit on every seat, looked through every window, and ran from the door at one end of the car to another, floating through all the hardwood luxury.

TRAINS
KIEV, UKRAINE, THE 1950S

The trips to Moscow with Babushka took the whole night and half-a-day until the new fast and extravagant train called "The Blue Arrow" cut it to twelve night hours. Victoria loved the suppers of cold chicken, hard-boiled eggs with fresh tomatoes in the summer or pickles in the winter, which Babushka packed for the train. She loved sweet tea in thin clear glasses with metallic glass holders that the conductor served at night and in the morning. There were thin mattresses and some linens for the wooden shelves and it was more comfortable to make a bed and to sleep on the lower shelf. However, Victoria loved her upper shelf. She could watch forever-fleeting landscapes and small stations with the villagers selling ready-to-eat young corn, tomatoes and hard-boiled eggs. Sometimes, Babushka would splurge and get the tickets for a compartment when you even could close the door at night.

TRAINS
KIEV, UKRAINE, THE 1960S

"Mama, see 'K, I, E, V'" said excited Dima after Victoria finally settled in their compartment and got out together with Dima to the long hallway facing the Railroad Station. Dima waved his hand to seeing them out Felix, who had to work, while they were leaving for Crimea on vacation.

In the train window, large printed letters started to move and three-year-old Dima wanted to read. Especially, to impress the young navy captain standing next to him at the window. The Captain was happy to chat with the boy. He was their neighbor in the compartment for four and Victoria suspected he would much rather talk to her.

"You are right, boy! Kiev. Do you know that Kiev is a capital of … what country?" The Captain squatted to meet Dima eye to eye.

"Ukraine, of course," smiled Dima. He knew this game all too well. That is how his grandfather, "Dedushka", demonstrated his prodigy Grandson to friends.

Then, he countered, "What is the capital of Liechtenstein?"

"What a boy!" smiled the Captain taken aback. He turned to Victoria, "Where did you get such a smart son?"

Victoria was not amused knowing exactly what was coming.

"What is the smallest country in the world?" Dima was not easy to dismiss; he loved this game.

The Captain measured his opponent. "It is easy, smart guy! Monaco!"

"Wrong, you are wrong!" Dima loved to win. "It is Andorra! "

Victoria interjected trying to stop the humiliation. "Dima, look, the Captain is a navy man, and he does not care for your capitals."

"Then he should know where is the deepest place in the world," her son was delighted with the new avenue for exploration.

The red-faced Captain did not bend over anymore. He stood in his full navy height and wanted to squash this three or whatever years old redhead, who was happy to report, "Mariana Trench in the Pacific."

As the conductor helped the captain change his compartment, Victoria herself was ready to kill her son. Their Crimean vacation was not as memorable as their ride on the train.

TRAINS
SPAIN, EUROPE, THE 1990S

Victoria was puzzled as she looked at the tickets. She and Felix disembark from the ship that took them from London to Barcelona for their twenty-fifth wedding anniversary and they had train tickets from Barcelona to Madrid, which the travel agent bought for them in the USA.

According to the tickets, they had seats at the car #146.

"Did you ever see a train with one hundred and forty-six cars?" Victoria turned to Felix who was busy with their four suitcases from a three-week- cruise.

"You got to be kidding," Felix was not smiling as a regular length train slowly pulled to the station. There was no car one hundred and forty-six, of course; no car forty-six and not even car fourteen. They pushed into the sold-out carriage with the last ring of the station bell, arguing with the conductor who did not understand English. The head conductor was summoned immediately, "You cannot stand on the moving train!" It followed by "You cannot block the door with your luggage!" and "I will fine you and threw you out of the train; your tickets are not valid!" in a loose translation of his Spanish screaming.

Victoria, who believed in humanity, was convinced that there is always a kind soul on every train and in every situation. This time the soul materialized in a handsome Spaniard with five word English vocabulary, "Restaurant, go Restaurant, seven cars ahead!"

They left their suitcases on four different high shelves along the car and walked seven cars to the Restaurant. They found a great window table and ordered Spanish wine to suit the Spanish landscape. They were all set to have a good time for the next few hours.

They did not expect an angry waiter at their table every thirty minutes. It turned out; they had to continue to order food or wine, or coffee, because the restaurant on the Spanish train was for eating not for sightseeing.

They spent their Spanish pesetas on Spanish wines. By nightfall, they arrived in Madrid drunk but safe and with their entire luggage.

*****

I could string a few more "train stories" on the necklace of my memory when Felix pulled in to our hotel at Hot Springs. We got lucky; the hotel had some public relations promotion and smiley welcoming ladies in the white aprons served delicious food and offered free drinks.

In the Grand Lobby, a pianist played some longing tune, and I brought my loyal laptop to write a nightly travel blog. I was all set, but my heart was beating in the strange rhythm of the moving train. I did not know if Dima, who is over fifty-years- old now, remembered his first train, but I certainly did. Decades later, we traveled Europe on Orient express and climbed to Machu Picchu on Hiram Bingham train. And I would never forget the last train from Russia. I cry whenever I tell this story, even four decades later.

To Nashville, Tennessee tomorrow.

DAY 45, OCTOBER 11
NASHVILLE, TN
RENAISSANCE HOTEL

We left Hot Springs, AK early in the foggy and windy morning and had four hundred miles to drive to Nashville. A chilly rain met us on the highway making visibility a problem.

We were in the mountains of Arkansas, which after driving through Wyoming, Utah, and California, we disrespectfully called "the hills." Finally, the sun got off the clouds somewhere in the middle of the road. It settled comfortably on my right shoulder, lighting up lush green hills and reflecting off the long polished roofs on the farmhouses.

My hands shook when we had to change our GPS disc to "Eastern States."

The view from our room on the twenty-fifth floor was fabulous. We got out of the hotel and soon realized that Nashville's bars and restaurants were loud, crowded and smoky; way too crowded and way too loud for us.

We hurried back and practically ran into Elvis! He was a perfect "look alike," young and friendly, and I was smitten and shaken as if he were the real McCoy. I took a deep breath and gathering all my courage asked him for an autograph and a picture. I pushed the camera into Felix's hands; I desperately needed this picture with Elvis; and luckily, he was happy to oblige. I touched his shiny sleeve and smiled for the camera, and I was as anxious if I were sixteen again.

"Remember the Grateful Dead concert, Felix?"

GRATEFUL DEAD
MAINE, USA, THE 1980S

It was a cold and snowy New Year's Eve in Kiev when I had my first musical encounter with Elvis. On American made tape, I could hear "Love! Love" and a diabolical roar of the dancing audience unable to resist Elvis's beat.

Elvis, o, sweet Elvis, at this moment, I could run to you barefoot on new snow, all the way from Russia. Thank God, I did not grow up in the blessed USA to become a groupie.

Twenty-five years later, I seriously considered should we or should we not accept an invitation from our sons to a Grateful Dead concert.

We were not fooled; we knew that as a part of the deal, this invitation carried extensive financial obligations. The kids could survive without us at the concert, of course, but then, who was going to rent for them and their friends this much-needed van to drive to the state of Maine? Who was going to buy these all-necessary tie-dye uniforms? So much for the unconditional love!

I was about to decline their well-plotted invitation when in the background of my memory, caught on the tape of my youth, rose the tremendous beat of raving crowds at all those concerts that we missed. I did not plan to be cheated out again.

So on the hot July day, Felix and I found ourselves in a long line of cars trying to park in a God-forsaken place in Maine where the old racetrack was the epicenter of culture and civilization. We followed the kids' rented van but lost it in a six-hour-traffic for the concert.

Our new silver Volvo was an overdressed outsider among beat-up pickups, dying Chevys and motorcycles. We made it to the track from the nearest available parking two miles away.

All the way to the track, Felix continued to complain that we were the oldest couple in the crowd, that we parked too far and that he was just about to die of thirst. A sweet woman-biker in a sweaty worn-out bandana overheard him and thrust a half-empty foamy can of beer into Felix's hands. It was a warm and thoughtful gesture of friendliness; however, it did not make Felix any happier or less thirsty.

He was right; we were well above age limit for this concert. It was not funny to be an ancient relic at forty-five. All those young wide-open eyes were looking at us with poorly hidden surprise. We were the oldest spectators in the crowd of sixty thousand where everything was new and unknown to us.

We had never been to a concert like this. We wanted to absorb the reality with all our senses, to make up for the losses of our youth when the communists cheated us out of freedom and fun.

We wanted to remember every face, every sound, and every move. It was surreal! It was so unlike the concerts we knew in the old country. Those were filled with washed and ironed shirts, haircuts approved by the school, and a well-behaved seating down crowd.

A light Maine wind spread the air, impregnated with smoke, above the racetrack. I felt incredibly happy! Kind of light and fluffy; I had never felt this way before. I was eighteen again, and I danced with Elvis! Twenty-five years later, this was my second, more intimate, encounter with American music.

Men! Why are men never happy? I think, being happy is against their religion; emotions, affections, and delights are mortal sins in their faith. After horrible traffic with hours of driving, a two-mile walk and politely declined beer, my husband was thirsty, hungry, unhappy and grouchy. He accused me of being "high" just breathing the air filled with marijuana smoke.

We had never smelled marijuana before, partly because we grew up in the fifties and partly, because we grew up in the Soviet Union, how he could know what was in the air.

Along with my kids and their friends, I was dancing on the bench and wished Felix would join in the fun. He would not cave in, "I did not eat all day, and the music is too loud! I lost my last pack of cigarettes, and we are too old for all this!"

In my slightly influenced mind, I found a quick solution. "Maybe you should try marijuana, it would take you right back to the sixties and would improve your experience," I suggested with a mischievous smile.

I think Felix felt guilty spoiling my fun. He followed my advice and, trying to please me, took two puffs from the pipe offered by his neighbor on the right, a young man clad in tie-dye under his leather jacket.

The change came right away; Felix smiled and joined me dancing on the bench, however, it did not last. He sat down and clutched his fists to his chest; he looked rather miserable and pale. Alarmed, I sat him down. Just a few weeks before Felix had a stress test, which he had passed with the flying colors. "Roger Staubach is less fit than you," said Cardiologist at the end of the test. In spite of this verdict of a "low probability for the presence of coronary artery disease," Felix became pale green and promptly fainted into the lap of our younger son, who was sitting right behind him.

Dave was terrified. Thanking fortune that I was not Elvis's groupie, but a well-trained internist instead, I tried to find the carotid pulse on my poor husband's neck.

Music was blaring, and the racetrack was shaking with rhythmical "woo" of the raging audience. Never mind carotid pulse, I could not even figure if he was still breathing.

"All normal husbands are dying in their beds and mine … mine is dead at the Grateful Dead concert!" was the only one frantic thought in my head. At this moment, I could not remember any of the useful techniques of cardiopulmonary resuscitation.

The young leather-clad owner of the pipe probably felt guilty as he dashed downstairs with the scream, "I am for the rescue" and disappeared. My right hand acting exclusively on its own made a full swing and delivered a few loud slaps to Felix's cheeks.

"Mom! What, the hell, are you doing?" screamed my two sons in rare unison. "He is sick! Stop slapping him!"

However, all this screaming and beating had a positive effect on Felix. He woke up looking startled and still green, but not missing a beat, jumped on the bench and started to dance. I was in pieces, just about to faint myself.

To our surprise, the rescue team arrived immediately, but looking for the body; they missed Felix, who was now dancing like a lunatic. They eventually found him, but Felix refused medical attention for many reasons. First, he explained, "he had his own doctor on site", and second, he did not want to jeopardize his security clearance or to lose his job designing "Patriot" missiles for a date with marijuana. It would not be a good idea at all.

We left the kids and the concert during the intermission. After all these planning, preparations and a long drive, we left after only half of the concert. Never mind, I was happy; my husband did not die at the Grateful Dead concert. We had survived all the excitement and I we had a hotel reservation in Portland, Maine.

I was so wrong; the night was still very young.

On our way to the car, Felix stopped at the ice cream booth.

"You do not like ice cream," I reminded him gently after he returned with six ice popsicles. Their poisonous pink color could easily beat any tie-dye.

The sun was still up when I started the car. Felix, in the passenger seat, was enjoying his ice. For some reason, the dashboard remained dark.

We had serviced our new Volvo before the trip; however, something was wrong.

Outside lights were OK, but it became dark fast, and I could not see any indicators inside the car. I stopped at the gas station, but no one could help me. We got gas and Felix went to pay while I waited in the car.

I was not concerned after the first twenty minutes; it could be the line at the cashier, a crowded man's room, long hand washing. The second twenty minutes, however, I tried to convince station manager to escort me to the men' room.

Suddenly, in the heat of the argument with the manager, I noticed Felix devouring two bags of potato chips in the dark corner of the station. He was very quiet and agitated simultaneously, like the bomb waiting to explode.

Back in the car, he continued to empty potato chips bags with incredible concentration. Bored, I put on radio only to catch the end of the concert we had left.

A long wailing cry tore through the car. Astonished, I lost control and almost drove into the side rail. "What? What happened?" I screamed terrified.

"It is so-oo beautiful," continue to wail Felix with tears of a true music lover on his face. "I love this music!"

I did not know that it takes two puffs of marijuana, fainting and two bags of potato chips to wake up the emotions in a real man; add six ice popsicles and what a lethal cocktail you would have.

Two hours later, we safely checked into sleepy Portland hotel. It was close to midnight, but we went to the deserted bar downstairs, where we ordered drinks in hopes to get some munchies. Both of us were tired and hungry now. The sleepy bartender generously offered an extra olive in our martinis.

Disappointed and still hungry we slowly walked the long hallway to our room on the sixth floor. Suddenly Felix disappeared! Familiar panic overtook me; I was too exhausted to look for him now.

A dark shadow moved ahead of me on the floor of the hallway. Still alarmed, I found Felix hovering over the tray waiting outside for the room service. A few lonely cheese cubes were on a dirty plate under the used napkin.

As a hungry hawk, Felix grabbed the cheese. Losing all my composure and dignity, I mouthed, "I am hungry too!" It was too late; the cheese already disappeared in his mouth.

In our room, an old Elvis's movie played on a glowing TV screen.

We looked at each other and laughed in relief. Finally, our day was over. My husband extracted two small cubes of cheese from his pocket and fed me with two precious tidbits, leftovers of somebody's fiesta.

Grateful, I hugged him, and we made a few passes on the shiny parquet of the room.

I danced with Elvis again! Even better, I danced with my husband who survived his first encounter with marijuana, big American concert and all the unfulfilled dreams of our youth. We were grateful he was not dead!

*****

Nashville was loud and smoky. Blasted with music; we took cover at the restaurant. I tried potato cheddar soup and fried green tomatoes; dinner had enough of the local flavors for both of us. Tomorrow, through stormy forecast and two hundred miles, we will drive to Walland, TN for three days of R&R. We were puzzled why Caroline decided to send us to the Farm.

DAY 46, OCTOBER 12
WALLAND, TN
BLACKBERRY FARM

Somewhere in the hills of Tennessee, my heart skipped a beat. I wondered what did it mean as the road was straight and nothing was wrong. Then I saw the clock on the car dash. Everything was wrong. We had returned to the Eastern Time! We were back to getting up with the first news of the day, still late compared to Europe, but the first in the New World. We could not wait to stop; we giggled and, exchanging conspirators' looks, fixed our watches while still driving.

We were already done with all the beauty around us; the sky was still incredibly blue, and the sun was still summer-warm. We were bored with clean houses and immense fields. Felix tried to nap every minute he was not driving, and I already knew by heart every song on our CDs.

Heading for a three-day stay on the farm seemed like a good idea as we had another nine hundred and fifty miles to drive home. I was happy I still had my memories and my stories.

BABUSHKA
KIEV, UKRAINE, THE 1960S

Vika was almost sixteen when her Babushka became sick. She was still the same feisty Asya everybody knew, but something had changed. She started to forget how to get to Lenya's place and would not show up for a few days. She forgot to change her dress or did not remember to take her purse.

Initially, they blamed it on high blood pressure and the age, of course. She was only 65, but by the standards of the time, she was a very old woman, and memory problems did not surprise anybody.

She managed to survive a recent small stroke and did not tell anybody for days about the weakness in her arm. When Lenya noticed that she was slightly limping and holding her arm, he got upset with her. It was apparent that she could not live alone anymore. She spent more and more time sitting in the chair, but still pretended that she was okay. Lenya insisted, and she moved in with the family.

Slowly she stopped talking; it was difficult to find the right word. She needed help to get dressed and forgot how to tie the laces of her large shoes. She did not remember how to eat, how to use a fork or knife and she stopped eating.

She smiled at Vika. Although she did not remember who Victoria was, she still remembered that she loved this girl.

On her sixteenth birthday, Victoria was shocked, when her grandmother, who always remembered everybody's birthday, forgot hers. Victoria was especially excited about this birthday. She just could not wait to become sixteen. Herself, with Mom's help, she baked all the deserts; she laid the table for the celebration and waited for her girlfriends and classmates to come. She came to bring her grandmother to the table, but Asya just waved her thin hand in utter despair, her cheeks were wet with tears of agony. She was lost for words; she was lost in this world.

Sixteen-years-old Victoria would not give up; she did not want to celebrate without her Babushka, and she could not understand why old age had to be so cruel.

The table was amazing and the guests loved all the cakes and pies that she made. Her dad surprised her with a wonderful present, the real adult photo camera that was hard to get. It was very expensive, and Victoria was thrilled; she dreamed about this camera for a long time. She showed the camera to her silent Babushka, who just sat there not touching anything. Babushka did not recognize the food on the table and did not know how to eat these things. She safely hid her thin hands, with their webs of prominent blue veins, under the tablecloth.

Babushka died next month. It was a hot summer day. Victoria graduated from high school and was full of plans and hopes. She was in love and on the top of the world. Her boyfriend was the only thing she could think about.

The funeral was at Babushka's room at the drab brick building of the liquor plant. The smell of sour borsch rose from the workers' diner. The family and the neighbors paid respect; Victoria sat on the windowsill between the second and the third floor with her cousin Zoya. She could not cry.

"Remember, my Babushka?" asked Zoya. Babushka and Zoya's Grandmother were sisters. "She was so sick all the time that I was happy when she died!" Zoya tried to be helpful.

"Auntie Yaha was also sick and old." They looked at each other, at the dirty, dusty window they leaned on, the muted sunrays, the ugly staircase; and suddenly the girls were so happy to be young and healthy and not dead yet, they laughed!

They felt guilty to be happy, but the new exciting world was waiting for them. They did not have time for the past, for childhood dreams and nightmares, for the shadows of the war and Babushkas.

A few years later, on the hot June day of the anniversary of Asya's death, married and pregnant Victoria brought Dmitry to Asya's grave. She told him the story about her Babushka.

"Do not worry," assured her Dmitry, "next time we will come here to tell her about our child." He was very wrong.

*****

As we drove east, the sun slowly descended in my back view mirror, and I pushed my sunglasses on the top of my head. Felix smiled; he thinks it is funny that I always wear sunglasses while driving, no matter rain or snow.

"A little property on the backside of the Great Smoky Mountains," said Caroline about our next stop. The unassuming sign "Blackberry Farm" surrounded by pumpkins and gourds confirmed the statement.

We drove up a long, winding unpaved road not prepared for the four-thousand- acres grand Estate with beautifully appointed suites, fireplaces, state of the art bathrooms and spectacular dinners at "The Barn".

A note, "jackets are required for dinner" and that a car would pick us up to drive to the Barn, surprised us.

The place was magnificent. By its size, it could be a hangar for the planes; however, the chandeliers, massive fireplaces, and elegant tables transformed it into a spectacular restaurant.

We could hardly understand the names of the dishes on the menu; even though, we had eaten at plenty of famous, fancy Michelin starred restaurants.

The wine list was five-hundred-pages long, and we congratulated ourselves on being Scotch drinkers. We got half of the radish with the greens still attached, on a bed of something white and crunchy as the "Complements of the chef" and a lonely cookie with a matching lonely candle and a "Happy Anniversary" sign for a desert. The ambiance and the menu were more memorable than the food.

The enormous custom-made Lexus SUV, which had a look and the feel of the Presidential car "The Beast," took us back to our suite. O, the joy of not getting up early or driving tomorrow.

Every night of our trip, we tried to convince ourselves that we had made it to the fiftieth anniversary. Now, the surprise and delight started to fade as Felix said "Only four more days to home."

DAY 47, OCTOBER 13
WALLAND, TN
BLACKBERRY FARM

E very time we left our room, even for a very short time, it gets made up. Yet, we never saw anybody in the hallway or a vicinity of the place. I put my bet on the hard-working elves, and Felix smiled approvingly. Not only the bed is freshly made, but there is also a thank you card or a lovely note on the cover and chocolate cookies and bottle of Italian mineral water on the bedside tables. Now I am not so sure I want to go back home.

Felix got tired just reading the daily ledger of all available farm activities. We would not take horseback riding, golf, gardening or truffle hunting; we were out of our league here.

Instead, we had breakfast with a lovely couple from Indiana. They were also celebrating their wedding anniversary, and four of us indulged in champagne on the terrace over the lake under the morning sun in the Smoky Mountains. I loved the farm life!

ELLA
KIEV, UKRAINE, THE 1950S

Victoria met her sister for the first time on a cold winter night. Well, she had heard about her sister for the first time on a cold winter night.

Victoria enjoyed her girlfriend's birthday party when the doorbell rang and Aunt Rose, swaddled in a knitted Siberian kerchief, walked in the room.

"Get dressed, Victoria," she said without as much as a hello. "You are going home. You have a new sister, and your Dad sent me to fetch you."

Victoria was not excited. "I can walk home by myself later," she tried to negotiate with Aunt Rose. It was useless. Aunt Rose was a determined woman, "I would not leave without you, Victoria."

When a few days later, her parents brought home her new sister, Victoria was upset. "Why could not I stay until the end of the birthday party, if she did not come home right away?" she looked at her sister accusingly. It was all her fault!

Her parents named their younger daughter Ella, in memory of Sarra's father Efim who died in the Babi Yar. The wounds of the war were healing; however, they left large and painful scars. The girls' both grandfathers died during the war. There were no cemeteries to attend, no graves to bring flowers or place a stone; there were only two little girls to carry the names and the memory.

The winter was no longer boring for Victoria. This winter was almost as busy and exciting as the summer; only the weather was freezing.

Aunt Rose was Sarra's aunt, a sister of Sarra's Mom Clara. She helped Clara when Sarra was born, and now she move in with Sarra and Lenya to help with a new baby.

Babushka made more noise with pots in the hallway kitchen and mouthed under her breath, "Nobody is asking me! Thank you very much!" She was not very happy with a new woman in her household, which until now she ruled single handedly.

It was a winter of "new." New snow that had never melted and a new baby. Ella with her huge dark eyes was a happy baby. Aunt Rose took care of her and Ella almost never cried. Sarra was delighted with her new ally, and Victoria made new friends at her new school in the first grade.

"We are moving!" The door flew open, and Lenya's hat landed on the table. He could not stop smiling. He picked up Victoria and danced with her.

"It is a beautiful room and just one more family to share a kitchen and a bathroom." He put Victoria down and waltzed with Ella now. "A real kitchen and a bathroom with a real bathtub!"

"I got a job at the new clinic," he added as an afterthought.

It was such a vast improvement, just five of them in the room! They were thrilled, and nobody noticed tears on Babushka's wrinkled cheek. They would be far from her, almost an hour first by trolley and then by tram.

Sarra got a new job too. With Aunt Rose taking care of Ella, Sarra went to work at the local hospital. She was a beautiful thirty-year-old, tall and thin, glowing with that special light of new motherhood and her new patients loved her. She was a caring and kind doctor, loving wife, and great mother. She navigated her complicated household with a grace and a smile.

At her new school, Victoria was doing well; she was a fast and easy study with plenty of friends, yet she still had ample free time for a constant war with Aunt Rose.

Aunt Rose adored Ella and had little love or patience for Victoria. Not that stubborn Victoria cared to compete for Aunt Rose approval; independent and spoiled, she had her Babushka to fight for her.

Now, Victoria had a much bigger problem. Her Dad, her love, and hero, was writing poetry not only for Victoria but his youngest daughter as well. Ella had to go!

Sisters

There were not too many holidays in the Soviet Union. The hospital, where Lenya worked, held big Holiday concerts three times a year, on the May Day-the Day of the International Workers' Solidarity, on the day of the Great October Revolution and the New Year. Since she was a little girl, Victoria always recited her Dad's holiday poems at these concerts. Now, she had to share a spotlight with Ella who was cute and smart, never forgot a line, and looked just like a smaller version of Victoria.

After the holiday concert at the hospital, the girls stood tightly together in the rowdy and happy holiday crowd, almost falling with each move of the tram full of partygoers. Victoria held the pole with one hand and Ella's hand with another; she was the older and responsible sister after all.

"You know," started Victoria, "I hate to tell you this, Ella."

Ella's frightened eyes turned up at Victoria, "I did not mess the lines, Vika, did I?"

"It is not about the lines, Ella. I did not want to tell you, it is a big secret, but I think you should know."

Ella became all ears; she would love to be a friend and a confidant of her much older sister.

"You're not my sister, Ella; you were adopted." Victoria was as dramatic as she could master in the crowded tram.

Ella's huge dark eyes became round with surprise as she tried to understand the implications. "How do you know that, Vika?"

"I overheard Mom talking to Dad at night," lied Victoria. "I think that is why Babushka loves me so much and you can have Aunt Rose, who is not even our Aunt, all to yourself!"

She watched Ella's eyes slowly filling with tears. The tram brakes screeched, and Victoria could hardly hear Ella's whisper, "Now I understand why nobody loves me."

Seven and a half years were hard to beat. They did not have the same friends, they did not go to the same schools, and Victoria did not have clothes to pass down to Ella.

Victoria was a busy girl; she was singing in the student chorus, performed in school plays and emceed every concert. She ran for every position in the school election and was on every committee and every council. She was a President of this and the Chairman of that. Her schedule had no place for her younger sister.

Contrary to Victoria's adoption plot, Ella was the joy of the family; she was funny and kind, always in a cute new dress as soon as they started to appear in the stores. Sarra insisted on ballet school for Ella and twice a week she and Victoria took Ella for the lessons to The House of Scientists.

"Why do I have to go, Mom?" whined Victoria. "I have homework to do, and I do not need to wait for Ella doing all these funny steps."

She hated to admit how much she loved the mirrored room, the music and, most of all, the short and puffy pretty ballet skirts. She was too old and too big for those.

"This is for Victoria," Babushka made it clear when she bought a piano. Nevertheless, Lenya decided that both girls would learn to play.

He was speechless that after a year and much money, Ella could play only one children song about "Two Happy Little Gees" and Victoria happily banged out all the popular songs "by ear." She did not like her teacher, and she hated written music.

ELLA
KIEV, UKRAINE, THE 1960S

They moved in two rooms with another two families cooking in the shared kitchen. For the first time in their sixteen years of marriage, Lenya and Sarra had a private bedroom.

In the other room, Ella and Victoria shared a sofa bed and Aunt Rose slept on the folding cot. Depending on the time of the day, this room was a bedroom, dining room and living room in turns.

The room was hot in the summer and cold in the winter, and Ella hated when on cold winter nights her older sister came back home late from the date and stuck her cold feet right into Ella's warm legs on her warm side of the bed. She did not like the light in her eyes when late at night Victoria feasted on the cookies and milk that Mom would leave on the stool next to Victoria's side of the bed. Ella was thrilled when Victoria finally left for the medical school. Now Ella could have the sofa bed with a French name Recamier all to herself.

Life was back to crazy when Victoria would return for vacations with a constant procession of short- and long-lasting boyfriends.

Ella and Mom loved Sam the best. Sam always had a funny story and knew how to tell it. They met at the friend's birthday when Victoria was home on vacation, and he waited patiently for her to come back to visit her parents on rare weekends. However, this summer Victoria transferred to Kiev Medical School, and Sam became a constant fixture at her parents' home.

"Ella, would you, please, clean the room today," started Victoria.

"But it is your turn to clean, Vika! I am busy." Ella looked at Victoria in her new black fur coat all ready to leave. "I love this coat! You look great Vika. Of course, I will clean," Ella was still bright eyes good-natured teenager always ready to help.

"I have to go to the hairdresser and Sam has to come in the evening. If you clean the room, we will stay home; otherwise Sam and I would go somewhere else," blackmailed Victoria.

Ella could not miss the opportunity to listen to Sam's stories. She liked his dark wavy hair and long curly lashes above his piercing blue eyes. He played soccer professionally and was built for it. However, the most, she loved the evening when she, Mom and Victoria just laughed to exhaustion.

The three of them had the same laugh; as Dad usually said, "they laughed in stereo."

"We went to see this incredibly funny movie The Ransom of Red Chief based on the Story by American writer O'Henry," Victoria returned from the date red-cheeked from the winter cold. "It was hilarious, and I laughed the whole movie," she still could not hold her smile, just thinking of the movie. "As we were leaving, an usher said that the movie was so funny, some crazy woman was laughing two showings in the row!"

"What movie theater did you go to?" Sarra was suddenly suspicious.

"Dad and I went to see this movie at the first showing, and obviously, you saw it at the second showing, Victoria" she laughed an infectious laugh like a silver bell.

No one laughed when one evening Lenya said categorical "Nyet," when instead of a story, Sam asked Lenya's permission to marry Victoria.

Lenya always had a final "Nyet" for his older daughter who, much like himself frequently fell in love.

*****

The lazy afternoon sun on the farmer's porch was warm, and Felix was napping when my telephone vibrated, and Ella's smiling face took the screen.

"How timely," I thought walking away from the porch trying not wake up Felix. He could never understand our long daily talks.

We were sisters, but the age difference made it hard to be friends and confidants. We added another gap to the age difference when Ella came to the United States eight years after us.

It was Ella who fulfilled our father dream and brought the family together again.

Years later, when Sarra was about seventy-five, the first

symptoms of Alzheimer's disease became obvious. She laughed about misplacing her keys. She dismissed as "silly" to mix up days of the week. She was still a beautiful, stylish woman and it was easy to think that at her age everybody forgets occasionally. She was a doctor, and she did not want to know the diagnosis. She fought as long as she could, but a few years later, she needed constant help and supervision.

Sarra could not fight anymore. She did not want to be in the nursing home, no matter how much care or comfort it could provide. She did not want to be there, and she used the only available weapon, she went on a hunger strike, she refused to eat. Only her girls could make her eat, and only when they cooked for her.

For years, our days started with a telephone call planning who would go to feed Mom and what food to serve. For years, Ella and I, two busy doctors, planned our days, our vacations and our lives around Sarra's. In the end, it was two of us at her bedside; we held her hands in the final embrace, and it was the two of us, she saw before closing her eyes forever.

Since then, for many years now, we call each other every day. I am sure our parents smile from above, happy that "the girls" are not only sisters, but, in spite of all the age difference and all the circumstances, are friends and confidants, and matriarchs of one large and beautiful family. I walked back to the sunlit porch where Felix was still napping.

So far, it was a perfect day on the farm. I slept, ate, took a bath and ate again. We were catered to and served and came back to our yet again freshly made up bed. I did not want to hurry back home.

DAY 48, OCTOBER 14
WALLAND, TN
BLACKBERRY FARM

There was nothing new in my dream this morning. I just needed to share it. "We were cruising," I said as soon as I felt Felix stirred up.

"You are always cruising," mumbled Felix.

He did not like to wake up to the conversation. He did not want to wake up, period. I never met another person who loved to sleep that much, in the car, in the dental chair, in the theater, especially, if it was a musical. He loved classical operas, but not musicals; however, most of all he loved to sleep.

It was nine on a sunny morning in the heavenly bed on the farm, "We should behave like real farmers and get out of the bed," I started to get up.

"It is not always 'cruising,'" I continued at breakfast. Felix did manage to wake up, and we enjoyed our eggs on the veranda overlooking a beautiful lake.

"Sometimes, we are on the boat or the lake, and sometimes we are just looking at the water, but it is always a body of water." The water in the lake was shimmering under the sun tickled by the light wind; it was the most placate and soothing view.

It was always water in my dreams, every single night since the cold and rainy July day when Dima drowned.

The first thirty days I lived through the shock and relentless terrifying nightmares when we stood holding hands in the yellowish water of Dnieper River right before Dima made his last fatal step. Every night for thirty days, he continued to hold my hand pulling me with him deeper and deeper into the waterhole with no bottom.

That was not what happened in reality. We were happy; the baby had kicked that morning for the first time, and we held our hands together to feel it. We still were holding hands when Dima took the step. He lost his footing, and he let my hand go, his dark curly hair vanishing into the water. Ever since, I dream my water dreams every night for over fifty years.

VICTORIA
PTSD

The trolley was crowded, there were no free seats, but Victoria was almost home. Her stop was next, and she got ready to exit.

She and a little Dima lived with her parents in a brick building across the street from the trolley stop. Sarra and ageless Aunt Rose watched Dima while Victoria was at work. It was a sizeable four-room apartment on the third floor with a long hallway and three balconies.

Dima was a beautiful red-haired boy with bright eyes and incredible energy. He ran non-stop along the hallway from one balcony to another, wearing out both, his Babushka and Aunt Rose.

Victoria took another breath and shook off her trembling hands. For a second, right before the stop, she saw her parents' apartment in flames, a crowd under the balcony where her precious little boy was lying dead on asphalt. She heard the sirens of ambulances and firetrucks, and she begged the ambulance driver to take Dima to hospital.

"I am a doctor," she screamed at the top of her lungs through her tears.

She turned and got a glimpse of the building through a narrow slit between the passengers on the trolley. Everything was quiet on the beautiful Boulevard framed by flowering chestnut trees. She took a deep breath and exited.

No crowd or ambulances. Victoria crossed the street sweaty and pale with her heart still pounding wildly.

She called these episodes "the visions" and they tormented her almost every day. She lived through plane crashes and cars smashing, falling in the deepest ravines, and dying again and again. She called ambulances; she screamed and cried over sick and dead. She did not pay attention and did not tell anybody. "What could these two seconds do to me?"

The fancy term "post-traumatic stress disorder" was not coined yet.

In reality, there was always something to worry about, the kids driving and coming late, sick patients, jobs lost, Felix not feeling well, or money.

She lived through her Dad's death at sixty-five in Kiev, thousands of miles away from her broken heart.

She tried to be brave, holding her head high and building the best life for her family. Sometimes she doubted her self-made diagnosis of PTSD. Maybe she was just a typical Jewish mother.

*****

We took a tour of the farm that had its produce, livestock, and fish. There were ponds and lakes, forests and gardens, fields, foot passages and roads. We did not dig, did not plant, did not harvest and did not attend the horses.

There was a library, a music room, and elegantly appointed living rooms. It did not look like European castles or country manors; it had a distinctly American style and charm.

Felix sat on a low stool in the music room quietly strumming a six-string guitar.

Back in Russia, he had played a seven-string guitar, and like everything in our lives, it had to be changed and re-tuned to a new, American style.

He looked good with the guitar in his lap, back to the dashing smiling husband of mine some fifty years ago. I had no regrets.

DAY 49, OCTOBER 15
KESWICK, VA
KESWICK HALL AT MONTICELLO

The gorgeous morning was warm and sunny just as many other mornings on our trip, but I could feel the cold breath of fall. The vast Ukrainian fields surfaced in my memory as they always did in the early mornings of fall as they did on the morning we had left on our trip. We were almost home; we had to drive only four hundred miles from Tennessee to Virginia and a few more miles tomorrow. After adding to our odometer nearly nine thousand miles for the last forty-eight days on the road, we were on the final stretch.

I am so superstitious; I am afraid to say, "We did it!" even to myself. First, we still have a few hundred miles to drive.

Somebody said that the mystery of boredom is in finishing everything. I would not mind getting bored.

THE TIMES

I see my life as a huge quilt. Stitched of myriads pieces different in size and color it is amazing. Some pieces are damaged or worn out; some are almost new; there are pieces of dirty tarp and ruff canvas next to the gorgeous swatches of silk and lace; a black piece is next to a one that is heavenly blue; some pieces are huge, and some are very, very small.

Each piece is a place or a time in my life, some are a person or a relationship, and some are music, poetry or a trip. I know every piece in this quilt; I remember every stitch, every hole, every place and every stretch of time.

I had never counted the childhood years, did not understand how precious the time was, I could not embrace this sweet and innocent swath of time. "Get older Victoria!" I hurried up, eager to learn, to experience, to live through. It was easier to manage the months; they were branded by important holidays or birthdays. Each month looked and smelled differently and, for me, the year started with December.

The sparkling white month smelled of snow and a New Year tree and began with Dima's birthday. To celebrate his amazing arrival, we celebrated Dima's birthday every month for the first year. The life that overcame the death, the victorious little red-haired baby who had to live the life for two, himself and his dead at twenty-five father.

December was jingly, glittery, and full of the promise of the important day, Dad's birthday on December 25. A few days after his birthday, Ella arrived as a slightly belated present to the family.

My grandmother Clara was born on New Year night.

The New Year was a fantastic holiday free of Soviet slogans. Of course, my year starts with December.

January comes with much fanfare, with the bells of Kremlin currants. It is sweetened with the candies in the presents from Uncle Frost at all morning festivities for the kids; it is cold with fresh snow and icicles hanging everywhere.

The coldest day, however, is Tatyana's Day on the twenty-fifth, religious holiday for the Saint Tatyana, a Christian martyr in the third century Rome. The girls born on January 25 were usually named Tatyana, as was the young woman who made and embroidered my first dress.

It was January when at the River Port Restaurant Felix and I danced our first dance over fifty years ago.

February used to be a gloomy month with short shadowy days. Everything was dark and dirty, melting snow, bare trees, and wet coats. It was Sam's birthday. He was drafted to clean up Chernobyl and miraculously survived. We called him every year to say Happy Birthday until he died last year in Germany from the consequences of those days in Chernobyl.

February is not a gloomy month anymore. The new country added a new dimension, a new holiday and our firstborn, the first generation American grandson. February is a great month!

March is purple with the first crocuses and gentle with fragile branches of mimosa. Mom adored its small yellow flowers and leaves that would fold defending themselves when touched but would re-open a few minutes later. The sun is shy. Everything is waiting.

The first comes the International Day of Women with all its craziness, the stores filled with men looking for the presents, the girls filled with hopes for the flowers and invitations to the parties.

Then comes Mom's birthday with invited friends and the best of Mom's culinary delights on the table; Ella and I conferring with dad about a present for mom, and the beautiful love poem that dad would read at the table, for everyone to know how much he loves his wife.

Felix added yet another birthday, right after Sarra's. However, the full glory and fun of the day came only in America. Felix's birthday is a fun day when, fittingly, everybody cheers, drinks and celebrates; plenty of green and Irish luck.

April is a very pregnant month, soft and ripe, smelling like fresh bread just out of the oven. It is a month of my parents' anniversary.

They were a great couple by any measure. How sad that Lenya did not get to age and Sarra had to do it alone, without her perfect half.

Even after fifty years, I am still not convinced that Felix and I are as perfect a match as my parents were.

The pinky-white May would storm in with thunders and smell of lilies-of –the valleys. On my birthday, Felix would bring me a basketful of intoxicatingly fragrant small white bells. The chestnut trees would light up their graceful white candles and I, no matter how old, would smile loving my May birthday.

In Kiev, the May Day parade would paint the streets red and a military parade on Victory Day would reverberate a thousand times with my name; everybody is exclaiming proudly, "Victory! Victory"!

The summer would roll in quietly, emptying schools' hallways and bringing in heat and dust. The easy summers of my childhood became more complicated.

June comes with military song "The Sacred War" and sound of marching armies, with the voice of Levitan and Dad's war stories. Babushka died in June and Dmitry, and I went to the cemetery; we were sad but full of hopes for a new life growing inside me.

I see two large black holes in my quilt; maybe I did not notice these before or perhaps I did not want to see.

My Father died in June. The warm night in Massachusetts was thousands of miles away from Kiev. Alone, I sat in my American living room on my American sofa with a huge hole in the place of my Russian heart. There was nothing to do, nobody to call, no shoulder to cry on. Felix and the kids were sad and supportive, but how do you help the tree that lost its roots, the bird that lost her song, the woman who lost her heart.

There was another hole in the center of the quilt, the large old hole with frayed edges burned by my tears and fears. I hated July, with its heat, beaches, dangerous waters and sad anniversaries.

I was mortally wounded, but I did not die on the terrifying July day over fifty years ago. I learned how to survive, and I had managed to rebuild my life.

Now July is a beautiful, warm and generous month; it gave me two fabulous grandsons, and I have loved this month ever since.

August was a lazy, yellow round month with pioneer camps and seaside resorts. The reminders "The fall is coming, the school is about to start" lurk around every corner, and kids free themselves from the ruts of the summer, ready to delve into the new academia.

Finally, refreshing September rolls in with still long days and starry nights, exciting possibilities and even more exciting love life.

We got married. Felix got a new ready-made family, a wife and a son.

There were seven years that we did not celebrate our anniversary, another dark piece somewhere on my quilt. However, the fabric was never torn, we mended it slowly and meticulously, and it is hardly visible now.

Just like my Babushka used to mend my Dad's torn socks. She would put the hole over her favorite cooking wooden spoon and place four horizontal lines with thick thread across the edges; then she would turn the spoon and place vertical lines with the same thick thread skipping one thread at the time. The sock looked almost new. The mending called "shtopat'" and I did plenty of it with my life.

September gave us an anniversary gift, the final say on our marriage, a beautiful granddaughter.

October comes in glorious burgundy diadem. It is framed in gold leaves and perched above delicious chubby cheeks of the golden child. It is Dave's Birthday.

Dave is like October itself, warm and brilliant, kind and generous, my golden baby. However, cold rain is not rare. And like every autumn, occasional snow would freeze the ground and kill the late flowers.

Winter arrives on the sleigh. It races on the new snow, fast and fearless, loud and obtrusive. It starts with the day of Great

October Revolution at the beginning of November. Freshly painted red flags and slogans would cast the red shadow on virgin snow; the not intended reminder of a communists' terror lasting hundred years. It was always a cold day, good for the winter boots if you were lucky to have them.

Then, with December, my year would start again.

*****

We drove about four hundred miles not only in the space but in the time as well.

Tennessee, which we had left this morning, had all the abundance of greenery in the world. The forecast was eighty degrees by the weekend, and the Great Smoky Mountains were as green as they could be. By noon, still in eastern Tennessee, we saw a couple of yellowish spots among the universal greens.

Suddenly, a few miles and a few hours later, in pastoral Virginia, we were transferred into autumn, with its beautiful reds and yellow. It was not complete foliage, of course, but a close reminder, that fall is coming.

Our suite in Keswick Hall at Monticello was another example of American heritage at its best. Surrounded by the Blue Ridge Mountains, the hundred –year- grand old dame of a hotel was elegant and inviting. There was an intriguing story of the two "easterners," a Virginia University medical student and a daughter of the Newport Yacht club Commodore who built the eight-thousand-square-feet Italian villa.

The view and the interior were equally superb, and we ordered a room service. It was strange to think that we would have dinner home tomorrow and would sleep in our own bed. Not the elegant four-poster bed from the Laura Ashley Estate.

Felix opened a bottle of red, and we celebrated our last stay in the hotel on our behemoth trip. We did not need sleeping pills; we slept before our heads touched the fancy pillows.

DAY 50, OCTOBER 16
FRAMINGHAM, MA

I reloaded our GPS with the home address and got dizzy with the numbers. We drove about ten-thousand miles, crossed the Continental Divide six times, stayed forty-nine nights at the most exciting hotels, ate at glorious restaurants, charming cafés, and authentic American diners, spent innumerable hours talking, singing, thinking and sleeping in the car, and amazingly managed not to kill each other!

I planned to add another statistic later; the names of the National and State Parks we explored, the names of the many mountains we climbed and the names of the states we traveled through.

Just today, in a span of about six hundred miles, we would cross Virginia, DC, Delaware, Maryland, Pennsylvania, New Jersey, New York and Connecticut into Massachusetts.

"Imagine, Felix; we are in a time machine!" I was anxious we would be home tonight. "It is pretty green here, and by night our backyard would be all red, yellow and maroon with the real foliage."

"It is not that important what colors would be leaves in the backyard." Felix refused to get excited about such a silly thing as the leaves' color. "After all this driving, I just want to be home."

"You see, you said home."

"What is the difference? Try to translate 'house' to Russian. Now, translate 'home,'" Felix smiled mischievously.

I could come up only with one word "dom." Great mighty Russian language did not make any distinction between "house" and "home."

But I did.

THE PLACES
KIEV, UKRAINE, THE 1940S

The room was all that little Vika knew, a small room with wooden floor. She could not possibly remember a dugout behind the front line where she and her parents lived during the war. She remembered vaguely a military hospital, which was a big name for any undamaged house where her parents treated wounded soldiers. As the Russian Army advanced toward Berlin, baby Victoria dispensed small pieces of chocolate from America to wounded soldiers for every killed fly; her Dad's hospital was the best, clean with no flies.

The wooden floor in their first apartment after the war was almost bright yellow because Babushka washed it every day. Not merely washed, but scraped it with a big kitchen knife standing on her knees. When doing this, Babushka did not allow anybody on the floor, and it was one of Victoria's favorite times. She was permitted to sit on her parents' bed with her feet up. The narrow bed made of aluminum tubes and covered with a thin blanket was the coziest place for Vika. It was warm and smelled like her Mom, the narrow island among the shiny yellow floor. That was the home.

THE PLACES
KIEV, UKRAINE, THE 1950S

When they moved to Podol, the lower part of the city next to the river, the floor in their room was painted. In the room with built-in white bookshelves, which stored Lenya's friend Boris's library, the floor was painted dark red.

These books by Balzac, Maupassant, Dumas, Flaubert, and Zola were all that Victoria was interested in; she would never part with the book.

In the morning, when she had to get ready for school, she laced her boots reading the open book on the dark-red floor. These books were her home.

THE PLACES
KIEV, UKRAINE, THE 1960S

Victoria was in medical school when her parents moved out, and she got her very own room. She loved everything in this small room. The old sofa bed now belonged to her alone, unless she was in love. The small almost empty wardrobe held a few things that she or her mom managed to buy. The bookshelves were jammed-packed with her old books and medical textbooks. A small dressing table had long elegant legs and a broken mirror, which she accidentally broke when Dima called her for the first time. The piano that took most of the place in a small room; she loved her piano, the present from her beloved Babushka. She could never be lonely or bored in a room with a piano. It was her home.

THE PLACES
KIEV, UKRAINE, THE 1960S

The sun filled a sprawling four-room apartment on a boulevard up-town; it was a dream. You could hear Lenya's beautiful baritone singing his favorite songs taking long showers in his own bathroom, not shared with other families. You could breathe fresh air from all three balconies and read the cut newspaper from the lonely pocket in the private toilet for as long as you want. Sarra and Aunt Rose had a kitchen all to themselves unless after a dinner Lenya was in a great mood and wanted to do the dishes. It was a happy household until one Saturday in July when Sarra and Lenya brought back from the beach crushed and destroyed pregnant and widowed Victoria. And everything had changed forever.

She did not move back to her old room; she slept in her parents' bed. Lenya gave up his favorite place at the kitchen table. The rain cried at the big window, and the trees on the boulevard were trimmed almost to the naked trunks. They looked like the black crosses on the cemetery where Victoria went every day. She sat at the window, listening to her baby kicking gently, and that was her home.

THE PLACES
KIEV, UKRAINE, THE 1970S

Matvey, late Dima's uncle was a sensible man. When his brother died in the war, Matvey promised to take care of his family. Now, that he lost his nephew, he loved little Dima as his own. His wife was a pediatrician, kind and gentle she took care of both Victoria's boys.

"Lenya, Dima should live with his parents," Matvey tried to talk senses to Lenya. They became friends at Victoria's wedding, and their friendship was stronger than ever, cemented by the tragedy.

"I am designing a new building for the TV studio at the center of the city, and I would be able to get a condo for Victoria. You would have to pay for it, but at least, with two rooms there would be enough space for both children." Dmitry's uncle was a reasonable man, and he liked Felix.

The whole wall in Victoria's new condominium was a big window, which continued to the balcony; it had an exotic name "erker".

After walking up six floors to their new condominium, Victoria and Felix were short of breath; the elevator did not work yet. They looked at the hospital garden under their balcony, inspected their own two rooms, and checked out not working gas stove in the kitchen. They were elated with their new apartment, their own. They were sure they would be happy here with their two sons. They embraced and kissed congratulating each other. The clothes came off; the floor still smelled with new polish, nothing yet worked in this empty apartment, but they loved each other, and that was their home.

THE PLACES
HAVERHILL, MA, THE 1970S

The myriads of lights under a plane's wing were Boston. Americans dined, and there was a warm light for every family, but theirs. They left everything, their family, their home, their life. They stayed the first night at the hotel and early, the next morning, on Sunday, looking outside at the deserted downtown of a small New England town Victoria said, "Finally, I am home."

*****

They bought their first and the only house five years later, and they loved it. They took a two-day course on "how to buy your house" and followed the advice. Victoria's best girlfriend loaned them a thousand dollars to put into their empty bank account.

The friend, who helped them to move, examined every room of their modest split-level. "When I was at pioneer camp in the summer, the whole camp was in a house like this; there were forty of us. Now you are the true capitalists!"

Victoria was not happy to become a capitalist; she noticed things she had not looked at before. "Felix, did you see all the cracks in our driveway? You will have to call somebody tomorrow. Please, call the town hall; they would have to fix these."

Felix's jaw dropped down, "We are responsible for our driveway, Vika." However, Victoria was sure somebody from the town would have to take care of the old windows and the cracked driveway to her new house.

She covered old windows with lace panels, which previously, in another life, covered their "erker". She had to wear sunglasses to protect her eyes from the shiny reflective wallpaper in the bathrooms (now that she had all three of them for her four-person family); they destroyed the vegetable garden and cleared the backyard for a majestic water view. She joined an all-male private practice; they sent Dima and Dave to private schools and colleges and made beautiful friends.

Eight years later, Sarra with Ella and her family made it to America. Victoria did not see her Mom for eight years, and she met her eight-year-old niece for the first time. For the first year, they all lived together. And that when the house became a true home.

*****

As I predicted, our backyard was a beautiful pastel of rose, yellow, gold, and maroon. Our home, lit by the setting sun, was warm and inviting. We started to unload our car, and suddenly we both stopped overwhelmed by the sense of pride for what we did. We kissed and hugged, but this time our clothes stayed where they were. The first year of the next fifty was upon us.

About the Author

Nadia Shulman grew up in war-torn Soviet Union facing all the hardships of state-sponsored anti-Semitism. She and her husband came to the United States with two sons, two suitcases and $90. Doctor Shulman practiced internal medicine for over forty years. She is an avid traveler who visited over 100 countries, and a frequent guest on a local TV travel show. DOUBLE EXPOSURE is her first biographical book about her family's tragedies and triumphs.